‖‖‖‖‖‖‖‖‖‖‖‖‖‖‖‖‖‖‖

GAY SCIENCE

Between Men ~ Between Women   Lesbian and Gay Studies

||||||||||||||||||
GAY SCIENCE

THE ETHICS OF SEXUAL
ORIENTATION RESEARCH

Timothy F. Murphy

 Columbia University Press   New York

Columbia University Press

Publishers Since 1893

New York   Chichester, West Sussex

Library of Congress Cataloging-in-Publication Data

Murphy, Timothy F.

    Gay science : the ethics of sexual orientation research / Timothy F. Murphy.

    p.   cm. — (Between men ~ between women)

    Includes bibliographical references and index.

    ISBN 0–231–10848–6

    1. Homosexuality—Research—Moral and ethical aspects.

2. Homosexuality—Research—Social aspects.   3. Sexual orientation—

Research—Moral and ethical aspects.   4. Sexual orientation—

Research—Social aspects.   I. Title.   II. Series.

    HQ76.25.M87   1997

306.76'6'072—dc21   97–16308

                                                      CIP

⊗ Casebound editions of Columbia University Press books

are printed on permanent and durable acid-free paper.

Printed in the United States of America

c 10 9 8 7 6 5 4 3 2 1

Between Men ~ Between Women   Lesbian and Gay Studies

Lillian Faderman and Larry Gross, Editors

Advisory Board of Editors

Claudia Card
Terry Castle
John D'Emilio
Esther Newton
Anne Peplau
Eugene Rice
Kendall Thomas
Jeffrey Weeks

Between Men ~ Between Women is a forum for current lesbian and gay scholarship in the humanities and social sciences. The series includes both books that rest within specific traditional disciplines and are substantially about gay men, bisexuals, or lesbians and books that are interdisciplinary in ways that reveal new insights into gay, bisexual, or lesbian experience, transform traditional disciplinary methods in consequence of the perspectives that experience provides, or begin to establish lesbian and gay studies as a freestanding inquiry. Established to contribute to an increased understanding of lesbians, bisexuals, and gay men, the series also aims to provide through that understanding a wider comprehension of culture in general.

CONTENTS

|||||||||||||||||||||||||||||||||||||||||||||||||||||||||||||||||||||||||||

ACKNOWLEDGMENTS

In the 1995–1996 academic year I had the privilege of a fellowship at the Institute for the Humanities at the University of Illinois at Chicago, during which time I wrote the greatest part of this book. Given the robust competition for those fellowships, I gratefully acknowledge the institute's support of my project. I also want to thank David Barnett, J. Michael Bailey, Norman Gevitz, James Miller, Joe Sartorelli, Edward Stein, and Marguerite Vallance for their admonitions, counsel, and suggestions, though they will no doubt continue to disagree with me about many matters. I also appreciate the diligence with which two anonymous reviewers examined the initial manuscript for Columbia University Press. I want to say last that I appreciate the generosity of David E. Tolman and Keith Kissee in letting me think things through for a time in their grand house at the corner of Monument and Strawberry.

||||||||||||||||||||||

GAY SCIENCE

||||||||||||||||||||||||||||||||||||||||||||||||||||||||||||||||||||||||||||||||||

INTRODUCTION

As many commentators about sex research are fond of pointing out, in the fourth century B.C.E., the philosopher Plato offered a fanciful account that attributed the origins of erotic desire to divine punishment. Zeus punished the first human beings for impious and willful misbehavior by splitting them in half.[1] Erotic love, the desire to reunite lost halves, is the legacy of that punishment. Plato's mythology described not only the erotic entanglements of men and women but of men and men as well as women and women. Since then, the debate about the origins and meaning of eroticism, and especially same-sex eroticism, has only grown more contentious. Some twenty-five hundred years and a great deal of failed research later, questions about the origins of erotic interests still enjoy considerable prominence, though lately it has not been philosophers but scientists who have taken up the inquiry, and they study not *eros* but *sexual orientation*. Genetic loading, fetal hormone exposure, and cerebral lateralization have supplanted gods, divine wrath, and mortal longings as the categories used to investigate and explain erotic desire.

Since scientific efforts to account for sexual orientation commenced in earnest in the nineteenth century, researchers have reported differences between gay and straight people in their fat distribution, metabolism, hair quality, height, lisping, lipid levels, the angles at which they carry their arms, susceptibility to paranoia, and an almost indefinite number of biophysical and psychodevelopmental traits.[2] From these alleged anatomical and behavioral differences between gay and straight people various competing conclusions have been drawn about the origins of erotic desires: that they result from events in psychosexual development and are therefore primarily psychological in origin or that they are hormonally or genetically influenced and are therefore largely independent of psychological events.

Regardless of its vocabulary and assumptions about causality, scientific research is thought to have considerable significance in judging the psychological integrity, the morality, and the social accommodation of various sexual orientations. For example, taking the evidence to show that homoeroticism was a psychic disorder, perhaps having roots in heredity, many psychologists in the past two centuries investigated treatments and cures. Researchers and the public alike once routinely looked to biomedicine and the health sciences to rid society of a trait they judged psychologically if not also morally and socially offensive. By contrast, rarely—and only rarely—have there been people wanting to move from heteroerotic to homoerotic interests and identities.[3] Against this historical backdrop, some commentators worry that current sexual orientation research can only reinvigorate pathological interpretations of homoeroticism, as philosopher Eric Juengst has cautioned might happen.[4] Commentators of this persuasion believe that, spurred by beliefs hostile to homoeroticism, research may be used against gay people in a variety of ways. They worry, for example, that a primary objective of sexual orientation research is a therapy for homoeroticism. They fear that objectionable consequences will befall gay people not only in authoritarian states where gay people are especially vulnerable but also in advanced democratic states that manifest exclusionary and discriminatory policies toward gay people, with the United States being no exception among the latter.

Some commentators go so far as to raise this worst-case scenario: sexual orientation science is laying the foundation of a genocidal campaign against gay people. Less alarmingly, and more frequently, other commentators raise a vision of a future in which gay people are greatly diminished in number rather than altogether extinguished. For example, in commenting on the results of a genetic study of homoeroticism, Thomas Stoddard, attorney and director of the Campaign for Military Service, observed, "One can imagine the science of the future manipulating information of this kind to reduce the number of gay people being born."[5] So prevalent are assumptions of this kind that it has become a media convention to conjoin news reports about sexual orientation research with speculations about expected ill effects for gay people. Just after the latest scientific findings are reported someone is typically quoted to the effect that this research may work to the detriment, even to the extinction, of gay people.

Other commentators take a much more sanguine view of sexual orientation research. In fact, some see sexual orientation science as a formidable bulwark of protection against moral judgments that reflect ill on gay people. They see in sexual orientation research the foundations of a social transformation that will fold gay people seamlessly into the prevailing currents of moral and civic life. They argue this point variously, but in the main they contend that to the extent research shows that sexual orientation is fundamentally involuntary and explicable in terms of biopsychic development, no moral account can properly blame people for having the sexual interests they have.[6] Some commentators go even further and conclude that science can show that homoeroticism and its behaviors are natural in a morally significant sense. Seeing homoeroticism as "natural," they not only reject claims that it is psychologically, morally, or socially undesirable, they also argue for a broad social accommodation of gay people. Commentators of this persuasion believe that research undermines individual and social heterosexism and thereby improves the standing of gay people in the eyes of the public and the law.

The 1986 Supreme Court decision of Bowers v. Hardwick, which denied the existence of a fundamental constitutional right to sexual relations between people of the same sex, seems to have foreclosed the utility of research that could affirm the centrality of homoeroticism to gay people and their private, consensual sexual relations. In that case the court held that homoerotic interests did not have the kind of fundamental centrality to human life that would trigger constitutional protection. Sexual orientation research may nevertheless sway people and courts from unfavorable judgments about homoeroticism in other ways, for example, by showing the need for heightened judicial protection from hostile laws. Whether or not this latter event occurs will depend, of course, on what research uncovers, how these findings are received in public opinion, and how courts reach decisions about cases involving gay people. Nevertheless, if sexual orientation research leads to greater social accommodation of gay people and perhaps even to specific protections under the law, these outcomes would be an ironic commentary on worries about genocide.

It is not my intention to offer here an account of why people have the sexual orientations they have or to assess how sexual orientation is grounded in one's biological heritage or psychological history. That task belongs to empirical researchers in the relevant life and social sciences, in the fields of genetics, endocrinology, neurology, psychology, and so on. Neither will I offer an account of the history of sexual orientation research; much of that story has already been told by neuroanatomist Simon LeVay in his 1996 *Queer Science: The Use and Abuse of Research Into Homosexuality.*[7] My goal here is to offer an ethical overview of sexual orientation research and, more specifically, the meaning of that research for gay people. In this project it will be necessary to describe representative research in the area, but, again, it is not my goal to defend any particular account of the origins and development of erotic desire or to offer any definitive overview and assessment of the science currently being done in the field. In regard to the specific causal mechanisms by which people have the erotic interests they have, I profess myself agnostic. I write not as a lab scientist or sexual sociologist but as a philosopher of medicine whose primary concerns are ethical in nature. There are purely speculative moments in what follows; there are practical suggestions as well. I speculate, for example, what would happen if the earth were visited by extraterrestrial beings interested in our sexual lives, but I also offer recommendations that ought to govern privacy and control of biological samples and records. At the very least, my project here maps the issues that are relevant to the ethical analysis of sexual orientation research. I will use the remainder of this introduction to describe the general contours of the project as I have organized these by chapter.

In chapter 1 I countenance the question of what sexual orientation research can hope to achieve, namely, what it is that this sort of research legitimately takes as its object of inquiry. Historically a great deal of research has been conceptually flawed given that some researchers quite wrongly assumed in their investigations, for example, that homoeroticism is a single, uniform, and reifiable trait abidingly present or not within any given human being and that the trait constitutes whether a person is "a homosexual," just as its absence, by default, would constitute someone as "a heterosexual." Against assumptions of this kind I understand human eroticism to encompass a broad array of capacities and interests that are not best understood as the sorts of properties akin to, for example, blood oxygen levels or body mass. Human eroticism always encompasses biopsychic dispositions, cultural possibilities, and personal choices. Accordingly, it is highly misleading and reductive to believe that there could be a single cause of complex erotic interests and behaviors. If two women have a sexual relationship, it is not necessarily because there is something biologically manifest in them that is absent in women who never have this kind of relationship. To the extent two teenage boys have a sexual encounter, it is not necessarily because their genetic endowment fates them to that erotic relationship. Nevertheless, I hasten to add, some people may very well be disposed toward one kind of erotic interest over another, whether that interest is homoerotic or heteroerotic, whether those dispositions are biological, psychological, or cultural, or something else. These dispositions cannot by themselves, however, be decisive about an adult human being's erotic interests and behaviors. The nature and extent of those dispositions and their interplay with cultural possibilities and personal choices in producing actual erotic interests and behaviors are exactly the domain of sexual orientation research.

For illustrative purposes I review research that links homoeroticism to neurological structures in the brain, to prevalence patterns in siblings, to a genetic region on the X chromosome, to finger skin ridge patterns, and to psychic injuries sustained during childhood. My goal here is primarily expository, but I will offer some global comments about the value and limitations of these studies. By the end of the chapter it should be clear that while I think that factors influencing the emergence of erotic interests can be studied scientifically, there are still more questions about the causal determinants of erotic interest than there are answers, both because science in the area is preliminary and because there is more to eroticism than can be discovered in studies of these kinds.

In chapter 2 I consider arguments regarding the value and some of the purposes of sexual orientation research. Sociologists Dorothy Nelkin and Laurence Tancredi once observed that "deeply rooted beliefs about the moral and political neutrality of science tend to preclude debate about the interests served by science."[8] For many gay men and lesbians, however, there is no such expectation about the neutrality of science and medicine with respect to matters of sexual orientation. On the contrary, among many gay people there is deeply entrenched suspicion about ulterior motives in sexual orientation research. Some commentators claim, for example, that such research is necessarily heterosexist and continuous with the oppressive lineage of science that had as its goal the eradication of homoeroticism. I therefore consider whether sexual orientation research must be always of a piece with pathological or disciplinary interpretations of homoeroticism or whether it can have liberating effects. In particular, I consider one commentator's recommendation that a moratorium be imposed on this line of research in countries where there is still social discrimination against gay people. I will try to show that sexual orientation research need not presuppose that homoeroticism is pathological and that it can have important liberating effects. Even apart from this kind of effect, this sort of science has its own value. There are many reasons to strive for a confirmed theory of human psychosexual development in all its manifestations. To be sure, a science that aimed only to know the origins of homoerotic interests to the exclusion of all others would be a lazy and crabbed science. Scientific efforts to account for the emergence of human erotic interests in general would, however, be an ambitious and fertile effort. Moreover, it would hardly be desirable to leave the research field in its current state if there are major errors in the work that now dominates scientific and public understandings of human eroticism. If sexual orientation research works to lift erroneous judgments, it would be an egregious oversimplification to say that it must of necessity stigmatize gay people. To say that sexual orientation is plausible and interesting in its own right is not, however, to say anything about what sort of priority it ought to have. It will remain a separate question for the research community and society to answer about what priority to attach to sexual orientation research compared to all other theoretically interesting and socially useful projects vying for intellectual talent and funding.

After the foregoing discussions I begin to take up some of the ethically troubling issues that attend the expected uses of sexual orientation research. In chapter 3 I address the question of sexual orientation research and therapy for homoeroticism in adults. Therapy for homoeroticism no longer has the formal backing of major Western medical associations, but the practice has not altogether disappeared, and it may very well happen that sexual orientation research will ascertain some mechanism for recasting erotic interests in adults. Then again, it may not. Even if a therapy did emerge, it would not likely be a threat to gay adults uninterested in its use. In the main, most gay people are entirely content with their erotic interests and would not change them even if ways of ways of doing so were available. In democracies states may not impose therapy on adults against their will except under circumstances so extraordinary that they would never occur with respect to sexual orientation therapy. The most pressing question in regard to the future of sexual orientation therapy is not, then, one of involuntary application but whether any future therapy would respect the ethical standards that elsewhere govern therapy. It does appear that some forms of sexual orientation therapy could be formulated in ways that are ethically accountable, the grave deficiencies of history in this regard notwithstanding. This is not to say that I look favorably on efforts to alter homoerotic interests, for I certainly do not. It is to say that so long as therapy of this kind abides by the ethical principles that govern treatment and research elsewhere in biomedicine, especially standards of informed consent and protection from undue risk, this kind of therapy may be pursued by those people interested in it. Adults should be entitled to make their own mistakes here as they do elsewhere in the pursuit of therapies they believe important to their lives.

In chapter 4 I look at the meaning of sexual orientation research for children. Some researchers and commentators alike have speculated that sexual orientation science could produce methods of prenatal diagnosis that would permit parents to undertake prenatal diagnostics and interventions in order to avoid having lesbian or gay children. Perhaps some diagnostic test could alert parents to the likely sexual orientation of their children, opening the possibility of the abortion of pregnancies likely to end in children with unwanted traits. Prenatal interventions for sexual orientation might take the form of hormonal or genetic treatment during specific stages of embryonic and/or fetal development. In order to analyze the ethics of these practices, it is first necessary to consider the extent of parental rights over the traits of their children. These rights are grounded in the expectation of parental beneficence toward children and in the profound effect children have on the lives of their parents. I will try to show that parents have no right to a child of a specific sexual orientation or a duty to secure only heteroeroticism in their children. For their part, children have no duty to exhibit a specific sexual orientation, and neither do they have the right to a specific sexual orientation. Nevertheless, because of the importance of respecting parental rights and the significant effect of their children's lives on them, parents should generally have the right to try and control the sexual orientation of their children so long as those efforts end in no harm to children and are not contrary to their interests. This is certainly not to say that parents may do anything to control the sexual orientation of their children, because children clearly have some rights to protection against parental interventions, especially as they mature. The moral latitude I defend, it is worth saying, would protect those parents who wanted to have gay and lesbian children, should techniques emerge offering that possibility. These parents ought to be free to select for gay children, even if others find such decisions profoundly objectionable.

In chapter 5 I use a number of speculative scenarios to flesh out the possible uses of a test for sexual orientation, namely, a test that could differentiate people according to their likely erotic interests. This is, again, an entirely hypothetical discussion, but my goal is to assess whether such a test would always work against the interests of gay people. Fearing prejudicial applications, one researcher has said that he would use the intellectual property rights that attach to his genetic studies to prevent the development of any such test.[9] To be sure, such a test would not be without its attractions. The U.S. military, for example, has a long history of interest in tests that can be used to exclude gay people from service. Despite invidious practices like this, I will try to show that the results of a test for sexual orientation need not be uniformly antigay. Toward that end I describe scenarios involving the use of a sexual orientation test in criminal and civil trials, in media reports, in establishing civic benefits, in establishing cultural identity, in medical records, as well as in military service. While there may be motives to use a sexual orientation test for exclusionary purposes, there are other purposes that might make the test important to gay people. The best manner to protect against unwarranted uses of sexual orientation tests would be, then, not to foreclose the science that would produce them but to establish the kinds of confidentiality and antidiscrimination protection that will be required in the age of advanced biological research, in an age that confidently expects to be able to predict all manner of human traits and dispositions from biogenetic tests. Toward that end I offer some guidelines about the standards of confidentiality and informed consent that ought to prevail generally for biomedical testing, including tests for sexual orientation.

Insofar as the idea of "nature" undergirds a great deal of debate about homoeroticism, it is important to be clear on what sexual orientation research can and cannot do in regard to clarifying human nature. In chapter 6 I discuss what sexual orientation research means for ideas of human nature and for the standing of gay people under the law. Research can very well illuminate the facts of human eroticism, studying both the causes and effects of sexual orientation, so far as they can be meaningfully ascertained. In that regard, sexual orientation research can go a long way in dispelling errors about why people have the erotic interests they have. Insofar as nature represents a philosophical ideal rather than the totality of scientific facts about human beings, sexual orientation research may prove fairly useless in arguing against the proposition that homo-eroticism is contrary to human nature. Philosophical views of nature can only be falsified by scientific research to the extent they are dependent on false empirical assumptions. To make this point, I describe one philosophical view of the nature of human sexuality, a view that is unfavorable to homoeroticism, and describe why it is immune to repudiation by scientific study. I nevertheless go on to criticize that view of human nature as inadequate both in its characteri-zation of human sexuality and in the public policy conclusions that are said to be implicit in it. It is in assessing the effects of social attitudes and public policy that sexual orientation research can be eminently useful in clarifying the "nature" of sexual orientation.

To judge whether sexual orientation research helps protect gay people by triggering certain protections under the law, I consider its implications for the legal doctrine of suspect class. I try to show that while there are some arguments to be made in favor of this approach invoking heightened scrutiny for laws dis-criminating against gay people, it is unclear that sexual orientation science is in a position to confirm that sexual orientation is immutable in the way legal doctrine requires. While seeking suspect class status is one strategy for protect-ing gay people, it is not the only one, and its utility may have been surpassed by the logic of the 1996 Supreme Court case, Romer v. Evans, that struck down the part of the Colorado constitution that forbade extending antidiscrimination laws to gay people. Whether courts come to the conclusion that gay people are entitled to heightened protection and whether they find the science of sexual orientation informative for their purposes will depend on the cases they are asked to hear and the judges sitting on the bench at the time. In any case, it seems to me that most of the laws that burden gay people should be struck down regardless of why people are gay, because those laws fail to bear a rational relationship to a legitimate state interest, and such was the logic that prevailed in Romer v. Evans.

In chapter 7 I speculate about the future of gay people in an age of advanced sexual orientation science. Against worries that sexual orientation science will work to the detriment of gay people, I ask whether other forces might not favor and protect gay people. In particular, I suggest that there may be social devel-opments that favor the emergence of openly gay people regardless of whether, for example, parents have the ability to choose the sexual orientation of their children or whether adults have a therapy available to change their sexual orientation. Certain social developments, immanent in existing social and economic developments, may enlarge the freedom to pursue sexual interests outside the context of reproductively oriented family relationships. Granted widely across a society, this freedom may produce more and not fewer gay people, just as it has to this point, even if a subset of parents was so worried about the sexual orientation of their children that they would abort a pregnancy rather than face the risk of a lesbian daughter or gay son, even if some adults chose sexual orientation therapy for themselves.

Claims like this are speculative, of course, and it might just as easily happen that the total number of gay people will fall in the future, for reasons currently unforeseeable. This need not be the end of gay people properly speaking or the final nail in their social coffin. Society might entertain discussion about whether and to what extent it has an obligation to sustain gay people for reasons, for example, that have to do with damages society endures because there are fewer gay people. Social programs to ensure a certain number of gay people in society would be politically volatile, and while they could work, they would be ultimately unwise. They might also be unnecessary, for I do not foresee the conditions under which gay people would come to be extinct even in an age having control over sexual orientation. The central question about the future of gay people is, finally, not one of total numbers but of moral standing. Regardless of how many gay people exist in the future, will they enjoy social equality or will they suffer an increasingly abject social state? If there is a remedy to worries about sexual orientation science, it is to be found, I believe, in securing equal standing in society for gay people.

Achieving a world in which gay people suffer no unjust discrimination will be difficult, just as it will be difficult to sort out the meaning of sexual orientation research for that project. Social tolerance of the ill-treatment of gay people has an ancient lineage and is sustained in a variety of conscious and unconscious ways, though it is not always clear why or at what cost to those responsible for the ill treatment. I wonder, for example, why homoeroticism and heteroeroticism are not seen merely as morally equivalent scions of a larger sexual denomination or as children of the same erotic god, with their own purposes and value, their differences vanishingly small against the backdrop of their common goals and purposes. Instead, differences of erotic interest have all too often been pitted against one another in portentous and historically significant antagonisms. These antagonisms are deep and intertwined with personal and cultural identity, but identities can be imagined in other ways and need not incorporate an antigay psychology or its moral equivalent. The future can be imagined as something other than an endless continuation of an unreconstructed and antigay present. En route to a better world, it seems to me that the best strategy for protecting gay people is to secure their social equality in the law and, more important, in social attitudes. Banning or censoriously monitoring sexual orientation research will not provide the kind of protection that gay people ultimately need, and neither would these measures always provide desirable models about the way in which social heterosexism should be countenanced and amended. The law is often a poor substitute for a sense of justice that prevails unspoken in the hearts and attitudes of a people.

Before I conclude this introduction let me say something about the terminology I use. While the terms *homosexuality, heterosexuality,* and *bisexuality* hold an entrenched place in both popular and scientific language, I believe they are misleading to the extent that they connote an unambiguous behavioral referent or psychological character, something akin to physical traits like hair color or bone density. By using the terms *homoeroticism* and *heteroeroticism,* I mean to suggest that people can range by degree and intensity within erotic interests just as people range within other "isms" such as liberalism, patriotism, or fanaticism, even if there is a hard-to-define-but-somehow-still-obvious core around which such isms revolve. I use the terms *homoeroticism* and *heteroeroticism* in order to get past the erroneous assumption a trait exists that is homosexuality or heterosexuality itself and that defines sexual identity independent of context. This is not true in regard to liberalism, patriotism, or fanaticism, and the same caveat applies to eroticism, to sexual orientation as well. The terms *homosexuality* and *heterosexuality* also lack transhistorical merit. Being very much products of the nineteenth century, their application to periods outside that time can be ambiguous. The terms *homoeroticism* and *heteroeroticism* have the advantage of being untied to medical conceptions of pathology or to moralistic conceptions of sodomy. Moreover, as critics in the wake of philosopher Michel Foucault are fond of pointing out, homosexuality has come to designate not only a reifiable trait but also a kind of person, whereas the truth of the matter is that social designations of sexual orientation in any particular society probably have more in common with categories like Democrat and Republican than with discrete transhistorical species in nature, even if there are biopsychological contributions to them. That said, I will nevertheless occasionally use the terms *homosexuality* and *heterosexuality* in order to preserve the language others have used in their discussions. The American Psychiatric Association did not, after all, first pathologize and then later declassify homoeroticism; it made its judgments about homosexuality.

Throughout this discussion I use the term *gay people* to refer inclusively to men and women with substantial homoerotic interests, whether or not they acknowledge those interests, act on them, or use that term to describe themselves. People with substantial homoerotic interests can identity themselves, for example, as *queers* or *nongay homosexuals,* depending on how they view the meaning of their erotic interests. I use *gay people* more as shorthand than as a commentary on the merit and utility of other labels. In those instances in which a distinction by sex among gay people seems justified by the context, I will advert to *gay men* and *lesbians.* I should also acknowledge that although I identify as a gay man I do not use the terms *we* and *us* when referring to gay people in the following discussion. I do so not to hide behind impersonal third-person usages but because I do not want to suggest that my views about who "we" are or how scientific research will affect "us" are universally shared by gay people. My goal here is not to serve as any kind of plenipotentiary ambassador having full diplomatic privileges to negotiate treaties on the relations between researchers and gay people but simply to offer my own considered views about attempts to locate and describe the determinants of human sexual interests, paying special attention to the meaning of those attempts for gay people. I fully expect that certain of my arguments will be controversial. Even where they are controversial, I hope that they will force more considered and reflected judgments about the meaning of science for gay people than have sometimes occupied public discussion. I hope that they will help stave off, for example, all-too-easy assessments that sexual orientation research is a kind of erotic phrenology doomed to failure from the start, that it is necessarily benighted in its motives, and that it must necessarily render the future of gay people more abject.

Biomedical research and its social applications are almost always worthy of sustained critical scrutiny. History is replete with all sorts of unfounded scientific projects and claims regarding matters of race, gender, intelligence, and sex. Science has been prejudicially applied, that is, to categories central to how people make judgments about personal and social worth. Prejudice and calumny are always looking for support from the sciences, and whole cultures have gambled on social experiments grounded in scientific reports having every appearance of truth. Later analysis and the critical reflection time and distance make possible have often shown, however, that there has been maleficence in the motives and malfeasance in the science. Given the comparative social powerlessness of gay people, sexual orientation research deserves as much scrutiny as meets the latest study of, for example, the comparative intelligence of human races. Some sexual orientation research has been as bad as research has ever been, and it has been driven by iniquitous motives often masked by the face of medical compassion. Whether sexual orientation research can be rescued from that historical legacy and whether it can go forward without prejudicing the social standing of gay people are the questions now at stake.

1 ||||||||||||||||||||||||||||||||||||||||||||||||||||||||||||||||||||||||||||||||||||||||

SCIENTIFIC ACCOUNTS OF SEXUAL ORIENTATION

Most morphological males have a dominant erotic interest in morphological females, and most morphological females have a dominant erotic interest in morphological males. This is not to say that human beings are always male or female in any uncomplicated way, for even that simple division has fluid borders in anatomy and genetics; people may be apparently male or female in anatomy but apparently the opposite in genetic endowment. Neither is it to say that those erotic interests are dictated by bodily morphology. It is merely to say that most human beings have these erotic interests and not others. Common usage designates such people as heterosexuals. There are nevertheless significant numbers of people whose sexual orientation does not fit this profile. Some males evince erotic interest only in other males and some females evince erotic interest only in other females. Common usage designates these people as homosexuals. To complicate the mix even further, some people range across both males and females as objects of erotic interest—if not simultaneously then at least serially during their lives. By default and linguistic convention, these people are bisexuals.[1]

The effort to account for this cleaving of erotic interest has a long and contentious lineage. For example, there has been considerable debate about the distribution of erotic interests in a given population and also about whether the categories underlying their study make sense. Homoeroticism has been alleged, for example, to be more common in certain nations than others, and in some cases was even attributed to the climate of those places, as was the case in the last century when languid Mediterranean countries were thought given to homosexuality. In fact, homoerotic interest is not necessarily more prevalent in countries where it is simply more visible or socially accommodated.[2] As for the adequacy of the concepts at stake, sex researchers from zoologist Alfred Kinsey to anthropologist Gilbert Herdt have cautioned against taking the terms *homosexual, heterosexual,* and *bisexual* to stand for natural and mutually exclusive kinds of people.[3] They note that human erotic lives are often plastic in a way that defies easy categorization. What is the sexual orientation of an male adolescent who, for example, has sex with both male and female farm animals? What is the sexual orientation of a male who enjoys having sex with a woman in the presence of other sexually aroused men? Because of the variability of human sexual expression, some researchers believe that sexual orientations are distributed across a population in a way that could be mapped onto a bell curve between poles of homoeroticism and heteroeroticism, with most people having some measure of bisexuality in their erotic lives. Others argue that sexual orientation is bimodally distributed, with most people lumped as heterosexual or homosexual at opposite ends of a continuum, with very few bisexuals in between.[4]

These cautions and debates are emblematic of the considerable problem in documenting the numbers of people with gay, straight, and bisexual orientations and determining why people have the erotic interests they have. Although there are obstacles to counting people according to their sexual orientations, social research can study sexual practices, labels people apply to themselves, fantasy content, and household arrangements, and thereby offer useful if not perfect generalizations about the way in which erotic interests divide.[5] Whether science can identify the *causes* or determinants of sexual orientation depends in part on what sexual orientation is and what science is capable of describing about the causes of sexual orientation.

Sexual orientation science in this latter sense has its own skeptics and prophets, respectively vilifying and defending attempts to offer causal account of erotic desire. The most serious challenge to the conceptual possibility of sexual orientation science is that such research is doomed from the start if erotic interests and behaviors are far removed from immediate causal roots in biology and/or psychology and are explicable only in terms of personal choices and social scriptings. By social scriptings, I mean something like the imprint of social forms on human erotic capacities that are otherwise blank slates. The "causes" of sexual interests would be thus akin to the reasons why people are interested in a particular film, not because root causes in human biology or psychology have ineluctably made it popular but because forms of social organization make it so—it is well marketed, it is released at a time of year when many people go to the movies, it has star power, and so on. In short, one could not explain the attraction of the film by the study of its physical properties, the physical mechanisms by which it came to be a film. Some commentators maintain that erotic forms are social constructions in roughly this way.[6] By contrast, researchers in the biological and life sciences typically contend that while erotic desires of human beings are complex, there is no reason to think that some kind of generalized explanations about the origins and development of those desires are entirely beyond causal accounting, no matter if the categories used in those explanations must be tentative and remain open to revision.

In this chapter I will first describe the ways in which science can meaningfully study sexual orientation. I will describe the domain of sexual orientation science and then offer an argument about why it is conceptually coherent to study the biopsychological determinants of sexual orientation even if there are social components to erotic development. Second, I will review some of the 1990s research that has described traits of people with homoerotic interests, traits thought to be suggestive of causal origin. I do not intend to offer an exhaustive overview of the state of sexual orientation science here. My purpose in discussing these reports is primarily expository, to show the kinds of things that are being done by researchers, but I will also describe some of the limitations of these studies to indicate what they do and do not mean about the causation of erotic interests.[7] I will conclude the chapter with a discussion of the sorts of scientific conclusions that are possible in regard to the determinants of erotic desires in general and, since it hogs the limelight, homoerotic desire in particular. It turns out that science has yet to rise to the many challenges it faces in regard to explaining why people have the erotic desires they have. Far from being an archaic nineteenth-century project, sexual orientation science appears to have a rather daunting and meaningful set of challenges ahead of it. Whether sexual orientation science is necessarily heterosexist and prejudicial or whether it is scientifically important are issues separable from its conceptual possibility; I do take up those questions, however, immediately following in chapter 2.

THE DOMAIN OF SEXUAL ORIENTATION SCIENCE

The most accepted usage of sexual orientation defines it in terms of the sex of the object of one's erotic interests. For example, psychiatrist Richard C. Pillard and psychologist J. Michael Bailey describe sexual orientation as many researchers do, as "the sustained erotic attraction to members of one's own gender, the opposite gender, or both—homosexual, heterosexual, or bisexual, respectively."[8] Contrary to the practice of most sex researchers and moralists, I think there is value in specifying both a broad and a narrow sense of sexual orientation. In its broad sense the term *sexual orientation* should probably be understood as referring to the entire range of a person's erotic interests and responsivity, to the full complement of a person's sexual dispositions and behaviors across a lifetime. It would thus include all practices and patterns of erotic fantasy, forms of intercourse, sexuoerotic play, arousal-cue responses, and some patterns of interpersonal affection. In fact, it is possible that erotic interests may blend sex traits and gender traits. For example, a man might be attracted to another male only insofar as that man or boy exhibited behaviors typically associated with females in mannerisms and dress. Sustained erotic attraction toward a given sex is only one part of the constellation of features that compose an individual's sexual orientation. In defining sexual orientation merely in terms of a "sustained" or dominant erotic interest defined around sex traits, the narrow definition fails to acknowledge aspects of sexuality that are just as important to eroticism as attraction based on sex traits.[9]

It would be just as interesting scientifically to know why people have attractions, interests, and behaviors that are no less erotic for being nondominant, nonsustained, and unrelated to the sex traits of one's sexual partners. How is it, for example, that some adolescent boys can lustily engage in sex with male peers but then go on to lead a life altogether lacking in homoerotic relationships? How is it that some women can embrace sex with men until later in their lives, when they find their erotic interests turning toward women? How is it that otherwise straight males and females can be influenced to depart from their accustomed erotic patterns by their circumstances, for example, in what used to be called the "facultative homosexuality" of sex-segregated prisons or military service? How is it that for some ostensibly straight men and women homoerotic sex is merely two or three stiff drinks away?

Sexual patterns that prevail for a short period of time are no less part of a person's sexual orientation than those that endure across even the largest part of life. It may be that the categorization of people according to their dominant sexual interests serves important social and political purposes, but it does not follow that those categories exhaust the domain of sexual orientation, properly speaking, from a scientific or moral point of view. The effort to categorize people into a binary or triadic system of sexual orientation may be a residual effect of a dichotomous understanding of human sex: as there are only two ostensible sexes, the number of possible sexual orientations will be a small integer: one, if everyone is heterosexual; two, if people are either heterosexual or homosexual; and three if people are either heterosexual, homosexual, or bisexual. Sexual orientation science should not, however, assume in advance that people should be studied only in regard to their sustained, dominant erotic interests.

Because of the way I am defining it in terms of sexual responsivity, the broad meaning of sexual orientation is not only complexly constituted, it will not be an invariant trait enduring across a lifespan. Philosopher Frederick Suppe has pointed out that—because of the combinations possible with regard to patterns of sexual fantasy, behavior, arousal-cue responses, and patterns of interpersonal affection—there are hundreds of sexual orientations.[10] The sexual orientation of all human beings will change as they develop, mature, and grow senescent. Each person will see significant changes in sexual orientation across his or her lifetime. The thirteen-year-old boy who has an erotic interest in his gym classmates most often has no interest in thirteen-year-old boys by the time he is fifty. At thirteen this adolescent would have found the notion of sex with fifty-year-old people entirely revolting, but at sixty he might well cast a longing eye toward the fifty-year-old neighbor returning his glances across the garden fence. In fact, if one takes into account such elements as age interests, hair interests, musculature interests, erotic practices, and so on, there are probably thousands of sexual orientations. Interests in particular sex traits are just one component of erotic interests. Sexual orientations do not neatly cleave into two or three anthropologically universal categories.[11]

In the broad meaning of the term, *sexual orientation* is not something different from *sexual preference,* a term favored by some commentators for its connotations of choice and control in one's sexual life. For example, in her book, *Lesbian Choices,* philosopher Claudia Card gives a great deal of credence to the role of choice and options in the emergence of one's sexual interests and commitments, and she is not wrong to do so.[12] Her account captures the way in which choices in different contexts could have ended in different sexual interests, in roughly the way omnivores could have become vegetarians had their lives and the options they had and the choices they made been different, to use one of her examples. Understood as the domain of behaviors that are not "caused" involuntarily in any morally significant sense by biological or physical determinants, choice does play a role in sexual orientation because choices are always required in regard to one's behavior ("I will try to begin a sexual relationship with that blond-haired guy standing languidly at the end of the bar.") and fantasies ("I'm not too busy with work right now and will therefore go ahead and daydream about having sex with a raven-haired football player in a canoe."). As I see it, however, there is nothing contradictory about incorporating this notion of choice into the definition of sexual orientation I am adopting. Paying attention to choice in erotic interests and behaviors may reveal that people differ in their capacities to choose, which matter would be scientifically interesting in its own right.

Philosopher Edward Stein's account of sexual orientation stresses not the voluntary aspect of eroticism but its manifold parts. He says *sexual orientation* refers to erotic desires and dispositions broadly construed according to gender (though not including self-conscious labels or actual sexual practices) whereas *sexual preference* refers to "more fine-grained erotic desires such as desires for sorts of people (e.g., large-breasted women or muscular men) or for particular activities (sadomasochism or being "passive")."[13] This distinction is ultimately arbitrary, for it is unclear why a sustained erotic interest in muscularity is any less part of one's sexual orientation than one's interest in morphologically male human beings. There is no one who could not be characterized in regard to interest in muscularity or breast size; these traits *must* figure in erotic interests in one way or another. Not having a strong interest in the muscularity of a man's buttocks is as much a trait as having a strong interest in that same muscularity. It seems, therefore, unuseful to distinguish between sexual preference and sexual orientation in the strict way Stein has suggested.[14] By drawing all erotic responsivity under the same umbrella, the broad meaning of sexual orientation I am urging here avoids the sorts of border problems that bedevil distinctions between primary and secondary components of erotic interests.

A broadened understanding of sexual orientation has a final advantage over its competitors for an additional reason: its geographical connotations: how one is oriented relative to the points of erotic interest and gratification that are more or less fixed—or perceived as fixed—in a given culture. I take it for granted that no one has a "natural" sexual orientation in the sense that there is a biologically or psychologically inevitable sexual orientation uninfluenced by familial and cultural circumstances, just as no one has a "natural" intellect or language uninfluenced by developmental conditions such as nutrition, family dynamics, enriching stimulation at the right moments of infancy, formal education, and so on. By the same token, I take it for granted that no sexual orientation belongs to people simply by virtue of their culture. Any culture will have visible, dominant, and influential forms of sexual orientation, and societies do inculcate and foster certain sexual orientations at the expense of others. In practice, however, most societies exhibit a range of sexual orientations, regnant mores and official pronouncements notwithstanding, and people are often able to evade dominant sexual codes in one way or another. There will nevertheless appear—and all the more so to children—a fixity to gender roles, to approved sexual behavior, to regnant notions of the purposes of sexuality. There can also appear a near-metaphysical fixity to acceptable gender and sexual behavior. In addition to whatever contributions these social elements may have in a causal sense to the emergence of a given individual's sexual orientation, they will also function as compass points by which a person may be said to be oriented one way or another. A geographical image of sexual orientation thereby reduces the temptation to collapse erotic interests into two or three kinds; on the contrary, there are many points by which to take the measure of sexual orientation.

Acknowledging the breadth and the flux of sexual orientation does not put it beyond the purview of scientific inquiry. It merely follows that sexual orientation science will be complex and that one cannot assume that human beings are robotic biological puppets. It does not follow that because erotic responsivity is mutable across a lifetime or that it involves some degree of choice that there are no biological or psychological determinants of sexual orientation. Even if one assumes, outlandishly, that sexual orientation is only and always the result of choice and that it has no significant causal determinants in psychological development or physiology, it does not follow that it could not be studied scientifically. Population studies might well reveal that socioeconomic factors could predict quite accurately what sorts of sexual practices people in a given population will "choose" and how those patterns are linked to various cultural matters like job availability and venues for socializing, the ultimate metaphysical freedom of individual choices notwithstanding.

Of course, the study of *all* the elements that constitute erotic life would be a broad and ambitious undertaking, and any such undertaking would have to be broken down into manageable parts in order to make meaningful progress. For that reason I will adopt in the rest of this book the narrower and more familiar meaning of *sexual orientation* and restrict my analysis to erotic interest dependent on male and female sex traits of other people. It should be understood, though, that I take erotic interests directed toward male and female traits to be only one subsection of human sexual orientation, and even the narrow sense of sexual orientation cannot mean being interested in males or females and nothing else. One will always be interested in males or females *of a certain kind*, and that kind will vary according to age, muscularity, hair color, and so on. Even the most erotically promiscuous human beings are not interested in males or females undifferentiated in kind.

The questions for science are thus whether there are determinants that cause sexual orientation in the sense that they influence the emergence of one set of erotic interests where others might have otherwise occurred and whether those determinants are within meaningful reach of a testable general hypothesis. Since the last century there has been no shortage of confidence in the ability of science to offer exactly these reckonings.

SCIENCE AND SEXUAL ORIENTATION

In 1905 Sigmund Freud insisted that heterosexuality is as much in need of explanation as homosexuality; he did not think heterosexuality a self-evident outcome of psychological development.[15] Indeed, as a matter of scientific logic heteroeroticism is every bit as legitimate an object of scientific inquiry as homoeroticism. Part of the reason homoeroticism took center stage as an object of scientific inquiry is that, contrary to Freudian counsel, heteroeroticism was assumed to be perfectly obvious and natural, so much the order of things as to be in no apparent need of explanation. By reason of its sheer prevalence and instrumentality in having children that assumption has a psychological plausi-bility to it. But prevalence, familiarity, and reproductive instrumentality do not exempt heteroeroticism from scientific reckoning.

Some commentators, notably feminist critic Adrienne Rich, have turned this standard assumption on its head and gone so far as to characterize heterosexu-ality as being derivative of a fundamental homoerotic inclination in all human beings.[16] In this kind of view heterosexuality is a secondary phenomenon and, as such, is *more* in need of an explanation than the homoeroticism she says is the bedrock relational impetus of all human beings. Rich seems able to make this claim only by eroticizing *all* social relations, which seems unfair because it is better to recognize that human beings have different kinds of emotional rela-tions even if there are sometimes fuzzy borders dividing them. By the same token the idea that heteroerotic identities and relations are constructed around—by defending against—homoerotic impulses is highly suggestive and certainly merits scrutiny. To make the point plain, it may be asked: what do all of society's functionally heterosexist norms protect against if not some degree of homoerotic interest that would otherwise bubble to the surface? It would make no sense to put in place pervasive barriers to homoeroticism unless there existed in fact some corresponding pervasive homoerotic interests to obstruct. Rich offered her argument primarily to describe the way in which social struc-tures and identities work to the disadvantage of homoeroticism; she does not appear especially interested in an empirical assessment of the position. While I am unaware that any researchers in the life or social sciences have taken Rich's account seriously and while it is difficult to see how the proposition might be tested, her theory of heteroeroticism could be subjected to scientific analysis to determine whether heteroeroticism is a primary or secondary phenomenon.

To say that heteroeroticism and the whole domain of human eros could be objects of scientific analysis is not to say that researchers will as a matter of course be drawn to studying what is perceived as obvious. In fact, much scien-tific inquiry is directed toward matters considered deviant in one way or another, toward the phenomena that seem somehow outside the expected order of things, to phenomena unaccountable within accepted paradigms of explanation, to use the familiar analysis of philosopher and historian of science Thomas S. Kuhn. Like people elsewhere, researchers are drawn to the novel, to the odd, to the apparently inexplicable, and for many researchers homoeroti-cism fits that profile exactly. Nevertheless, the impetus to study homoeroticism and other less common sexual interests should not leave the impression that heteroeroticism is *un*caused and immune to the kinds of explanations science is looking for elsewhere. In fact, the study of homoeroticism might well have implications for understanding the pathways of heteroerotic development.

How a human being moves from a single cell at conception to a complex adult human being with erotic interests of a highly specialized kind is a legitimate question whether the orientation that emerges is homoerotic, heteroerotic, or something else. Sexologist John Money has said that "people become homosexual, bisexual, or heterosexual because of what happens to them partly in their prenatal history and partly in their postnatal history."[17] It is the task of sexual orientation science to describe the specific mechanisms of that history and to do so across the entire domain of human sexuality—to the extent that it is possible.

In order to permit sexual orientation to proceed with a clean conceptual bill of health, it is necessary to meet an important objection: that sexual orientation cannot be meaningfully studied by the life sciences. As I have mentioned above, there are camps of thought holding that sexual orientations do not exist in nature in the way, for example, mineral deposits of silver and gold exist in nature, as objective forms unsusceptible to historical and cultural permutations. They cannot therefore be meaningfully studied by the life sciences because sexual orientations and identities have more in common with the roles in a play than with entities in nature.[18] Any number of scholars have, for example, drawn attention to the way in which societies have quite different sexual identities and forms of sexual expression. Some cultures, for example, easily incorporate homoerotic behaviors into their social rituals, while others do what they can to banish all manifestations of homoeroticism.[19] It is not even apparent that what we think of as homosexuality has been the same phenomenon in all cultures and historical periods. The temptation here is to think that culture in its structural norms and implicit values determines what erotic interests will be available to people and what of those interests will prevail. According to this line of thought, it is the cultural forms of a society that determine the warp and woof of erotic interests and identities. It is society that, for example, determines whether the homoeroticism of an era will emulate the pederasty of Attic Greece or the adult relations that prevail in capitalistic democracies around the globe today. To take a strictly social constructionist view, as these sorts of views have come to be known, there are no sexual orientations independent of social practices that produce and sustain them: they are artifacts of culture and therefore inexplicable by the life sciences, which presume that a specific sexual orientation such as homoeroticism is a transhistorical biological phenomenon existing discretely in nature, uninfluenced by social forms.

It would be wrong, however, to infer from cultural plurality and differentiation that sexual orientation is wholly "constructed," i.e., causally dependent on the norms of any given society and causally independent of human biology.

Philosopher Richard D. Mohr has offered some convincing criticism of why social constructionist accounts fail as causal accounts, noting especially that they offer no coherent explanation of how socially prevalent concepts in fact produce the erotic desires manifest within a particular culture or individual.[20] That is, the thesis of social construction—that erotic forms are a function of prevailing cultural norms—cannot also be its own evidence. Social constructionists must show better than any one of them has done specifically how cultural notions of, for example, homosexuality cause people in the culture at large to have and express homoerotic interests and behaviors or any other erotic forms for that matter. Specifically, this reckoning should also be able to explain why one individual rather than another comes to have the erotic interests that he or she has. So far, explanations of this kind have been wanting.

Moreover, even if there are social contributions to the expression of erotic interests, it does not follow that various erotic forms share no common aspects traceable to biology or psychology. Literature professor David Halperin has said that erotic preferences seem no more fundamental than dietary preferences, and he notes that no one seems to be interested in the causes of differences in what people eat. He goes on to say that "sexual preferences should not be thought of as intrinsic constituents of the personality; rather, sexual categories based on preference should be considered culturally contingent."[21] Yet certain aspects of dietary habits are explicable in terms of fundamental human interests in proteins, fats, and sugars—even if the foods available to deliver those dietary elements vary widely from one culture to the next. This does not mean that science, to be meaningful, need describe the necessary and sufficient causality by which Joe Smith, thirty-three years old and self-employed as a building contractor, while standing on a train platform in Chicago on Tuesday afternoon at 3 p.m., has a sudden craving for a bowl of chocolate marshmallow ice cream. In order to be meaningful, sexual orientation science need not either explain exactly why Mr. Smith has, later that same afternoon, the desire to be whipped to orgasm by a midget dominatrix. The science of erotic interests can be meaningful if it describes general patterns of sexual development and expression, even if it cannot enter into the particular forms of each and every sexual desire and behavior.

Mohr has also pointed out that social constructionist accounts have no conceptual basis for the contention that sexual orientation cannot be studied as a culture-independent matter:

> Indeed, most social history is simply irrelevant to the question whether there is an innate biological drive in some people to have erotic encounters with members of their biological sex. Simply showing that different cultures give a different importance to same-sex relations (in some cultures held sacred, in others profane) or

showing that same-sex relations manifest themselves differently, are differently structured between cultures (in some cultures men fuck boys, in others boys fuck men), is completely compatible with the naturalistic claim that there are root biological drives and that they are shaped this way and that by cultural forces and given this and that social importance, just as is done with biological drives to eat or sleep or drink.[22]

Even if it takes manifold forms, there may still be some root drive that determines the general patterns of a person's erotic interests. More radically, science need not suppose the existence of an innate biological drive that is sexual interest itself and that is "in nature" like iron ore is in nature. Science can just as easily proceed on the assumption that there is no fixed homoerotic or heteroerotic drive, no drive in nature that is homoeroticism or heteroeroticism trying to break through, or that this drive is caused in any simple way by anatomy or genetics. Sexual interest might be, to speculate here, epiphenomenal to other biopsychological processes, not a separate "life force" unto itself. It is not the goal of science to demonstrate that there are transhistorical, transcultural sexual orientations and root drives of same—unless there are such sexual orientations and root drives. The goal of science is to explicate the development of erotic interests no matter where and how they occur. Science may discover that certain biogenetic traits dispose people toward one set of erotic behaviors rather than another, but this is very different from saying that sexual orientation exists as a root drive set apart in human nature and that is itself the proper object of causal research.

Ultimately, a thesis of social construction of sexual orientations and identities has value not as a causal account but as an axiom of science this way: that sexual orientations and identities cannot but be influenced by the social context in which people develop and mature. There is nothing in that axiom that rules out scientific investigation of the origin and development of erotic interests by the life or social sciences, since such an approach could in fact accommodate the influences of culture in accounting for the variety and distribution of actual erotic interests.[23] This is why Halperin is wrong to say as he does that "if it turns out there actually is a gene, say, for homosexuality, my notions about the cultural determination of sexual object-choice will—obviously enough—prove to have been wrong."[24] Even if there is a gene "for homosexuality," that erotic interest must of necessity be influenced by culture. The outcome of a gene for homosexuality will be very different for people in societies that accommodate homoerotic interests than in societies that do not. It is ultimately mistaken to cleave biology and culture so strictly, as seems to have been done in most of the "essentialist" vs. "constructionist" debate.

We have long ago given up the idea that human beings spring from a homunculus compacted in sperm; it is time to give up the equivalent idea that there are also fixed erotic forms buried intact inside human beings, that homoeroticism and heteroeroticism are simply sexual interests waiting to break forth apart from all developmental and cultural influence. But acknowledging the important role of experience and development does not disable sexual orientation science. Scientific questions about the ultimate origins of any given person's sexual orientation would remain intact even if no two people on the planet had the same culture and if no two people had the same sexual orientation. It would also be perfectly meaningful to inquire about the causes of phylogenetic diversity in regard to sexual orientation. Were adaptive purposes for the species as a whole being served in the emergence of various social forms of homosociality and homoeroticism?[25] Are human reproductive interests served or hindered by diversity of sexual orientation among its members? Are the interests of human survival served by broad patterns of erotic adaptability? In all these instances the question of why some people evince one sexual orientation or another is a legitimate scientific question and not one that requires the assumption that sexual orientation is explicable in terms of root drives or that it is entirely the doing of culture or biology alone. The answers to be found in a science of this kind may suggest that there are many pathways in erotic development and that determinants of erotic development are subject to a principle of uncertainty. Even so, it is a scientific advance to demonstrate why there are domains of uncertainty where we once only blankly confronted the uncertainty itself.

RECENT REPORTS

Studies about the determinants of sexual orientation bear scrutiny to varying degree. I have selected for discussion here some of those that have attracted a great deal of public interest. I make no representation here that the survey that follows is exhaustive; I hope merely that it is illustrative.[26] The first four reports are in mainstream biological sciences, representing efforts in neuroanatomy, genetics, and dermatoglyphics. I will also discuss a fifth account because it is representative of a genre of sexual orientation study that often dominates the public imagination in regard to the causes of homoeroticism: it is a psychological account that contends that some young males are channeled into homoerotic interests by reason of events involving their fathers. In studies of this kind biogenetic factors are usually excluded as relevant or, less stringently, excluded as decisive with regard to adult erotic interests, and emphasis is put on developmental experiences rather than biological determinants. My goal in the following sections is to introduce the results of these studies and to identify their chief limitations. What studies like these mean for the future of gay people will be the subject of the rest of this book.

Study 1   In 1991 neuroanatomist Simon LeVay published a study of the human brain that reported size differentiation by sexual orientation in a certain neuron group. Before I discuss the specifics of this study, I want to note that it received considerable media attention in part because it used sophisticated microscopic techniques, was conducted by a reputable researcher, and was published in one of the most highly regarded scientific journals in the world, *Science*.[27] Since that time, LeVay has gone on to offer a more comprehensive account of sexual orientation and brain differentiation in *The Sexual Brain* as well as a history of the study of sexual orientation research, *Queer Science*.[28] LeVay has said that the motive for his research was to honor the nature of his relationship with his lover, Richard Hersey, who died with AIDS.[29] LeVay hoped with his brain research, he said, to clarify certain misconceptions about why some people are gay. Whether his research will have that effect or another depends on what the research uncovers and how it is socially received and interpreted. It is not my intention here to follow the course of sexual orientation research as it passes into and shapes public consciousness, though certainly that would be an important study in its own right. Such a study might show that a researcher's motives may not be honored in the breach between the pages of scientific journals and the public understanding of the technical reports given there. My goal here is more modest: merely to describe the central findings of the research and to identify its chief limitations.

In regard to his own interest in the origins of homoeroticism, LeVay has said that he was interested in reports of size differentiations in the brain according to gender, that is, reports that on average certain brain structures appear larger in males or females. In particular, he wondered whether the hypothalamus might not only be differentiated according to gender but according to sexual orientation as well.[30] The hypothalamus is part of the brain that is involved in instinctual and fundamental life functions involving circulation, respiration, metabolism, and so on. LeVay chose to study the interstitial nuclei of the anterior hypothalamus (INAH) because these nuclei occur in the brains of both men and women and are involved with sexual behavior: damage to this portion of the brain (by lesions from accidents, for example) impairs sexual behavior, though without altogether eliminating sex drive. Figure 1.1a shows a schematic representation of these cell groups.

To determine whether these nuclei vary in size according to the sexual orientation of the subjects, LeVay studied tissue samples from forty-one cadavers: nineteen homosexual men (all of whom died with AIDS), sixteen heterosexual men (six of whom died with AIDS), and six presumably heterosexual women (one of whom died with AIDS).[31] He dissected the brain tissue, prepared it, stained it,

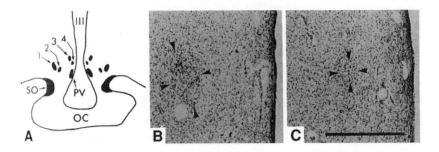

FIGURE 1.1

1.1a is a schematic drawing of the interstitial nuclei of the anterior hypothalamus (INAH). Figure 1.1b shows an INAH3 neuron group from a heterosexual male subject, while figure 1.1c shows an INAH3 neuron group from a homosexual male subject. Reprinted with permission from Simon LeVay, "A Difference in Hypothalamic Structure Between Heterosexual and Homosexual Men," *Science* (1991), 253:1034–1037. Copyright © 1991 American Association for the Advancement of Science.

and examined it microscopically. He found that in his subjects three of the nuclei (INAH1, 2, and 4) did not differ by volume. One did: the INAH3.

LeVay found that on average the INAH3 was almost three times smaller in homosexual men than in heterosexual men and that the smaller size was comparable to the average size of the neuron group in the heterosexual women studied. Figure 1.1b shows an example of a large INAH3, and figure 1.1c shows a smaller INAH3. The full results of LeVay's comparisons are plotted on the graphs in figure 1.2.

As LeVay was unable to identify any women as lesbian via their postmortem medical records, he did not offer any characterization of INAH3 size in women according to sexual orientation. In light of the average size difference between straight men and gay men, he concluded that the INAH3 is dimorphic with respect to male sexual orientation, which he thinks "suggests that sexual orientation has a biological substrate."

In his report LeVay tried to anticipate some of the criticisms that would meet his research, and in his *The Sexual Brain* he enlarged that commentary. Especially problematic was the possibility that because so many of his subjects had died with AIDS, including every gay man in the study, the differences he found were due to pathogenic processes unrelated to sexuality in any way. LeVay is not persuaded that criticism along these lines is sustainable because, as he says, (a) some of the heterosexual men with AIDS did not exhibit any diminution in INAH3 size, (b) no other nuclei showed a size differential, (c) there was no relationship between size of the INAH3 and the duration of disease in an individual, which

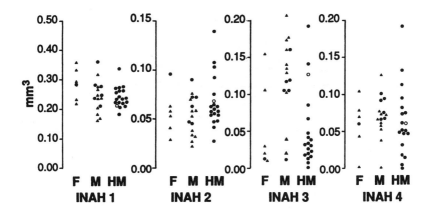

FIGURE 1.2

The four columns map the size distribution of INAH structures 1–4 in LeVay's study. Only the third column shows a distributional difference in the average size of the INAH3 neuron group. F = females. M = heterosexual males. HM = homosexual males.

would be expected if the effects of the syndrome were progressive over time, (d) there were none of the typical signs of cell death or degeneracy, and (e) an additional subject—obtained after the original study—who was homosexual but who did not die with AIDS also exhibited a smaller INAH3.[32] It may yet be the case that something about the course of AIDS in these subjects had an effect on INAH size; in any case, it would be hard to rule out absolutely.

LeVay also defended his study against charges that his sample of gay men was unrepresentative. By way of response, he says that given the commonality of gay sexual practices gay men with AIDS are probably not an unrepresentative sample of gay men as a whole.[33] It is genuinely difficult to know what would count as a representative sample of gay men for purposes of a study like this. Yet a more telling sort of criticism would be: we do not know in fact what the baseline species variability is in regard to INAH3 size. In a larger subject pool the kinds of differences reported here might vanish altogether because of the broad range of INAH3 size that occurs regardless of sexual orientation. Only further study will be able to shed light on this question.

Against media coverage to the contrary, LeVay himself protests that he did not prove that " 'homosexuality is genetic' or some such thing."[34] On the other hand, he has also said that "to put an absurdly facile spin on it, gay men simply don't have the brain cells to be attracted to women."[35] This statement, facile to say the least, invites exactly the kind of misunderstanding LeVay protests as an unfair characterization of his research. First of all, LeVay's findings are probabilistic in nature: they do not support a conclusion that INAH3 size is either a necessary or sufficient condition of sexual orientation. For example, the second-largest INAH3 belonged to a gay man; the third smallest INAH3 belonged to a straight man. There is no INAH3 size at which sexual orientation divides neatly into homosexual or heterosexual categories, with the single bisexual man in the study straddling a dividing point between the two. Sizes of INAH3 range, for gay men and straight men alike, over almost the entire gamut possible for that nucleus. That is, some gay men and some straight men exhibit small INAH3 sizes and some gay and straight men exhibit large INAH3 sizes. Plenty of gay men, therefore, "have the cells" for attraction to women, yet they somehow do not have that attraction. The INAH3 may contribute to the development of erotic interests, but if it does so, it does so in a way that is apparently independent of its size in adult life.

LeVay acknowledges that sexual orientation may not be the sole predictor of INAH size since there are exceptions to the general correlation, but in this regard he says, "It is also possible, however, that these exceptions are due to technical shortcomings or to misassignment of subjects to their subject groups." In other words, the distribution of INAH sizes may involve technical errors on LeVay's part or to misclassification of the men in the first place. If there were errors this systemic, though, it hardly seems reasonable to believe that they would have occurred only in regard to gay men outside their expected volume size. Errors of inclusion—taking straight for gay, gay for straight—would likely have occurred as well.[36] It may be that species-normal variations or, as LeVay notes, even sexual behavior are at work in influencing INAH size. It is entirely possible, as some critics have noted, that INAH size is an effect of actual sexual practices rather than a cause. LeVay is unpersuaded by this view, however, and believes it likely that INAH size is established early in life and influences sexual orientation rather than the other way around. Nonetheless, he does not attribute all erotic interests to the INAH3; he has speculated that it is not merely this neuron group that governs sexual orientation; he expects that a chain of nuclei will be involved.[37]

Developmental geneticist Anne Fausto-Sterling has criticized LeVay's study for mapping something as complex as sexual orientation onto a binary system that presupposes a rigid divide between erotic categories. She is certainly right to do so inasmuch as the terms *homosexual* and *heterosexual* are very rough categories.[38] LeVay does not know, for example, whether his homosexual subjects were functionally heterosexual at one point or whether his heterosexual subjects exhibited some homoerotic desire or behavior at some point in their lives.

Rather than putting people into Procrustean categories of sexual orientation, it might be better to see people as having some sort of general capacity for erotic interests but understand that that capacity varies according to age, situation, learned and entrenched habits, and maybe, yes, some dispositional influences. It may turn out that it would be better to speak of homoerotic interests as a threshold phenomenon rather than as a trait like bone density that exists in isolation—as both effect and cause—from all others. Because of age, situation, and existing erotic habits, some people may more easily have an interest in homoerotic practices than others. Some can be easily nudged over the threshold by circumstances, while others resist homoeroticism more stringently. LeVay's conception of a binary division of people biologically divided into gay or straight is thus of limited value because most of us, if given a different life history, could have had a very different array of erotic interests and not been "homosexual" or "heterosexual" in the rigid sense presupposed by this study.[39] There is a complexity to human erotic behavior that LeVay's anatomical cadaver study simply cannot express.

Neurobiologist and psychiatrist William Byne has noted that testosterone effects, medications being used by subjects with AIDS, and disease effects may have had an effect on comparative INAH size, as would difficulties in measurement of these tiny cell groups.[40] More important, he has even questioned the existence of the INAH cell groups themselves as meaningful units of brain function, a point also made by biologist Evan Balaban who has drawn attention to the way in which staining techniques can create biological artifacts.[41] These sorts of issues are certainly important to the integrity of the kind of research project inaugurated by LeVay and can only be assessed through further study.

Biologist Ruth Hubbard has criticized LeVay's study on a number of grounds, including moral grounds. She points out, first of all, that it is only because homosexuality is stigmatized that anyone looks for its causes, biological and otherwise. "Questions about the origins of homosexuality would be of little interest if it were not a stigmatized behavior. We do not ask comparable questions about 'normal' sexual preferences, such as preferences for certain physical types or for specific sexual acts that are common among heterosexuals."[42] She wonders why erotic interests in hair color, body shapes, and racial types are systematically uninteresting to researchers. She concludes that it is not biological theory that drives sexual orientation research but merely social disdain that was formerly extended to masturbators and other "perverts." In my account of sexual orientation, given earlier, the questions that Hubbard observes have been neglected would in fact be of legitimate conceptual interest. Being consistent in sexual orientation research, putting the whole inventory of erotic interests under investigation, would render these criticisms from Hubbard's moot, though that is not all there is to her criticism.

Apart from the question of the contentious selection of traits to be scrutinized biologically, Hubbard is unconvinced that patterns of erotic interests are necessarily more likely to have a biological basis than the Western trait of writing from left to right, the Semitic trait of writing right to left, or the Asian trait of writing from top to bottom.[43] This seems an overstatement. There may not be biological determinants of these writing patterns, but there may ultimately be biological capacities or dispositions that made it unlikely for any people to write in circles or triangles rather than in linear fashion. In any case, it would be interesting to know if different biological events were involved in learning *how* people learn to write in different ways. This is to say that biology may not be decisive with respect to particular behaviors, but they are not for that reason irrelevant either. Most people do not require substantive education in order to have erotic interests or to have erotic interests in males or females; biology seems therefore to be contributing something substantial to the mix even if one cannot say that biology fates men or women to particular erotic interests.

Hubbard also makes a criticism of biological studies of homosexuality generally. She says that complex traits such as homosexuality are variable and unpredictable in their determinants and will involve a wide range of biological and environmental factors. She therefore cautions against small sample sizes and study populations that all have the trait under investigation. Science needs to sample randomly, she says, and then determine whether or not a person with a given anatomical trait or genetic configuration manifests the trait in question. More mistaken and meaningless correlations will be drawn, she fears, if a researcher studies subjects with the same trait and then asks to what extent they share a particular anatomical trait or genetic configuration.[44] Certainly studies conducted in the manner Hubbard proposes would be more immediately convincing about any correlations they discovered. These kinds of study would be especially convincing if they were transcultural and showed that people from markedly different social backgrounds all showed a correlation between a particular biological trait and erotic interests of a specific kind. But, it must be admitted, the considerable and costly efforts involved make this kind of work much harder to accomplish. There is no denying, though, that this kind of study would be more convincing in regard to its data.

When all is said and done, the work of LeVay is more suggestive than anything else. It certainly does not show that there is a hard and fast correlation between INAH3 size and sexual orientation. The work might point to a biological pathway that is involved in sexual development. Whether or not that correlation holds up to further study remains to be shown. If it does hold up, there are still more questions raised than answered about how the INAH3 functions in regard to erotic interests. How exactly and to what extent does it control the development of one set of sexual interests rather than another? These questions are far from being answered by the current state of research.

Study 2   In a pair of similar studies psychologist J. Michael Bailey and his colleagues studied the likelihood that lesbian or gay twins had a gay or lesbian twin
or adoptive sibling.[45] They recruited subjects through publications directed
primarily toward gay men and lesbians. In the study on males the researchers
found that among their subjects there was a 52 percent likelihood that a
monozygotic twin would also have a gay twin. There was a 22 percent likelihood
that the twin brother of a gay dizygotic twin in would also be gay. The study also
showed that there was an 11 percent likelihood that an adoptive brother would
be gay. In the study on females there was a 48 percent likelihood that a lesbian
monozygotic twin would also have a lesbian twin. There was a 16 percent likelihood that the twin sister of a dizygotic twin would be lesbian. This study
showed a 6 percent likelihood that an adoptive sister would be lesbian.

The researchers believe their studies confirm a moderate to strong genetic
influence in sexual orientation. The adopted siblings were included in the study
to show that familial dynamics or patterns of socialization could not by themselves account for the sexual orientation of children in a given family, and sibling homosexuality was in fact less common when children raised in the same
family group were not biologically related. According to various socialization
theories, patterns of rearing should have roughly the same effect on all children
in a given family, but this hypothesis is not borne out by the results, given the
lack of uniformity in sexual orientation across all children. As pointed out by the
researchers themselves, there is a considerable discordance rate among monozygotic twins who do not always share the same sexual orientation. If genetics
were decisive in regard to sexual orientation, it would be expected that siblings
who have virtually identical genomes would share the same traits. There is, however, only a statistical rather than a necessary correlation between twins in
regard to sexual orientation. Monozygotic twins do not share identical sexual
orientation, and in the females of this study they do so less than half the time.[46]
Genetics cannot explain, according to this data, sexual orientation as a simple
common inheritance. Bailey and his colleagues conclude nevertheless that there
are very likely genetic influences on sexual orientation, and that these may
express themselves during prenatal development through, for example, genetic
influences on hormonal processes and/or neurological development. These
events are perhaps variable enough—that is, susceptible to variation in spite of
the common genetic endowment of twins—to explain the discordance rates
observed between twins in regard to sexual orientation. It is to be noted, too,
that genetics can account for so-called penetrance differences in the expression
of a genetic trait, because different alleles can be involved at the same genetic
locus, but the work establishing these sorts of penetrance effects remains to be
done. Though postulating genetic influences on sexual orientation, these stud-

ies do not offer any suggestion of what genes might be involved or the specific mechanisms by which they would operate. That work would remain for others to do, and work along exactly those lines was not long in coming.

Study 3   In 1993 molecular geneticist Dean Hamer and his colleagues published a report in *Science* that grew out of their interest in determining whether male homosexuality is genetically influenced.[47] They first carried out a pedigree study on 122 subjects, pedigree studies being commonly used in genetic studies to document the occurrence of a particular trait across generations. Their study led the researchers to the conclusion that homosexual men were significantly more likely than straight men selected at random to have male siblings, maternal uncles, and male cousins (related through maternal aunts) who were also homosexual. Figure 1.3 shows representative pedigrees illustrating the matrilineal distribution of male homosexuality in four families.

Hamer and his colleagues noted that female homosexual orientation follows different patterns of family aggregation, but they did not dwell on this topic because their focus in this study was male homosexuality.[48] One potential explanation for the prevalence of gay males in the patterns Hamer and his colleagues observed is that an X-linked genetic trait is involved. In males X chromosomes are heritable only from the mother, thus increasing the frequency of matrilineal X-linked traits in male descendants.

Using blood samples from forty pairs of gay brothers, thirty-eight of which were from the pedigree study, Hamer and colleagues conducted DNA linkage studies to examine the X chromosome for common genetic regions shared by the gay brothers. They found that thirty-three pairs of those gay brothers did share a common genetic region, Xq28. This finding was sufficiently strong, the researchers felt, to conclude that "our data indicate a statistically significant correlation between the inheritance of genetic markers on chromosomal region Xq28 and sexual orientation in a selected group of human males."

This study does not identify a "gene for homosexuality," as many ill-informed reports have had it. In fact, the chromosomal region in question is large enough to contain several hundred genes. Moreover, the genetic action at work is not decisive by itself because there were seven pairs of gay brothers in the study who

FIGURE 1.3
Represented by black boxes, homosexual males occur more frequently on the maternal sides of the families represented here than on paternal sides. Reprinted with permission, Dean H. Hamer, Stella Hu, Victoria Magnuson, Nan Hu, Angela M. L. Pattatucci, "A Linkage Between DNA Markers on the X Chromosome and Male Sexual Orientation," *Science* (1993), 261:321–327. Copyright © 1993 American Association for the Advancement of Science.

DH99002

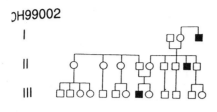

DH99017

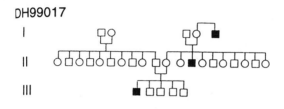

DH321

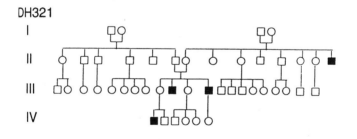

DH210

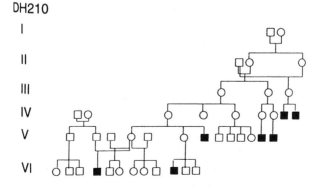

did *not* share the same genetic commonality at this region. The researchers did not despair of this discordance, however, noting that "sib-pairs that are discordant at Xq28 should provide a useful resource for identifying additional genes or environmental, experiential, or cultural factors (or some combination of them) that influence the development of male sexual orientation." In other words, the researchers do not assume that all male homoeroticism is the result of the same developmental pathway. If they are right about the significance of Xq28 involvement in male homoeroticism, their study is clear evidence that there *must be* multiple pathways to the same erotic outcome. Nevertheless, the researchers interpreted their study to suggest a strong genetic involvement in homosexual orientation even if that involvement is quantitative in nature and even if other nongenetic factors can also account for the development of homoeroticism. If there is a direct Xq28 genetic influence on sexual orientation, it will fall to researchers to explain exactly how it works and how homoeroticism emerges in males without that designated genetic region. In any case, a causal explanation of how males develop homoerotic interests because of a particular gene is not to be found in this study. As the researchers themselves note, "The proof for the involvement of genes in a human behavioral trait must ultimately consist of the chromosomal mapping of the loci and isolation of the relevant DNA sequences."

Like the LeVay study before it, this particular study received considerable media attention and, like LeVay, the principal author also went on to write a book about his research: *The Science of Desire: The Search for the Gay Gene and the Biology of Behavior.*[49] The book details the professional and biographical reasons Hamer undertook his study, in addition to offering details of the research project. It also tries to meet some criticisms of the research while sketching some of its social implications. The research itself is in fact of considerable importance for, if true, it establishes hard—if yet unspecified—evidence that sexual orientation in some people is subject to genetic influences. To date, there is still conflict about the meaning of Hamer's results. This study was criticized on a number of grounds, including a refrain familiar with all these sorts of studies: small sample size.[50] Ruth Hubbard also criticized the study for its failure to conduct DNA linkage with the straight brothers of the gay subjects.[51] A high concordance of the Xq28 region in those straight brothers would have strongly suggested that the DNA sequences in question were *not* responsible for gay sexual orientation. As the matter was not pursued, Hubbard contended that the concordance seemed to favor a genetic interpretation only because possibly disconfirming data were not collected. In addition, some other researchers have reported difficulty in replicating Hamer's findings.[52]

To meet these concerns, Hamer and his colleagues did conduct a follow-up study, one that involved both males and females.[53] That second study also showed a high degree of concordance among thirty-three pairs of gay brothers in regard to the Xq28 locus, a concordance that is significantly smaller for their straight brothers who were included this time as control subjects. On the strength of these findings, the researchers concluded that the data indicate that this genetic locus contains genetic influences that increase the probability of homosexual orientation in males. By contrast, the study of thirty-six sib-pairs of lesbian sisters showed no such concordance in the Xq28 locus; their straight sisters, moreover, showed only a degree of concordance at that region that could be predicted by chance. The researchers noted the way in which this study lent credence to the 1993 study of males, and they also concluded that pathways of development are different in males and females for sexual orientation.[54]

This second study notwithstanding, there is much more work to be done before it can be taken as an settled that genes at Xq28 decide the sexual orientation of some males. Evan Balaban has said of the first Hamer study that "they've shown little more than that a group of highly selected men who happen to be homosexual share among them a certain region of the X chromosome at a higher rate than would be expected due to chance."[55] In fact, there is a long way between finding genetic commonalities in a small group of people and making claims about the causal relationship of those commonalities to complex psychobehavioral erotic interests.[56] It may be that the correlation identified in this research holds up under further examination but that it is relevant not to sexual orientation per se but to some other trait that gay men share. Even if a single gene or set of genes were identified that seemed to dispose people to homoerotic interests, science would still have most of its work ahead of it in explaining how that particular mechanism acts and to what extent its influences are amenable to developmental modification.

Study 4   In 1994 psychologists J. A. Y. Hall and Doreen Kimura published a dermatoglyphics study whose findings, they say, are "consistent with a biological contribution to sexual orientation and indicate that such an influence may occur early in prenatal life."[57] Dermatoglyphics studies "the characteristics of ridged skin on the fingertips, palms, toes, and soles of primates and some other mammals." According to Hall and Kimura, dermal ridges are complete in humans at about the sixteenth week of fetal development; genetics are the primary determinants of their form, but they can also be influenced at certain developmental points by a pregnant woman's consumption of alcohol or certain anticonvulsant drugs. Maternal stress has also affected dermal traits in nonhuman primates, and hormonal variations may have similar effects in humans.

Hall and Kimura note that human beings seem to be governed by a rule of somatic asymmetry: where symmetrical body parts differ in size, they generally do so in favor of the right side in males and the left side in females in breasts, testes, and feet, for example. While most males have larger right feet than left feet, most women will have larger left feet than right feet. In regard to dermal ridge counts on the fingers, males have a higher total average compared to females. Yet both men and women generally have a higher average number of ridges on their right hand than on their left. This latter trait is not universally true, however, and there are minorities of both males and females with "leftward asymmetry," a higher number of ridges on their left hand than on their right hand. While females have a lower average ridge count compared to males, the prevalence of leftward asymmetry is higher in females than in males. Hall and Kimura wondered how these patterns would be influenced if their subjects were differentiated by sexual orientation.

Hall and Kimura therefore compared the dermatoglyphics of the thumbs and little fingers of 66 homosexual men and 182 heterosexual men whom they categorized by sexual orientation using the Kinsey scale and self-declarations. They found that gay men and nongay men did not differ significantly according to the total number of ridges present on all their fingers. Consistent with the general trend for human beings, moreover, most gay men displayed a rightward asymmetry, meaning that they had more ridges on their right fingers than on their left. But there was a significant difference between the number of gay men and the nongay men exhibiting leftward asymmetry, with more gay men than straight men exhibiting that minority trait. There was not a significant difference in the prevalence of leftward asymmetry, however, when the gay men in the study were compared to an archival group of 128 heterosexual women. The gay men and straight women showed about the same prevalence rate of leftward asymmetry, though leftward asymmetry was perhaps slightly more common in the gay men than in the women. Hall and Kimura conclude that "the dermatoglyphics of gay men are therefore composites of some male-typical (total ridge count) and some female-typical (directional asymmetry) characteristics."[58]

Hall and Kimura interpret their findings to be consistent with theories of an early biological contribution to adult sexual orientation in men. Like the other research reports mentioned here, their work establishes no universal correlation between a sexual orientation and a physical or behavioral trait. An individual gay man, for example, may have a rightward or leftward asymmetry in his ridge numbers. In fact most gay men share the same number of ridges exhibited by straight men; it is just that a greater number of gay men exhibit the minority trait of leftward asymmetry than would a population of straight men.

The interesting point here is that this study links somatic traits to genetic and possibly hormonal influences, influences that seem to transpire very early in human development. Whether that correlation will withstand further scrutiny remains to be seen. If it does, it may be that there are some genetic or hormonal influences that effect both sexual orientation and somatic development. This is not to say that these effects are causally linked to one another, because the effects could be mutually independent features of a more ulterior developmental process. Hall and Kimura do not identify any specific process whose operation influences sexual orientation or finger ridge patterns. They rightly confine themselves to speculating that there is a biological influence on sexual orientation, one that is somehow conjoined with the determinants of a somatic trait. To postulate this kind of biological influence is far from describing either the locus of that influence (in genetics, drug use, hormones, or all three) or its mechanism (how it brings about its effects). It is fast becoming necessary in sexual orientation science to refrain from speculating that there are early biological influences in erotic development and to start identifying those specific influences so that they may be tested in their own right. Indirect evidence such as dermatoglyphics cannot produce that sort of causal explanation, though it may provide clues about where to look for answers if it helps identify relevant common pathways of development.

Study 5   In 1991 Joseph Nicolosi attributed the origins of male homosexuality in adulthood to psychic injury suffered by a child in relations with his father.[59] It must be said at the outset that Nicolosi hardly sees homoeroticism as a neutral trait that may be studied disinterestedly. On the contrary, he describes it as a major psychological disability: "The homosexual condition, if understood properly, is always a barrier to developmental completion."[60] "I do not believe that any man can ever be truly at peace in living out a homosexual orientation."[61] Living in a gay relationship only compounds the problem: "There is not only an inherent anatonomical [*sic*] unsuitability, but a psychological insufficiency that prevents a man from taking in another in the full and open way of heterosexual couples."[62] It is not surprising that Nicolosi therefore says, "I do not believe that the gay life-style can ever be healthy, nor that the homosexual identity can ever be completely ego-syntonic."[63] Given this view of homoeroticism, Nicolosi has much to say about the psychological professions, which he believes have abandoned homosexual men and abrogated their responsibilities to care for people suffering from homoeroticism.[64] Nicolosi therefore calls for reopening the question of the pathology of homoeroticism and reconsidering the merits of gay-affirmative therapy. My interest in Nicolosi's work is not to assess the alleged deficits he attributes to homoeroticism or to engage the debate about whether the psychological professions should revive their previous judgments about homoeroticism as disordered, though surely there are many things to say about these issues.[65] I want merely to consider his account of the origins of homoeroticism. By any measure, this account fails to meet minimal standards of scientific credibility.

Nicolosi believes that "homoeroticism is a developmental problem that is almost always the result of problems in family relations, particularly between the father and son. As a result of failure with father, the boy does not fully internalize male gender-identity, and develops homosexually."[66] The primary cause of homosexuality is, Nicolosi says, "not the absence of a father figure, but the boy's defensive detachment against male rejection."[67] In effect, at an early age, in his second year, a boy experiences an alienation from his father, an alienation in which his mother may play a supporting role. The boy, therefore, fails to identify as male but forever after seeks to do so via an eroticization of other males, a task that is doomed to failure by reason of the inherent limitations of homoerotic desire: "Homosexuality is an alienation from males—in infancy, from father, and in later life from male peers. By eroticizing what he feels disenfranchised from, the homosexual male is still seeking this initiation into manhood through other males."[68] Nicolosi attaches only ancillary significance to biological determinants of sexual orientation. He says, "A review of the physiological literature demonstrates that genetic and hormonal factors do not seem to play a determining role in homosexual development." He nevertheless grants that "some predisposing factors may make some boys more vulnerable to gender-identity injury."[69]

Nicolosi wrote his book before the appearance of the reports by LeVay, Hamer, and Bailey mentioned above, and it is indeed true that there is little convincing evidence in the literature that anatomical, physiological, or genetic factors categorically play what Nicolosi calls a "determining role in homosexual development." By the same criterion, though, Nicolosi offers no evidence— beyond the conceptual plausibility of his claims—to substantiate the causal analysis he offers or the efficacy of the therapy he builds thereon. Nicolosi's account is of a kind familiar in psychological studies that purportedly draw on clinical experience to generalize about the origins of a particular behavioral trait. Accounts of this kind concern themselves with a retrospective determination of causality on the basis of various theoretical commitments about the nature and developmental processes of human beings and the contents of dialogue between subject and therapist. While the adequacy of theoretical concepts and the contents of clinical interactions can be studied in principle, Nicolosi offers no controlled empirical evidence to support any of his theoretical or interpretive contentions.[70]

Nicolosi's work is methodologically unsound in that it does not describe how he recruited his subjects or how he studied them in order to arrive at his conclusions. There is no effort made to achieve a random sample of gay men or even the subset with whom Nicolosi is dealing: men dissatisfied in one way or another with their homoerotic interests. At the very least, a comparison group might have revealed whether the reports of psychic injury at the hands of the father were widespread in the population (regardless of sexual orientation) or whether they were overrepresented in gay men. A comparison group of siblings could have shown, for example, whether brothers in the same family were subjected to the same sorts of psychic injuries and with what effect on their sexual orientation.[71] Problems of this kind are familiar to critics of psychodynamic accounts, but because they are familiar they may be avoided. Nicolosi has chosen to offer the same sort of unsubstantiated claims about psychic events that determine homoeroticism that clinical therapists have expounded all too often during the better part of this century.

It is also unclear why Nicolosi's theory is thought to be an improvement over any of its competitors at explaining the origins of sexual orientation in gay men. Many of these theories were reviewed in brief by Bieber and colleagues. Some of these are merely quaint, while others are more complex and demand close analysis as to their causal assertions about the nature of erotic development.[72] What theoretical or evidential deficits of any of these theories are improved upon in Nicolosi's analysis of homoeroticism as a defensive reaction against gender deficit? Even if we do not compare his account to others, Nicolosi's views run into trouble within the confines of his own claims. Suppose we improved on Nicolosi's science and took a random sample of gay men and did compare them to a random sample of their own brothers and the population at large. Suppose we found a common psychic injury in the gay men, an injury unlikely to be purely coincidental. Even if we had evidence of an injury of this kind, we would still have no evidence that the psychic residue of that injury is necessarily the key determinant of sexual orientation. It would still be necessary to sort out whether this injury was cause or consequence of some other factor disposing a child to homoeroticism. Nicolosi himself admits there may be biological dispositions in some boys to various sorts of psychic injuries. If so, this injury could be altogether epiphenomenal to the real causes of sexual interests. The psychological injury might be merely one element in a constellation of events that determine sexual orientation, and not necessarily the most important one, or it might even be simply a by-product of homoerotic development, a vulnerability typical in boys disposed for other reasons to homoerotic development. Nicolosi's attribution of causality to injurious psychic events is overstated even if no comparison to other methodologies or studies is made.

It is certainly possible to study psychological claims empirically—provided the key terms are specific enough to be framed in ways that can be tested. It is unclear that Nicolosi's key terms or conclusions could be tested this way. For example, he says, "Failure in relationship with father may result in failure to internalize male gender-identity."[73] One way this claim certainly should not be tested is to ask gay men if there was a failure in the relationship with their father, for it is hard to imagine that there are many children, regardless of gender, who do not experience some psychic injury in their relations with their parents. If, moreover, the respondents think that an affirmative answer will offer some explanatory benefit regarding their sexual orientation, they will be likely to offer up exactly such an injury. Or the injury may be real enough but causally irrelevant to the origins of erotic interests. If this study were to be meaningful, Nicolosi would have had to spell out in detail the nature of the alienating event he thinks key and tried to uncover independent evidence of this injury. As it is, Nicolosi leaves the nature of the alienating injury so general that it cannot be meaningfully tested; he retrieves evidence in favor of his thesis in a way that can only be prejudicial to impartial results.

There is, too, a glaring conceptual error underlying this account: Nicolosi assumes that what it means to have male gender identity is to express erotic interest in females. This simply does not follow. A child can well internalize a male identity—that is, to believe unequivocally in his maleness—and yet not express erotic interest in females. There is no inherent meaning of maleness that requires exclusive erotic interest in females; the most one can say is that most morphological males have erotic interests primarily in morphological females, for male gender identity is entirely compatible with erotic interests in males, females, and males and females. Not only do some cultures incorporate homoerotic interests in their notions of what it is to be a male, most men with homoerotic interests have entirely conventional gender identities. One might want to argue that as a matter of definition part of what it means to be male is to have erotic interest in women and to express certain sex-typical behaviors. It is unclear, however, why this normative and exclusionary definition should prevail when, anthropologically speaking, erotic interests and behaviors of men— and gender constructs of masculinity—range much more widely in male gender identity than Nicolosi's definitional fiat acknowledges. It should simply not be assumed that homoerotic interests fall outside the domain of male gender identity properly speaking.

In the end, Nicolosi's interpretive study of homoeroticism has more in common with aesthetic or narrative interpretation than it does with scientific research. I am not saying that the particulars of Nicolosi's claims are not true. It may very well be the case that gay men suffer some sort of psychic injury during their second year of life more commonly than straight men and that their fathers are to blame for it. This injury may well play a role in their psychosexual development. On these matters I profess myself agnostic. Nicolosi has, however, offered no credible reason for thinking these alienating injuries exist and have the consequences he describes, and the same limitation holds true when it comes to his claims about the ability of gay men to adopt more gender-typical roles and thereby develop and act on heteroerotic interests. The history of psychology is littered with psychological accounts that purport to offer a more or less definitive account of how men and women come to have homoerotic interests. Many of them could well serve as case studies in science gone badly wrong. Nicolosi's work represents a scientific improvement on none of them.

THE FUTURE OF SEXUAL ORIENTATION SCIENCE

It is not a conceptual mistake to think that at least some of the determinants of sexual orientation can be studied scientifically in an individual or population. Erroneous assumptions can, however, profoundly disable the worth of any such undertaking. At the very least, sexual orientation research should not go forward on the simplistic and erroneous assumption that there is a trait in human beings that is eroticism itself or that particular erotic interests and/or behaviors are determined only by a single and unitary set of preconditions. It may be that the origins of erotic interests are better traced to capacities, to dispositions that can unfold in a variety of ways than to traits that manifest themselves in a rigidly uniform way, even if at some point these original capacities become more or less petrified and resistant to modification. It is also important to understand that people can have erotic interests that defy categorization in a simple system of exclusive homosexuality and exclusive heterosexuality or even a system that adds bisexuality to the mix. It is not the end product that is of interest in sexual orientation science so much as the path by which sexual interests emerge and prevail over other possible outcomes in both individuals and populations alike.

In any case, because of the plasticity of human erotic interests sexual orientation science will likely find that erotic interests are underdetermined by biological contributions. To a certain extent people's circumstances and choices will decree their sexual orientation as much as their biology. It may be that part of the reason people have the sexual orientations they do is akin to the reason people end up living where they do, having the jobs they do, and having the entertainment interests they do: for biographical reasons rather than because of genetic, anatomic, or hormonal imperatives. It is unlikely that the male homoeroticism in the adult initiation rites of the tribal people Gilbert Herdt called the Sambia depend on those men having the smaller INAH3 neuron sizes Simon LeVay found in some of his gay male subjects in urban California.[74] Many of the men in LeVay's study did somehow find their way to homosexuality despite the fact that their INAH3 were as big as or larger than those of straight men. So too did some of the men in the Hamer study come to homosexuality without the expected genetic traits at chromosomal region Xq28. Even if it turns out that there are biological dispositions toward some erotic interests, they will be meaningful only in developmental context. If a male child with a biological disposition toward homoeroticism were born and raised in a context in which he had *absolutely no* contact with or knowledge of men, he could hardly develop homoerotic interests. Introduced after his sexual maturity to men, he might be utterly incapable of reconfiguring the ways in which he had learned to take sexual satisfaction. For similar reasons, children born without any putative disposition toward homoeroticism might be socialized into homoerotic practices if their environments offered that kind of sexual satisfaction as a legitimate and socially accessible option. As it is, human beings are sufficiently plastic in their development that many if not most of us could have learned a variety of different sexual repertoires if only circumstances had so required.

Sigmund Freud once observed that "it seems probable that the sexual instinct is in the first instance independent of its object; nor is its origin likely to be due to its object's attractions."[75] He therefore rightly rejected the "crude hypothesis that everyone is born with his sexual instinct attached to a particular sexual object."[76] One cannot know in advance—in any sort of innate or congenital way—the sensuous pleasures of, for example, touching a man's cheekbones or a woman's breasts; and neither are the physical properties of high cheek bones or shapely breasts sufficient to explain their erotic attraction or to explain why erotic attraction for them should be felt by men or women exclusively. For this reason the application of the term *heterosexual* or *homosexual* to a child immediately at birth would be meaningless because sexual orientation is as much about experience as it is about any dispositions that might be given in biology.

It is necessary to clear away other confoundings that obscure the goals of sexological research. In most studies, for example, sexual orientation has been significantly underdifferentiated as an object of inquiry, as Frederick Suppe has noted.[77] This failure to differentiate the various components of erotic behavior and gender roles is glaringly evident in regard to the frequent conflations of eroticism with other behaviors. For example, when asked about the origins of their homoeroticism, some men describe their childhood preference for playing with dolls, avoidance of rough play, and so on.[78] They point, that is, to nonerotic behaviors. Many researchers have understood homoeroticism in terms of gender or social nonconformity, even though activities that are perceived as evidence of male homosexuality—lisping, ways of walking, aversion to rough-and-tumble sports—are not properly speaking aspects of sexual orientation just as a preference for playing softball is not part of the erotic nature of lesbianism itself. Properly speaking, these activities do not constitute sexual orientation in the erotic terms I have stipulated above. Sexual orientation science should resist conflation of biological and social aspects of homoeroticism into an undifferentiated whole. Sexual orientation science should not mistake homoerotic interests for the behavioral roles in which they are permitted or for correlative behaviors that may accompany sexual orientations. That gay men are overrepresented at florist conventions and straight men overrepresented in the Pentagon does not mean that sexual orientation ordains people to particular social and behavioral roles. The social deployment of people according to sexual orientation and certain common behaviors of gay people may turn out to be better explained by mechanisms of social stratification than by root biological causes. It must be acknowledged, though, that some behaviors might be linked to sexual orientation because of common developmental influences. This is not to assume that these behaviors cause sexual orientation or vice versa. It is merely to acknowledge that traits may be linked in biopsychological development.

By observing these cautions, research is better situated to avoid the expectation that there is a single unitary cause of sexual orientation and to avoid mistaking effect and cause. To stress the importance of developmental experience is not to undercut the worth and significance of biological research. Research may well prove that there are genetic or neurological dispositions toward learning one set of erotic interests more easily than another. In such a view genetic or neuron groups would not cause homosexuality in any simple sense, but they might well be crucial to the pathways of early learning, memory, and social adaptation. These biological factors, decisive at early stages of development, would "cause" sexual orientation in the sense that they determine lasting adaptations that fundamentally control the way in which people can learn to take sexual pleasure. Some genes or brain structures might, for example, be responsible for the neurological organization of early social experiences and thereby entrench pathways of learning that are themselves more or less likely to end in one sexual orientation rather than another. A hypothesis of this kind would go a long way toward explaining why people, especially children, retain homoerotic orientations despite the formidable cultural obstacles put in the way of same-sex relations. If a hypothesis of this kind is borne out by further study, part of the answer to the question of why people have the sexual orientations they have would be something like this: some people are best suited to learn preferences for same-sex interests and less suited to learn erotic preferences for different-sex objects; in others the learning dispositions are reversed. These dispositions do not mean that other kinds of learning cannot occur, they would mean only that other learning will be more difficult.

Psychologist Daryl J. Bem's proposal about the origins of homoeroticism strikes me as a meaningful conceptual paradigm for conceiving of erotic interests as causally influenced by the interplay of biological and developmental influences.[79] Bem's proposal is less concerned with accounting for the existence of *classes* of persons based on their erotic interests than with the development of any given person's homoerotic interests. Bem proposes that biological features (genes, for example, or brain structures) code for temperaments in children. Gender atypical temperaments (reflected in interests and behavior) can produce feelings of difference from one's gender peer group in both males and females. Bem says these felt differences lead to "heightened nonspecific autonomic arousal that gets eroticized to that same class of dissimilar peers: Exotic becomes erotic." That is, children who feel themselves different in some important way from their peers come to eroticize those from whom they feel different, namely, gender-typical children of their own sex. This eroticization proceeds along pathways of psychological development involving the sexual imprinting process and opponent process, the latter process involving the production of certain psychic consolations associated with formerly anxious experiences. What once threatened (as in parachuting from a plane for the first time) now exhilarates.

Thus constructed, Bem's account takes biological effects for granted rather than offering any specific reckoning of how genes or anatomy code for different temperaments. In order for his proposal to be validated, it would remain to be demonstrated just how biological features code for particular temperaments. Indeed, it would need to be demonstrated that these temperaments exist in the way he says they do and that they are a primary developmental event in erotic interests and not an effect of other developmental processes that are themselves more causally responsible for erotic interests. It would also remain to be shown how many gay people do not have a strict erotic identification with gender-typical members of their same sex but in fact eroticize gender-atypical behavior as well. My purpose in mentioning Bem's account is not to defend it as true—for there are many unanswered questions in its proposals—but to illustrate the kind of conceptual unity between biological and psychodevelopmental processes that will be necessary to account for the determinants of sexual orientation. This account possesses the advantage that it does not suppose an opposition between biological determinants and social construction because it does not suppose that erotic forms are simply fated by biology independent of experience or impressed by culture on a blank biological slate.

It is worth repeating that there is nothing in an explanatory model of this kind that maintains that people disposed toward one sexual orientation rather than another are exclusively and forever bound to those dispositions and *unable* to take pleasure in different-sex objects. It is only to say people with these dispositions will be less able and therefore less likely to learn a preference for different-sex objects, and the same sort of situation prevails in regard to heteroeroticism. A young male with no real psychological interest in homoerotic relations may nevertheless learn to take sexual pleasure with males if he, for example, has sex with men in order to make money. He may learn that part of his disinclination toward homoeroticism is cognitively grounded, namely, he has *learned* that homoeroticism is repugnant, which lesson becomes incompatible with his own experience. Though not a "native speaker" of homoeroticism, he can learn enough of the "language" to serve him well.

It is true that a great deal of sexual orientation science belongs on the intellectual wreckage heap. Oddly enough, it is probably better for sexual orientation science that those reports molder there. It is to be remembered that one of the principle activities of science is falsification.[80] It would be worse for sexual orientation research if many prior accounts of the origins of homoeroticism had not been advanced and falsified, else we might still be tempted to ascribe homoeroticism to languid climates, the overeducation of women, or hypersensitive genitals. It is better that we do not believe that homoeroticism can be cured in males, for example, by testicular transplants or chemical and electrical aversive therapy.[81] It is better that we know that hatred of men does not "cause" lesbianism. This is not to say that any and all scientific guesses about the origins of sexual orientation are worth pursuing, even for purposes of falsification, for they are surely not. Joseph Nicolosi's account, for example, fails to meet even minimal standards in hypothesis formulation, evidence gathering, and corroboration. Accounts as ill-substantiated as his have more in common with folklore shared around the campfire than with hard science. At this point in sexological history we would be better off without yet another scientifically unsupported, usually untestable account of homoeroticism as the consequence of psychic injuries inflicted by a bad father or worse mother. Many of the worries about the ill effects of sexual orientation science could be avoided, I suspect, if science in the field were held to higher standards than those that sometimes prevail among even the most reputable journal and book publishers.[82]

What sexual orientation science discovers will depend on what is asked of it, the limits of its methodologies, and the extent to which erotic dispositions are amenable to causal explanation. Will science be able to determine why a given individual is disposed toward males or females as erotic choices? Will science be able to account for the distribution of erotic interests across a population? Maybe. Part of the reason for this hesitant answer is that there is no unitary meaning to the term *cause* in scientific explanations. Causal explanations can involve any of the following conjunctions: (a) invariant associations, (b) necessary and sufficient conditions, (c) contingent and necessary conditions, (d) functional dependencies, and (e) retroactive connections.[83] Explanations of all these kinds have been offered in regard to the cause of sexual orientation, and what they establish can fall far below the powers of explanation and prediction approaching metaphysical certainty or even the practical certainty human beings like to have in manipulating events in their experience. Though of late most researchers are rightly cautious in regard to claiming that their work establishes all necessary and sufficient conditions of human sexual orientation, some explanations of erotic desire have not been so circumspect, especially in those psychological accounts that have vastly overstated the significance of their evidence. Gradually, though, causes that are scientifically meaningfully may come to light in regard to the development of erotic interests, even if these causes do not fully establish necessary and sufficient relations between cause and effect.

As it is, science has not yet identified any definitive evidence that a particular person is causally destined to have a particular sexual orientation because he or she has a specific neuroanatomical, genetic, dermatoglyphic, psychological, or other trait. If some version of the disposition-and-learning hypothesis I have been describing is credible, depending on which capacities of learning prevail and depending on the way in which people are capable of learning erotic attachments, people may be strongly shifted by biology toward one sexual orientation or another without, however, being foreclosed in some capacity to learn other erotic pleasures. This position is speculative, of course, and it remains to sexual orientation science to examine the credibility of evidence that might be offered on behalf of the specific causal pathways involved and to determine how independent of those pathways human sexual choices finally are.

Another reason for hesitance about the ultimate explanatory power of sexual orientation research has to do with the complexity of the subject itself and the way in which it is connected to social values and debates. Sexual orientation science is vulnerable to distorting influences of superstition, quackery, and ill-substantiated science. The simple view of science as a body of knowledge entirely abstracted from embedded cultural beliefs is hard to credit, since science always transpires under the pervasive influences of morality, politics, and religion. Given those influences and the multiple meanings of causality, one can predict that science will almost necessarily incur error in its efforts and all the more so in a matter as complex and as contested as human sexuality. As it is, sexual orientation science has spent a great deal of time studying what have turned out to be stereotypes of gay men and lesbians. But in its commitment to the testability and refutability of its conclusions, the scientific process at least has the saving grace that it adheres as a matter of principle to a methodology that requires self-correction. In any case, though, a fallible process is predictable as a matter of course. Research into sexual orientation cannot therefore be objectionable simply because it cannot achieve infallible results in every research report.

The discussion above should make clear that the studies by LeVay, Bailey and colleagues, and Hamer and colleagues are not as the media headlines would make them out to be: enormous leaps forward in the attempt to uncover the causal mechanisms by which people have the erotic interests they have. Instead, the reports discussed above are but incremental additions to a fallible scientific literature, and researchers will have to toil long and hard to determine what ultimate explanatory utility is to be found in them, if any, or whether they are merely biological stereotypes. In some ways these reports are more significant as evidence about what we do not know than about what we do know in regard to the biology of sexual orientation. It is impossible to say whether sexual orientation research will be able to offer all the explanations demanded of it. It may well prove that research will uncover some domain of uncertainty that thwarts ambitions to explain every erotic interest and behavior. Research may well find that the causes of sexual orientation are too multiple and too unpredictable to be characterized in any easy way or that some of them are matters more suited to the methods of biography than biology. All other things being equal, there probably are describable reasons why some people systematically prefer strawberry to butterscotch flavorings, or vanilla to chocolate. At the moment, however, these reasons are too remote and of insufficient interest to be taken as important topics in gustatory and olfactory science. Sexual interests may be just as far away in terms of scientific capacity and research interest. Nevertheless, if there are limits to the powers of sexual orientation science, they will only become evident by looking for them and by making a lot of mistakes along the way. There is no logical obstacle, though, to thinking that we will eventually prove equal to the task of explaining the causes of sexual orientation—to the extent they can be explained.

The goal of sexological science in regard to sexual orientation is clear, even if the ability to approach that goal is yet unclear. John Money has said, "Sexological science has not yet advanced to being able to formulate a causal explanation of gender transposition, specifying all necessary and sufficient determinants in the degree of detail that would permit its prediction, induction, prevention, or reversal."[84] For Money homoeroticism belongs in the domain of "gender transposition," which he defines as "the interchange of masculine and feminine expectancies and stereotypes mentally and in behavior and appearance."[85] Whether homoeroticism should be seen in this way or not, if science achieved the goals Money sets out here, a scientific armamentarium would exist that has the capacity to (a) predict the nature of any given individual's sexual orientation, (b) to influence the emergence of that orientation, (c) to prevent the emergence of any unwanted sexual orientation, and (d) to reverse any unwanted sexual orientation that occurred. Given a history of heterosexist medicine in heterosexist culture, it is little surprising that some commentators worry about the extent to which a science thus perfected could be used as a political instrument against gay people.

Because of the powers that sexual orientation research might produce, some commentators have condemned it as necessarily heterosexist, which is something different from saying that it is impossible in principle. Even if sexual orientation science is possible, is there a convincing moral warrant for going forward with it or do worries about its ideological nature and prejudicial effects undermine its moral credibility? I take up this question in the next chapter and try to show that sexual orientation research being possible it is also scientifically meaningful and not inextricably linked to heterosexist impulses.

2 ||||||||||||||||||||||||||||||||||||||||||||||||||||||||||||||||||||||||||||||||

THE VALUE OF SEXUAL ORIENTATION RESEARCH

In the late nineteenth century and in a substantial portion of this century the opinion prevailed among a great many Western psychologists and medical practitioners that homoeroticism was a serious disorder of psychic and/or biological origin. For example, Richard von Krafft-Ebing's 1886 *Psychopathia Sexualis* gave homoeroticism considerably more attention than even his most macabre accounts of corpse mutilation, bestiality, flagellation, and fetishes.[1] Despite the widespread nature of that view at the time, psychological or medical interest in the nature and origins of homoeroticism is nevertheless a cultural artifact novel to the nineteenth century, not a transhistorical opinion. Before that century medicine scarcely noticed homoeroticism let alone considered it fit for investigation. For the greatest part of Western history the origins of homoeroticism held no scientific interest whatsoever. This is not to say that homoeroticism was without moral, religious, and legal significance, only that until the nineteenth century biomedicine did not find homoeroticism interesting or legitimate as the object of inquiry.

Starting in that century characterizations of homoeroticism as a medical disorder quickly joined and sometimes supplanted prevailing social and ethical characterizations of homoeroticism, characterizations that had been couched almost exclusively in the language of morality and religion. Discursively speaking, medical terminology displaced moral characterizations and became constitutive of homoeroticism itself: homosexuality was construed as inherently pathological as a disease in its own right or as a symptom of underlying disease. This historical shift of perspective did not occur in a vacuum. During the rise of *scientia sexualis* the social authority of medicine was beginning to coalesce into new forms and strengths. Invested with new authority and social prestige, medical judgments of pathology spread widely and quickly throughout a society already prepared on other grounds to believe the worst about homosexuality.[2]

Despite being long familiar in the social, moral, and literary traditions of the West as eros, homoeroticism as pathology was a new conceptual venture, permitting analysis in the rhetoric and tropes of biomedicine. With this pervasive transformation in discourse, medicine's attention to eroticism in general and homoeroticism in particular opened whole new vistas of scientific investigation and offered a highly saleable product to meet the need of its own invention: treatment for disordered sexual desires. This latter point is worth special emphasis: the characterization of homoeroticism as pathological created a great deal of theoretical and experimental problems capable of engaging a broad front of clinical practitioners and researchers. Most of this treatment and research went forward under the banner of protecting people from a grave psychological ill and moral disorder. It is not my intention to describe how homoeroticism emerged as the object of scientific inquiry at the time it did and with what social consequences, though that would be an inquiry eminently worthwhile in its own right. I make these observations merely to underline the artifactual nature of the inquiry and to indicate the kind of spur that drove biomedical investigation of homoeroticism.[3]

In this chapter I will look at some of the ways in which sexual orientation research is connected to its social contexts. I will argue that although pathological interpretations of homoeroticism have dominated sexual orientation research thus far, with plenty of villainous consequences, the determinants of erotic interest may be conceived and pursued independently of those interpretations, if difficultly so. That is, the origins of erotic interests and behaviors can be studied as phenomena in their own right without an overriding assumption of pathology. Contrary to some critics of sexual orientation research, I will try to show how attempts to explain the origins and manifestations of homoerotic interests and behaviors can be conceptually separated from the assumption of pathology. Even if science is value-laden in conceiving its projects and priorities, mechanisms for correction exist in reducing the effects of implicit and unrecognized values and assumptions.

An additional argument raised against sexual orientation research is that it is of scant scientific interest. No one should care, according to this view, why people have the sexual orientations they do, any more than anyone should care why people favor the use of their right or left hand in their daily tasks. Issues like these are simply not important from a theoretical point of view and were sustained in science as long as they were, so goes the argument, only because of discredited moral viewpoints that left-handedness and homosexuality are inherently inferior to their counterparts. On the logic of this position sexual orientation research should not be morally censored so much as abandoned amid the ruins of trivial science. I will try to show that there are sound theoretical reasons for conducting sexual orientation research, reasons that do not depend on outmoded moralistic viewpoints. Even if left-handedness and homoeroticism are fully approvable from a moral point of view, they may still be studied in worthwhile ways.

HISTORICAL CONTEXT

Conclusions about the pathology of homoeroticism—whatever its ultimate origins—pervaded and prevailed in even the most august medical organizations from the nineteenth through the better part of the twentieth century. In 1952, when it first drew up its diagnoses in a formal classification, the American Psychiatric Association (A.P.A.) characterized homosexuality as a sociopathic personality disturbance.[4] In a 1968 revision the A.P.A. declined to retain that exact classification but nevertheless characterized homosexuality as a mental disorder.[5] That judgment lasted until 1973, when the A.P.A. accepted a committee report recommending the declassification of homosexuality as necessarily a disorder of any kind, though it did as a matter of compromise retain the diagnosis of "ego-dystonic homosexuality" which provided a justification for treating those who suffered from their homosexuality. All others with homoerotic interests were, however, accepted back into the fold of the mentally healthy.[6] That 1973 committee decision was supported by a majority vote of the A.P.A. membership in 1974. Later on even the diagnosis of ego-dystonic homosexuality was discarded, but the A.P.A. still recognizes the diagnosis of "sexual orientation distress" to describe people who suffer from unwanted sexual orientations.[7]

Needless to say, where there is a judgment of pathology or dystonia there is a prima facie medical and moral justification to proceed with research aimed at identifying the origins of and possible interventions with homoeroticism. Even now, because there is a medically recognized category of sexual orientation distress, therapeutic research into homoeroticism (and other sexual orientations that potentially cause distress) remains a medically justified venture. This view is not idiosyncratic to U.S. medical organizations.

While medical professional groups in many countries have adopted views similar to those currently held by the A.P.A., there is not uniform agreement around the world that homoeroticism is nonpathological. At present considerable numbers of health practitioners around the world believe homoeroticism to be a disorder of one kind or another. A 1994 survey conducted by the A.P.A., for example, showed that most psychiatrists in Belarus, Brazil, China, India, Poland, Romania, Spain, and Venezuela still consider homosexuality to be an illness.[8]

Even medical personnel sympathetic to men and women with homoerotic interests have often found homoeroticism a failed sexuality—if not a disorder, then
at least a psychosexual immaturity—and therefore counseled various methods
of treatment and prevention, thus fueling continued research interest in the area.
For these medical professionals and those with unwanted erotic interests, the
origins of homoeroticism are very much a live and legitimate question. Indeed,
the whole weight of medical ethics is brought to bear upon this search inasmuch
as it counsels biomedical practitioners and researchers to relieve human disorders and suffering.

The lingering effects of judgments that homoeroticism is pathological or
disordered or stressful in one way or another continue, then, to drive interest in
the origins of homoeroticism. This is hardly surprising. What is surprising is
that even though major medical professions in the United States no longer clas-
sify homoeroticism as pathological in itself, there appears to be as much interest in the causes of sexual orientation now as there was during the time psychiatric and psychological professions formally declared homoeroticism disordered. One key difference between the past and the present is, however, the way
in which this interest is formulated and justified. For example, some commentators now defend patient preference—and not pathology—as the justification for going forward with research into the causes and treatments of sexual
orientation.[9] In this view one's erotic interests are no more or less than just
another trait, and there is no reason that an individual must accept that trait as
immutable. Sexual orientation therapy is thus the cosmetic surgery or liposuction of psychology and psychiatry.

In some ways it may now even be easier than, say, forty years ago to conduct
sexual orientation research because less social stigma attaches to the subject of
sexuality in general and to homoeroticism in particular. As J. Michael Bailey has
observed, not only are more and more graduate students expressing an interest
in questions of sexual orientation, but straight men are entering the field, which
he interprets as evidence that stigmas about homosexuality are dissipating.[10] It is
certainly now easier to recruit gay people as subjects for research involving sexual orientation. Some nineteenth-century American physicians thought gay people so rare that they identified them by individual case number in biomedical
journals.[11] Whereas gay people may have been difficult for researchers to locate
during the past century,[12] one 1995 study by researchers at the U.S. National
Institutes of Health solicited volunteers for a genetic study of siblings by posting
notices on internationally accessible computer bulletin boards devoted to discussion of gay and lesbian issues. Not only is it easier for researchers to recruit
subjects, there are also outlets for research reports in prestigious scientific journals and in the news media, often offering researchers opportunities for both

professional advancement and recognition as well as, it must be said, their Warholian fifteen minutes of fame. Scientists do not, after all, undertake their research apart from the incentives that fuel human accomplishment elsewhere, and researchers making major advances in the understanding of erotic development will gain important recognition and rewards. In short, there remain professional incentives to sexual orientation research even if U.S. and other national medical organizations have by and large abandoned views that homoeroticism is pathological and even if the community of people committed to the development of a sexual orientation therapy remains in the United States, as literature professor George Rousseau has called it, "dwarfish."[13]

THE VALUE OF SEXUAL ORIENTATION RESEARCH

There are plenty of objectionable moments in the history of sexual orientation research, not only in its practices but also in its goals. As much in reaction to the horrors of the past as in expectation of worse in the future, some commentators have either called for close oversight of sexual orientation research or even an outright moratorium. Usually these objections are voiced by gay commentators who worry about the history and fate of gay people in relation to biomedical research. A common refrain in objections to sexual orientation research is that it cannot be freed from assumptions of pathology and disvalue. Statements of benevolent intentions and goodwill by researchers notwithstanding, these commentators fear sexual orientation research is necessarily continuous with antigay ideology. It is also believed that such science will have a stigmatizing effect, effectively labeling gay people as deviant. Homoeroticism must be something biologically degenerate or otherwise deficient, according to this concern, else there would be no research into the matter. Very little research at all is done, after all, into the determining why people are straight.

The stigmatizing effects of sexual science in the nineteenth and twentieth centuries are not to be denied insofar as some people did adopt views of homoeroticism as inferior sexuality precisely because of medicine's assertions to that effect. Just one reminder of this cause and effect relation can be given in the example of U.S. immigration policies. These policies, crafted in the early twentieth century to exclude the psychologically unfit from the nation, were extended to cover the exclusion of gay people, and the medical conception of homosexuality as pathological was used precisely to defend that exclusion. So entrenched was the medical view in immigration policy that the momentum to exclude gay people as legitimate immigrants continued *even after* medical organizations began to reject the view of homoeroticism as pathological.[14] In view of stigmatizing effects like these, sexual orientation research has the appearance of a moral cloud that hangs over all gay people and perpetuates objectionable beliefs about them. Sexual orientation research is thus both cause and effect of antigay prejudices insofar as it creates and reinforces judgments about the inferiority of homoeroticism.[15]

Just as genetic science is sometimes hard to separate from the eugenic movements that embraced it, popularized it, and bastardized it, so too the meaning of sexual orientation research is hard to assess independent of the therapeutic movement in which it emerged. While "intelligence" was by and large the trait that spawned eugenics,[16] sexual orientation is no less a problematic and divisive trait. Presumptions about the merits of different sexual orientations are melded in almost seamless ways with moral, religious, and civic values, with the prevailing social assumption being that heteroeroticism is vastly superior to homoeroticism. That assumption is reflected in the comparative social standing of gay and straight people, with gay people lacking the equivalent rights and duties held by straight people.

Given a historical lineage in which researchers and physicians were interested in sexual orientation for reasons related to the cure and prevention of homoeroticism, many gay commentators are suspicious that contemporary science cannot be adequately unshackled from historical viewpoints. The most cursory review of sexual orientation research suggests that even if there were some exceptions to the rule most investigators in the field thus far have believed almost reflexively that the world would be better off without *any* form of homoeroticism. Certainly the forlorn patients put on display by, for example, the late psychiatrist Irving Bieber and psychiatrist Charles Socarides seem to indicate that "homosexuals" would be much better off being straight.[17] Although much contemporary sexual orientation research appears free of the most invidious assumptions about homoeroticism—that it is pathological or disabling or instrumentally valueless—it also remains true that of all questions that might be investigated in regard to sexual orientation homoeroticism remains disproportionately studied, unaccountably so given that there are many questions of sexual orientation unrelated to homoeroticism that might also be investigated. So the question remains: why is homoeroticism singled out as a topic for investigation except that the field is still carried along by the momentum of research projects and moral agendas that identified homoeroticism as irretrievably a pathology, disability, and social handicap? Is it possible, gay commentators wonder, for contemporary research to be logically and morally unlike the nineteenth- and twentieth-century research that unabashedly held out the elimination of homoeroticism as its goal? Or do its assumptions still hold, even if in muted and discreet form, assumptions that will reemerge armed with powerful genetic or biopsychic interventions and give full sway to heterosexist fantasies of a world in which there are no gay people?

In 1984 sexologist Gunter Schmidt observed: "As long as society has not made peace with the homosexuals, research into the possible causes [of homosexuality is] . . . potentially a public danger to . . . [lesbians and gay men]. Seen in this light, it is good that we know so little about what causes heterosexuality and homosexuality."[18] Literature professor Jeffrey Williams has put the matter this way:

> Some people are relieved by this minoritizing function [of sexual orientation research]: being gay is similar to being blond—it's according to genetics or the hypothal[a]mus. But on the other hand, as a card-carrying anti-essentialist, I worry that this move to minoritize gay men finally serves a negative ideology and perhaps even genocidal purposes in separating those minoritized.[19]

Literature professor Leo Bersani has also wondered whether the increased visibility of "the homosexual" will aid the nineteenth-century project of surveillance, disciplinary intervention, and eventual extinction of homosexuals; he worries about what he calls "gender cleansing," especially in the context of AIDS, which has made gay men more visible and thereby more identifiable and vulnerable.[20]

The patron saint of objections to sexual orientation research—understood as inquiry into the causal mechanisms of sexual orientation—is Michael Foucault, whose judgment that "between techniques of knowledge and strategies of power there is no exteriority" is the conceptual basis for a great deal of commentary about the meaning and purposes of psychological and psychiatric study.[21] By this judgment I take Foucault to have meant that both the goals and methods of, in this case, sexual orientation research must necessarily afford techniques of manipulation and control, even if only at the level of discourse. To select sexual orientation in general and homoerotic orientation in particular as an area of inquiry is to problematize those topics in terms of the interests of the researcher, even to create "the homosexual" as a subject out of discursive nothingness. According to this view, researchers have a literally *authoritative* position in regard to their subjects: they create them on a discursive level by the deployment of a scientific interest that differentiates them in kind from other people regardless of whether or not those alleged differences exist apart from the interests of the researchers. By reason of the asymmetrical power between the straight researcher and the putatively disordered homosexual subject, any emergent techniques of control over sexual orientation could only work to the advantage of the researcher and the disadvantage of the subject.

It is for reasons like these—the creation of "the homosexual" as a clinical type, the asymmetrical power relations between researcher and subject, the lure of biomedical control over "the homosexual"—that literature professor David

Halperin has said pointedly, "The search for a 'scientific' etiology of sexual orientation is itself a homophobic project and needs to be more clearly seen as such."[22] Bersani has echoed this worry: "The elaborating of certain erotic preferences into a 'character'—into a kind of erotically determined essence—can never be a disinterested scientific enterprise. The attempted stabilizing of identity is inherently a disciplinary project."[23] The discursive creation of "the homosexual" permits the creation of sexual orientation therapy as well. Sexual orientation science, on this kind of view, is merely erotic war carried out by other means.

Philosopher Udo Schüklenk has crystallized worries of this kind in a proposal that sexual orientation research be halted in societies where there is still discrimination against lesbians and gay men. He holds that not only is such research harmful, it is of no use to the majority of straight taxpayers.[24] Even if atrocious social applications were unlikely to occur in democratic countries observing rights of citizens to be protected from involuntary eugenic applications, Schüklenk fears that such research would nevertheless prove a boon to autocratic countries.

These claims have a certain intuitive appeal to them in the sense that they seem consonant with liberal values of protecting gay people from inimical treatment, but I believe they are overbroad, antiscientific, and ultimately inimical to the interests of gay people. While the coupling of historically invidious motives for sexual orientation research and contemporary social hostility toward gay men and lesbians does raise important questions about the social reception and uses of that research, it does not follow that sexual orientation science must by its very nature be inherently heterosexist or that its effects can only be prejudicial to gay people. I do not deny that the motives for sexual orientation research have often been heterosexist in the most undiluted way. Neither do I deny that some researchers, like endocrinologist Gunter Dörner or psychiatrist Charles Socarides, have hoped for interventions that could in fact reduce the numbers of gay people in the world. It is, though, mistaken to lump all sexual orientation research into one category and dismiss it as inherently heterosexist. Some sexual orientation research has worked against heterosexist effects and helped lift the social and moral cloud hanging over homoeroticism. Depending on the context, the conceptual categorization of persons according to their erotic interests can work as much to their advantage as to their disadvantage. At the very least, for example, Plato's mythical account put people with homoerotic interests on the same moral plane as people with heteroerotic interests even if it did separate the former from the latter as seemingly different kinds of people. Just as genetic research need not be confined by its ancestry in eugenics, sexual orientation research need not be confined by its therapeutically driven and morally hostile history.

Some sexual orientation research has served purposes that could be called nothing other than liberating insofar as it proved of unqualified benefit for lesbians and gay men. According to the standards of the day, Evelyn Hooker's work on projective psychological profiles, for example, was invaluable evidence regarding the psychological normalcy of gay men.[25] Her work served to falsify erroneous psychological claims about the nature of homoeroticism, about its necessary connection with disseminated psychological disorder. Hooker's work was not in a strict sense a study of the origins of homoeroticism, but it was sexual orientation research by any meaning of the term insofar as it compared gay men and straight for observable psychological differences. The research went a great way toward dispelling the prevailing but erroneous notions that gay men and straight men differed in fundamental psychological ways. She found that when gay men were compared with straight men, matched according to shared social characteristics such as years of education, and not just compared with random controls, it was impossible to distinguish a subject's sexual orientation from the projective test results. It would have been profoundly mistaken for critics to call for a moratorium on Hooker's research on the grounds that it might prove harmful to gay people at home and abroad.

There are many ways in which empirical study of sexual orientation, in its origins and effects, can prove beneficial to gay people. For example, one study showed that the children of gay parents were not more likely than other children to be gay themselves.[26] This kind of study is hard evidence against claims that gay people should as a class be considered unfit as parents because they necessarily visit their own sexual orientation upon their children. This sort of evidence is crucial to courts in making custody determinations in "the best interest" of the children, even if courts do sometimes ignore this evidence in their actual decisions and deny custody to self-identified lesbian and gay parents.[27]

Other studies offer the same sort of hard evidence in regard to false beliefs about homosexuality in, for example, the military: that it is "catching" and disruptive in the way its critics claim.[28] One such study showed, for example, that the global exclusion of gay people from the military is unsupported by data drawn from military archives and court cases.[29] Studies of age-of-consent laws are also meaningful and important to gay men and lesbians inasmuch as some nations have higher ages of consent for same-sex relationships than for opposite-sex relationships. Whether and to what extent this sort of difference is justified in the name of protecting people from sexual misadventures and predatory relationships can only be determined through empirical study. Yet another example of the utility of sexual orientation research concerns health. It is certainly meaningful and important to study gay men and lesbians in regard to their health needs as a class, and these studies may require inquiry into the psychological development of erotic interests, for example, the extent to which distress about sexual orientation is adventitious and how interventions can protect against that distress. In light of this information, one might modify existing sex education in order to make it more meaningful to gay people. One might also study the nature and origins of antigay prejudice, to learn whether and to what extent it emerges in response to unwanted homoerotic interests in one's self. Research of this kind must necessarily presuppose the existence of gay people as a scientifically meaningful class.

Given all the advantages that can come from scientific study of homoeroticism, it is not clear that an "improper" motive on the part of any one individual or group of researchers should disable all inquiry into the nature and origins of homoeroticism. For the sake of the argument, suppose that Irving Bieber and his colleagues' motives for curing homoeroticism in their patients were entirely indefensible insofar as they rested on empirically false presuppositions, were informed by stereotypical views of gay men and lesbians, and were wholly prejudicial and heterosexist. Would the "immorality" of these motives be a sufficient reason to raise an impermeable barrier to further inquiry into the nature and origins of homoeroticism? I do not think there is any easy way to defend such a conclusion. Freedom of intellectual inquiry is an important moral and scientific value, and its control may be worse than any single wrongful use on which it is wasted. Moreover, it permits others to judge the worth and significance of studies and motives, and such freedom—the freedom to analyze and test—is crucial to lesbians and gay men in protecting their interests against research projects having base motivations.

It remains to be seen, of course, whether the current crop of studies suggesting a biogenetic basis for sexual orientation will have the same liberating effect of research like Hooker's. It does appear that these studies offer some pragmatic benefit. J. Michael Bailey believes, for example, that research showing the involuntary nature of erotic interests will give the lie to claims that gay people continue to exist only through the predatory recruitment of young people.[30] Some people also seem more inclined toward approval and/or acceptance of homoeroticism if they think it genetically or biologically involuntary: it appears somehow more "real" if it can be read into a person's biological makeup rather than being something people "merely choose." The reality of homoeroticism might also be emphasized if sexual orientation research did produce a treatment for adult homoeroticism. If there were such a treatment, and people *did not* use it, which many would not for the reasons I describe in chapters 3 and 7, the reality of gay people might be driven home all the more powerfully. At the very least the view that gay people existed merely because there was no treatment for them would be called into sharp question.

These kinds of pragmatic effects may be superfluous in a moral sense since gay rights can be advanced adequately on grounds entirely independent of theories of biological accounts of sexual orientation. Nevertheless, it might well prove that this kind of research—preliminary, tentative, unconfirmed—may have the same political effect desired by gay advocacy, namely, the social and political accommodation of gay people on terms equivalent to those enjoyed by straight people. I do not see, therefore, that there is anything to be gained by denouncing sexual orientation research as inherently heterosexist and calling for something as serious and perhaps as counterproductive as a moratorium. Sexual orientation research did not by itself produce homophobia, and neither will heterosexism be brought to heel by curbing sexual orientation research. Sexual orientation injustice is not a creation of scientific research, and the fight against injustices toward gay people may very well depend on strong research programs capable of falsifying invidious and erroneous beliefs about the nature and origin of homoeroticism.

I also want to note that many of the most prominent researchers who are today conducting sexual orientation research identify themselves as gay men or lesbian. To the extent their public remarks are a guide, their research does not by itself carry any explicit presumptions that stigmatize homoeroticism. Rather than presupposing that homoeroticism is necessarily disordered or that the goal of research is to produce techniques of sexual orientation change, these researchers proceed in their studies merely in the expectation of posing and refining answers to the question of why some men and women have more prominent same-sex attractions than others. It is not merely straight researchers who are interested in the question of sexual orientation; it is not merely straight researchers who are imposing their authority on the field. I suppose that one could try and argue that gay and lesbian researchers have been captured by self-loathing and are caught up blindly in heterosexist projects. This would be an overwrought contention, however, because the dispute about the value of sexual orientation science will ultimately rest on the facts rather than on the states of minds of the researchers.

One can come to the subject of sexual orientation research without heterosexist axes to grind. Many sexual orientation researchers do not presuppose the pathology or moral villainy of homoeroticism. Even if they did think that "dissatisfied homosexuals" ought to have access to sexual reorientation therapy, sex therapists William H. Masters and Virginia Johnson, for example, held homoeroticism to be entirely within the range of normal and acceptable human behavior.[31] It may also turn out that sexual orientation research does more good than harm, in which case accusations of heterosexist motive or predictions of heterosexist consequences would dissolve. Schüklenk's recommendation that research be halted in societies in which there is still discrimination against gay men and lesbians could prove politically unwise if the public at large believed that a social minority was vetoing the work of science. The public at large might be convinced that lesbians and gay men objected to such science because there was in fact something unsavory to be found out there, that homoerotic orientation was the result of biological pathogenic processes, for example. The public might also believe that gay men and lesbians continued to exist only by reason of their stranglehold on free scientific inquiry. Conclusions of this kind could fuel heterosexism in important ways and be more counterproductive for gay people than free and unrestrained sexual orientation research.

Moreover—and I cannot stress this point enough—cessation of sexual orientation work would prove profoundly objectionable if current reports are wrong in important ways. If so, it would be undesirable to have reports like LeVay's and Hamer's as the last word on the topic. Sexual orientation research would be effectively frozen at the turning of this century or whenever a moratorium took effect. To use one example of how research has corrected erroneous views, it is to be remembered that a view once prevailed among certain clinicians and the public that female homosexuality was more common than male homosexuality. The 1948 and 1953 Kinsey studies were central in dispelling this factual error.[32] That no one holds this view today is due in part to empirical study in the area. The Bell and Weinberg study of 1978 and the Bell, Weinberg, and Hammersmith study of 1981 are also important factual studies of the nature and effects of homoeroticism in people's lives.[33] All these studies have clear limitations, but seen from the perspective of science as a process of measuring the adequacy of hypotheses and evidence rather than as a window opening on veridical truth itself, these studies are all eminently useful and important, incomplete and flawed though they might be.

How social opinions about gay people are connected to the contemporary state of sexual orientation research is a complicated question, but it is certainly unwise to have society frozen in possibly erroneous beliefs about the nature, origins, and prevalence of homoerotic interests. As psychologist John Money has pointed out, it is simply wrongheaded to assume that scientific research is necessarily prejudicial but that scientific ignorance has no prejudicial consequences:

> The fallacy of censoring basic homosexological science is that ignorance as well as knowledge of the origin, cause, or genesis of anything . . . can be used politically in a manner that is either ethical or unethical. The political struggle should be for the ethical application of knowledge, not for the suppression of research.[34]

Sexual orientation research may well prove a greater benefit to gay men and lesbians than a moratorium if it clarifies misconceptions and shows any errors currently circulating about the nature and determinants of sexual orientation.

It is also worth observing that erroneous beliefs about gay people are not only held by straight people. Most gay people hold views about why they are gay, even if those views are indeterminate and not fully articulated. In *The "Sissy Boy" Syndrome* the parents and boys interviewed and studied by physician and attorney Richard Green had no hesitation in describing their beliefs about why the boys came to be gay: none of them were puzzled by the question.[35] Although this matter has not been well studied, it seems fair to say that gay people probably incorporate just as many unsubstantiated views in their folk accounts of why they are gay as do even the most heterosexist straight people, even if the accounts of gay people are more congenial to their erotic lives. If erroneous beliefs about the origins of homoeroticism are held by gay people, it hardly seems an act of heterosexism to correct these views and offer a more accurate account to the people most vulnerable to social distinctions drawn on the basis of sexual orientation.

One striking aspect of research on the origins (if not treatment) of homoeroticism is that the vast majority of research of this kind has been carried out with male subjects. An astonishing fascination with male homoeroticism exists in the literature. Men have been overwhelmingly the subject of most sexual orientation research and therapy. Female homoeroticism has been researched and treated, to be sure, but not nearly with the same vigor as male homoeroticism. This skewing of research subjects reflects, first of all, a wider skewing of biomedical research on male subjects. In some instances, male homosexuals may have been easier to identify than females because of patterns of social visibility, including arrest rates, more open sites of social interaction, and so on. It is also highly likely that sexism played some role in selecting out men as worthy of interest more often than women. It may be that researchers saw homoeroticism in men as a greater damage than homoeroticism in a woman, because men had more to lose socially and otherwise from homoeroticism than women did, even though according to the diagnostic canons homoeroticism would be an equivalent disorder in both men and women. This is perhaps one instance in which women have benefited from invisibility before biomedical researchers. Less visible to researchers and therapists, women were often spared many of the cruelties of sexual orientation therapy endured by men.

I mention this research imbalance between men and women in order to underline the way in which ideological effects *are* embedded in sexual orientation research. The relevant question is, though, not how to produce an ideology-free science all at once but how to identify and overcome these ideological effects in the scientific process. This is not a question that is unique to sexual orientation research, and it would be wrong to object to sexual orientation research simply on the ground that it can be infiltrated by some ultimately objectionable ideology. The more relevant issue is whether that infiltration, that value intrusion must remain unrecognized and uncorrected. In a sense, the conjecture of pathological homoeroticism and the refutation of that proposition are evidence that these intrusions can be recognized and discarded, again, if difficultly so and even if voices outside science must help researchers identify the value-laden errors of their ways.

Foucault's observation may ultimately be trivial in the sense that it states what cannot be otherwise: that knowledge and power are coextensive. The relevant question is not, therefore, whether science can achieve some neutral methodology and goals—that have, for example, no disciplinary functions—but whether particular forms of discursive and scientific power are objectionable in their conception and effects. Certainly the history of sexual orientation research is replete with objectionable assumptions, interventions, and goals, but sexual orientation research is not undermined because of the potential for categorizing and disciplinary effects. The search for the determinants of sexual orientation—such as they are tractable to analysis—has all-too-often been a heterosexist project, but, ironically, the excesses of sexual orientation research are its best moral counsel about the way to conduct study that does not commit those errors, for those willing to heed the indelible message written there.

SCIENTIFIC UTILITY

To argue that sexual orientation research is not undermined by ideological effects does not by itself establish the importance of this research relative to all other areas of study that might be studied scientifically. It does not follow that any science that has empirical content is important science, as any tenure committee or granting agency well knows. Some commentators have objected to sexual orientation research not on grounds that it is conceptually impossible or because of inimical consequences but because it is scientifically uninteresting and sterile. Philosopher Frederick Suppe has, for example, argued that sexual orientation research represents moribund science driven by antiquated moral views. He asks, "Who cares what causes homosexuality? Only those who subscribe to the Victorian 'Theory of Normal Love,' its current day remnants, or some moral or political agenda. But insofar as we act qua scientists, not I nor, I would hope, anyone of serious scientific aspirations."[36] Biologist Richard Lewontin has echoed these sentiments:

> The asking of a scientific question has the property of saying that that's an important question. Otherwise you wouldn't spend your time and someone else's money on it. And asking the question 'Are there any genetic differences between homosexuals and heterosexuals?' is stating that the answer to that question is an

important answer. That's my problem: You've got to tell me why you believe it's an important question.[37]

Suppe's argument that many of the initial motives for research into the origins of homoeroticism were fueled by ideological views about familial and sexual relationships is altogether convincing. It also seems to me fair to conclude, as he does, that a repudiation of the ideological views behind that research undermines most of the reasons sexual orientation science was conducted in the past. If sexual orientation research were justifiable only on those ideological grounds, Suppe's account should be the last word on the matter and sexual orientation science should be left to wither on the vine. I do think, though, there is a justification that can ground sexual orientation research, moralistic concerns apart. That ground is that it is important and not just tangentially interesting for biomedicine to have a generally validated theory of human psychosexual development. This is not to single out homoeroticism as the sole or even most important aspect of psychosexual development; it is to justify interest in homoeroticism as just one instance of a more general account of human erotic interest and behavior.

Even if the history of sexual inquiry is thus far replete with instances of substandard and morally suspect scientific efforts, there is nothing inherently unscientific about inquiry into the phylogenetic or ontogenetic emergence of human sexual orientation.[38] Aliens visiting Earth from another planet might well pose the exact same questions that drive sexual orientation science today: why do human beings have the exclusivity in their erotic lives they seem to have, how fixed or fluid is that apparent exclusivity, do straight people differ from gay people in any biological or psychological traits, and are those traits causally related to the development of their erotic interests? These questions are not logically dependent on outdated moralistic views or necessarily homophobic perspectives. Alien visitors from the far reaches of the galaxy might well wonder how it is that people come to have the sexual orientations they have. As long as I have already crossed the border of imaginative excess, let me further speculate that these alien visitors might want to know about the origins of homoeroticism in order to integrate its erotic potentials into their own sexual repertoire. That would hardly be heterosexist.

Sexual orientation research need not be driven by expectations about the pathology or the normalcy of homoeroticism. Those who do not accept the scientific goal of having a general validated theory of erotic development will not be convinced that sexual orientation research is important and, in principle, able to be uncoupled from heterosexism. I think, though, the burden of proof is on them to show that having a well-confirmed theory of erotic development is an uninteresting scientific project. Certainly such a theory would be neces-sary to judge the accuracy of claims that erotic interests and classifications are no more or less fundamental than classifications of people according to the foods they might happen to eat, the view espoused by David Halperin. Is it really true, after all, that people may be scripted into erotic interests the same way they are scripted into dietary habits? To use another example, the study of the origins of homoeroticism are instrumentally important in validating broader biological theories of evolution. For example, sociobiology appealed to homosexuality as a test case for explaining how various kinds of sexual orien-tation could have instrumental value in the survival of parents, children, and kin groups. In one such version of this hypothesis, for example, homoeroticism was linked to altruism, which while reducing the reproductive fitness of partic-ular individuals nevertheless contributed to the overall reproductive success rate of a group. Testing this hypothesis seems to necessitate the study of homo-eroticism as matter of scientific course.[39]

I also think it can be fair to pursue a research question simply because many people are interested in it. For whatever reasons, people *are* interested in why some people have dominant, entrenched homoerotic interests and why those interests are often associated with behavioral traits and social roles. At the very least the conceptual default could be shifted against Lewontin here by noting that as a matter of social fact the origins of homoeroticism are not uninterest-ing. It would certainly be of interest to a great many people to know whether genes are involved in coding for sexual orientation and whether they do so as a matter of common inheritance or whether the matter is far more complex. Because of such interest, critics of sexual orientation research are forced, I believe, to show why it is an unimportant, uninteresting question, not merely that it was once driven by outmoded assumptions.

I might also add here that right- or left-handedness may be more scientifically interesting than would appear to be the case. It is certainly all to the good that educators have abandoned efforts to force children to use their right hands exclu-sively when writing, and certainly the study of handedness to revert to that state of affairs would hardly be worthwhile, but handedness can be an interesting com-ponent of the effects of hemispheric lateralization, namely, the division of neu-rological labor in the brain. Hemispheric specialization might well be responsi-ble for all sorts of behavioral effects, ranging from mothers cradling their babies on the left to attention deficit disorders to neurolingustic capacities. As a part of brain laterality studies, handedness seems fair game as an object of legitimate inquiry even if it is not the most pressing problem on the research agenda.

To say that there are nonideological and nonhomophobic reasons for having a general theory of erotic development is not to say anything about the importance of that science relative to all other possible lines of research. A society and research community might well place this particular issue at the bottom of any funding list if it were convinced that other topics were more important in terms of the conceptual vistas they promised to open, the technical applications they would make possible, or the priorities of a nation or community of researchers at a given time. If the nation were at war, for example, research priorities could easily and justifiably be shunted away from sexual orientation research and handedness. Even in peace time there is nothing inherent in sexual orientation research that would automatically give it priority over, for example, research into ontogenetic and phylogenetic development of language or even research into the engineering of sewers. Many worthwhile and valuable scientific projects are simultaneously vying for funding and the intellectual interest of researchers. According to the interests and best judgments of people making decisions about funding and the deployment of talent, they might or might not place a high priority on sexual orientation research. Under conditions of lush funding and abundant intellectual energy there might be many incentives to pursue sexual orientation research. Even if funding were meager and intellectual resources scarce, a society might decide that it had a particularly compelling interest in sexual orientation research at the expense of research on sewers. There are many considerations involved in determining an equitable distribution of money and talent in scientific projects, but there is nothing about sexual orientation research that would disqualify it from competing in that domain. Neither, though, is there anything that would automatically entitle it to priority. The value of sexual orientation research is, finally, a separate question from its theoretical possibility and its ideological complicity with heterosexism. There is no way to determine in an a priori way the value of a theory of psychosexual development to a society. That question will have to be asked and answered by each society facing questions of resource allocation under conditions of scarcity.

As mentioned above, Schüklenk raised the question of the utility of sexual orientation research not in regard to science itself but in regard to the interests of taxpayers; he says it is of no use to the majority of straight taxpayers.[40] This conclusion is unfounded or at least overbroad. Let me indulge in a thought experiment for the sake of the argument and say that some straight taxpayers might want such research funded if they thought it offered a pathway to a society *without* homoeroticism, especially if that pathway gave them control over the sexual orientation of their own children. Afraid as this commentator is of objectionable uses of sexual orientation research, I do not understand how he can argue that sexual orientation research is of no use to the society he foresees using its results all too freely. It is also true that a considerable amount of research supported by governments is of no "use" to a majority of taxpayers, their sexual orientation notwithstanding. Basic research is often of no use to taxpayers in the sense that it does not produce commercial products having immediate utility; it does, however, often produce conclusions useful to scientists for further research. Social uselessness might be an objection relative to the total amount of money divided between basic and applied research or to the total amount of money expended on research in the first place, but unless one wants to object to all basic research in kind this objection holds little moral force when singled out against sexual orientation research.

It is also not true that taxpayers always have control over the funding of research. Private foundations and corporations are the source of a considerable amount of funding for research. Cutting off government money—on the grounds of its uselessness to taxpayers—would not necessarily starve sexual orientation research if foundations, whose decisions are made more freely and in ways protected from taxpayer wrath, support the research. A good deal of research is also carried out without funding other than a public or private institution's support of professors' salary—professors with rights of free inquiry. In this instance, again, the question of taxpayers' rights to useful products as a return on their tax "investments" would be moot.

One last consideration from Schüklenk's commentary that is worth mention concerns his claim that sexual orientation research should be halted in those countries that still discriminate against lesbians and gay men. While he narratively links this discrimination with autocratic societies, his position would seem to close down virtually all sexual orientation science around the globe. He does not offer a definition of what counts as relevant discrimination, but the United States and United Kingdom, to cite just two examples, formally exclude gay people from military service. In virtually every nation of the globe gay people may not marry one another in rituals recognized by the state. The overwhelmingly vast majority of people in the world do not live in jurisdictions that outlaw antigay discrimination. Consensual homoerotic behavior is illegal for adults in approximately one-half of the U.S. states. Depending on what counts as discrimination, there is no country on the planet that is free of antigay discrimination. It seems to follow that Schüklenk's position would require a global shutdown of sexual orientation research. For many of the reasons cited above, the importance of respecting academic freedom, the liberating effects of this research, the need to keep research from being frozen at a given historical moment, Schüklenk's proposal should be rejected as censorious and counterproductive.

For those with a static view of humanity science about the causes of traits and behaviors will always be a threat, for science seems to require readjusting notions of humanity to changing empirical characterizations of the world and human beings themselves. If one accepts human nature, however, as something inherently dynamic, it does not follow that psychological, behavioral, or genetic science necessarily threatens the fate of humanity. On this latter view science abets human interests rather than thwarts them even as it requires continual modification of moral, political, and philosophical views. There have been many objectionable views that spurred scientific interest in homoeroticism. It is unclear, however, that a scientific abandonment of sexual orientation research would favor the interests of gay people in the long run. So long as there remain empirical questions about the nature and development of sexual orientation, these may and should be pursued by science, subject only to the constraints society must impose in order to attend to its manifold needs. It is perhaps a recognition of the defensibility of sexual orientation science that most commentators focus not on halting the science itself but on controlling its consequences. Many of the feared uses of sexual orientation research do not attach to the research per se, however, so much as they attach to matters of sexual orientation therapy, prenatal diagnosis, abortion, and screening carried out for employment and insurance and the like. The following chapters take up these matters in turn, and it becomes clear that the key question to be addressed is not censoring science but assuring that gay people are protected from potentially invidious uses of research results. Before moving to a consideration of these questions, I want here to address one last question about the merit of research: whether sexual orientation research is objectionable because it stigmatizes gay people.

STIGMATIZING EFFECTS OF RESEARCH

In the 1970s a former president of the American Psychological Association argued that sexual orientation *therapy* for homoeroticism stigmatized gay people and was therefore unjust.[41] Could a similar argument be made that sexual orientation *research* wrongly stigmatizes homoeroticism and that the research per se is therefore unjust? Whether sexual orientation research stigmatizes homoeroticism in a morally significant way will depend not only on its conceptual foundations but also on its interpretation and social reception. Does sexual orientation research necessarily presuppose that homoeroticism is a disorder, and does it have the effect of worsening the social fate of gay people? Frederick Suppe blazed the trail for analysis of this kind when he considered whether or not sexual reorientation therapy—offering the promise of cure or change—had objectionable stigmatizing effects.[42] The framework of that account may be usefully followed here.

The first question to be asked is whether the mere existence of sexual orientation research—understood as the effort to identify the mechanisms by which people have the sexual orientations they have—strengthens social prejudices and discrimination against gay people. If it is wrong for a society to permit research programs that have unjust effects, there would be a prima facie case against sexual orientation research when the mere existence of such research worsened the already complicated social standing of gay people by, for example, causing more injustice in employment and housing practices. It is an empirical question, however, about which virtually nothing is known at present, whether the mere existence of research programs like Simon LeVay's or Dean Hamer's generate or sustain antigay prejudice and discrimination.

If a researcher's efforts to prove the pathological nature of homoeroticism were widely *perceived* as reputable and convincing (regardless of the quality of the research or its degree of certainty), the research would in fact serve stigmatizing purposes, and such a state of affairs certainly prevailed during the rise of last century's sex researchers who held views inimical to homoeroticism. I do not want to minimize the extent to which gay people suffered social stigma by reason of the social implications of a view of homoeroticism as pathological and inferior in both a psychological and moral senses, but the relevant question here is not historical in character but conceptual. Can research into homoeroticism be conceptualized apart from imputations of disorder and inferiority and be free of stigmatizing effects for that reason?

It should be clear from what I have said above that I think the first part of that question can be answered in the affirmative: researchers can and do treat homoeroticism as merely one part of the repertoire of human psychosexual capacity. The second part of the question is more complex, but I think that stigmatizing effects need not follow from sexual orientation research. If a researcher's efforts to prove that homoeroticism were merely a developmental variant well within the domain of human normalcy were widely *perceived* as reputable and convincing (regardless of the quality of the research or its degree of certainty), the research would in fact work against the stigmatization of gay people. Whether sexual orientation research has stigmatizing effects will depend, therefore, in large measure on what assumptions it carries about homoeroticism and the way in which it is socially received. Moreover, it should be pointed out that the stigmatization of homoeroticism could be better served by *failing* to research the origins of sexual orientation. Where there is uncertainty, there will be speculation, and it might well prove that the perpetuation of folk accounts about the origins of sexual orientation could prove more damaging to gay people in the long run than any stigmatizing effects endured in the admittedly fallible and time-consuming process of scientific conjecture and refutation.

The social reception and use of sexual orientation research is a complex issue, but it is to be remembered that sexual orientation injustice is not primarily an artifact of research methodology. Sexual orientation injustice and stigmatization exist because people do not accept homoeroticism as morally valuable, for reasons that are both original cause and sustaining effect of that moral position. That is, discriminatory practices and moral beliefs mutually inform and sustain one another. Gay people will not advance in the cause toward sexual orientation justice until they begin to share equal status with straight people. This is not to say that research plays no role in the social forms and influence of sexual orientation injustice—it certainly has in regard to spreading the gospel of homosexual pathology—but it is to say that in the present century there are probably more stigmatizing effects for gay people in their systematic exclusion from the military, from marriage, from full participation in visible civic society than in research attempts to determine the role of genes, hormones, and anatomy in sexual orientation. It is unclear that sexual orientation research, under social arrangements like these, could serve as anything more than a prop to stigmatizing effects that exist pervasively and independently for reasons causally unrelated to the methodologies and findings of science.

If the existence of research projects does contribute to antigay prejudice, it likely does so by substantiating sentiments and values that already exist, however latent they might be, rather than creating them ex nihilo. Medical conceptions of homoeroticism as pathological could hardly have taken root so widely in the last century had the public been unwilling to accept them. It is imaginable that some people might be led by the very existence of sexual orientation research to conclusions that are inimical to gay people, but they would do so only in the way that some people think that anyone arrested by the police must necessarily be guilty of charges brought against them. If so, it would be a preexisting stereotype that caused sexual orientation research to be construed in a prejudicial way rather than the research itself that generated antigay prejudice.

It simply does not follow that because researchers investigate a human trait it is necessarily disordered. Most people seem quite capable of understanding and accepting the distinction between basic research into normal function and research driven by interest in eliminating a disorder. The subject of homoeroticism as a matter of investigation should, therefore, be intelligible without an assumption of pathology, deviance, or inferiority. Moreover, even if homoeroticism is judged abnormal in some biological or psychodevelopmental sense, it does not follow that antigay prejudice is justified. No one could legitimately appeal to pancreas research as a justification for prejudice against diabetics. This is to say that even if sexual orientation research does play some causal role in the emergence of antigay prejudice, it does not follow that this prejudice should be contained by shutting down sexual orientation research altogether, as against specifically addressing wrongful conclusions drawn about the meaning of that research. In any case, it appears that research into the ori gins of homoeroticism can be conceptualized and practiced without stigmatizing gay people in an inherently unjust way.

Before leaving the topic of ideological motives for sexual orientation research, I would like to point out that research often undercuts its own assumptions. Advanced genetic research, for example, has revealed a rich and expansive range of genetic subunits such that it is unclear that the gene remains the most interesting unit of analysis in molecular biology. This is not to say that the notion of the gene has outlived its utility, rather that advance genetic research has made the notion of "the gene" less useful as a unit of scientific investigation and explanation than hitherto expected. Alleles, exons, introns, base pairs, and other gene subunits now dominate the methodology and conclusions of molecular biology. It is always difficult to predict where research may lead, but advanced sexual orientation research might conceivably led to a repudiation of the core concepts now holding sway. Already in this book, for example, I have had to restrict my discussion to erotic interests based on sex traits when it is clear that sexual orientation includes a great deal of other erotic interests involving, for example, hair color, race, age, and preferred contexts for intercourse.

Advanced sexual orientation research might show yet that it is biologically meaningless to cast people into the equivalent of sexual races: homosexuals, heterosexuals, and bisexuals. What sexual orientation research might discover is that erotic development is far more textured and variable than current understandings allow, that there is no single causal touchstone of sexual orientation. It is unclear how this sort of outcome would be necessarily disciplinary or homophobic. On the contrary, to use the kind of language favored in Foucauldian analysis, this kind of outcome might help subvert the hegemony of binary systems of sexual orientation. That we now appreciate better than in the last century how erotic interests cannot be read off biology in any simple way does not mean that there are no biologically observable differences between straight and gay people or that the search for such differences is now officially over. Even if there are no stark differences, still there may well be some constellation of biological or psychological traits that give gay people a family resemblance to one another and straight people another kind of resemblance. Finding such differences would only be discriminatory if they were falsely alleged or put to objectionable uses. The proved existence of such differences ought to be an absolute defense against charges that science looking for such differences is inherently defamatory. It is the work of the rest of this book to examine questions related to the objectionable use of any discoverable biological differences.

One more remark about the legacy of suspicion that attaches to sexual orientation research is in order. If one were to construct the debate about sexual orientation research in political terminology, one could characterize gay advocacy groups as the political left and forces in favor of the status quo as the political right. In a pitched conflict every success of the right is to be construed as a loss to the left, and these successes are all the more grievous because they are not balanced by some sort of political gain by the left. An advance toward understanding the causes of homoerotic interests seems to offer the gay left no gain comparable to the gain achieved by the right in its potential power over human sexual orientation. To put this in an extreme way, imagine that instead of undertaking the Human Genome Project[43] governments around the world had instead invested millions of dollars in the Sexual Orientation Project, which had as its goal the identification of the causal elements and mechanisms by which people came to have the sexual orientations they have. A project of this kind, orchestrated on an international scale, would undoubtedly provoke terror in gay people, even if a portion of that project's budget were devoted to a consideration of its ethical, legal, and social implications. Politically speaking, sexual orientation science will continue to seem a terror to gay people so long as it has a closed agenda (limited to finding the causes of homoeroticism), with only one commercial product (therapy for gay people), and indistinguishable from the science of the status quo (belonging to the party in power).

The relevant philosophical question is whether sexual orientation science need be confined by these conceptual parameters. Can there be a significant difference in purpose between research of the past that presumed the pathology of gay people and methodically planned their extinction? Can there be a sexual orientation research that overcomes these limitations? There are a few remedies that can be offered to offset fears of this kind. It is not my purpose to describe these in detail, but I can sketch out the conditions under which a science ought to proceed. First of all, sexual orientation research should proceed without any explicit or implicit assumptions about the inferiority of homoeroticism. For scientific purposes it should be a matter of utter moral indifference whether people are gay, straight, or something else. The goal of this science would be an inclusive account of the general pathways of human psychosexual development. All erotic desire would thus be the proper topic of investigation, and there would be no stigmatizing effect because the umbrella of science would include homoeroticism only alongside all other erotic interests. Research efforts in this area might also make clear to the public that they are continuous with animal behavior research even if there are important differences between human beings and other animals.[44] Sexual orientation science would also have to have gay people visibly present in its research teams, this as an assurance that the research is not simply an extension of heteronormative privilege.

The passage of research results into public consciousness is often problematic, and—as bioethicist Arthur L. Caplan has pointed out—the effects of that passage can be volatile and prejudicial.[45] One can imagine that there might be some reason not to proceed quickly with this research, certainly not on the scale of the Sexual Orientation Project I described above. In a climate of acute antigay prejudice, evidenced by the passage of state laws prohibiting any sort of legal protection on the basis of sexual orientation, a gay-friendly researcher might well decide to forbear from research for fear of the social misuse to which it might be put. The research community is obliged to consider the way and pace at which it proceeds with sexual orientation research, but the existence of antigay prejudice should not be used as an outright bar to such research, for there is no society in which there is no antigay prejudice. The most important task in response to antigay uses of sexual orientation research is not a reining in of that science but a direct confrontation and emendation of the social attitudes and policies inimical to gay people. It would be mistaken not to look for genes contributing to cancer in human beings out of the fear that tests for such genes will be used to the disadvantage of people carrying those genes. The relevant issue to be addressed for both genetic and sexual orientation research is the fitness of social structures to absorb this information in just ways.

Because of the all-too-real existence of antipathy toward gay people and because people are not yet protected as a matter of policy in the ways they will need to be protected from biomedical testing, maybe it is better that sexual orientation research remains a comparatively low-level, loosely organized scientific venture and not an ambitious international crash project. I should remark here, however, that it is often difficult to predict the successes of research. We do not know how much time lies ahead in which to prepare society for the results of sexual orientation research because that research may surprise us all and jump forward in big leaps rather than in modest incremental steps. The ethical, legal, and social preparations necessary for those leaps are imaginable now even if science is far from completing its self-appointed tasks. Rather than try and stave off the advances of sexual orientation researchers, it would be better if critics and commentators started thinking through the exact sort of protections that gay people—and others—would need if science accomplishes what it is trying to achieve. I describe some of the features that will be necessary in this regard at the end of chapter 5.

At any rate, I have tried to show it is hard to frame a convincing argument that sexual orientation research is necessarily homophobic. I do leave open, though, the question of the pace at which this science should proceed and what priority the research ought to receive for funding. Those issues cannot be settled except by a consideration of all competing inquiries and how social resources and intellect should be apportioned among them. Sexual orientation has no automatic claim on priority, but neither should it be left off the list of fundable research.

Before leaving the topic of the social effects of sexual orientation research, I do want to make clear that the quest for the determinants of homoeroticism has hijacked many important questions, the very deflecting of which has left considerable gaps in our knowledge about the "nature" and meaning of homoeroticism. The origins of erotic desire are not necessarily the most interesting questions to be asked in regard to homoeroticism. On the contrary, one might just as profitably ask why it is that homoeroticism is seen as a danger to family, religion, and society. Why is homoeroticism seen as a condition of failure and not simply a behavioral variant to be accepted as an essential part of the human sexual panorama? Why is homoeroticism constructed as an object of moral, religious, and medical opprobrium? Why do schools, legislatures, television, the military, and advertising presume and enforce heteroerotic ideals? Why is it permissible to exclude from employment and fire people solely on the basis of their sexual orientation, as is true in most parts of the planet? How has homoeroticism come to be a damning metaphor for degradation and worthlessness, and why is it used as a pretext for unaccountable violence against those accused of being gay? How is it that anyone could believe AIDS to be a punishment from God for homoerotic immoralities?[46] How is it that a majority of U.S. Supreme Court justices could find a moral distinction between a homosexual and heterosexual blow job, permitting the criminalization of one but asserting a constitutional right to the other?[47] The understanding of homoeroticism that might come from sustained inquiry into these questions does not lie in explaining its biogenetic origins, whatever they might be. A richer and deeper understanding is to be found in asking what society has made of homoeroticism and why. And these questions have little to do with the size of brain structures, antenatal fetal hormone balances, the X chromosome, or the density and distribution of finger skin ridges. These questions are, by contrast, questions about the origin of public morality and social conscience. We would do well to spend as much time on them as on the origins of homoerotic desire, else there risks being more heterosexism in the questions that we do not ask than in the ones we do raise and pursue.

3 ||||||||||||||||||||||||||||||||||||||||||||||||||||||||||||||||||||||||||||||||||||

THE PRACTICE OF SEXUAL ORIENTATION THERAPY

When asked whether he thought genetic sexual orientation research would be of benefit to people coming to grips with homoerotic identity, psychiatrist Richard Pillard said that "one thing I think it will do is get psychiatrists away from trying to convert sexual orientation."[1] While the practice of sexual orientation therapy is minimal in North America and developed Western countries, there is no reason to think it will ever entirely disappear as a matter of clinical and public interest. Around the world and in the United States there continue to be practitioners and advocates of sexual orientation therapy.[2] Until it closed in 1994, for example, the Masters and Johnson Institute in St. Louis was the most well known clinic offering a reorientation program for men dissatisfied with their homoerotic orientation. Other programs have filled the void left by the closure of that clinic, some of them fueled by longtime advocates of sexual orientation therapy, others promoted by therapists newer to the field. In addition to offering views about the relationship between society and homosexuality, psychiatrist Charles Socarides continues to advocate sexual reorientation therapy.[3] Some religious groups now sponsor programs they believe will help both men and women abandon their homoerotic interests and identities. Because sexual orientation therapy is not reported to data-collecting agencies, it is difficult to know to what extent it is currently practiced, though it is clear that there are both practitioners and clients to be found in psychiatric, psychological, and religious fields.

Given that interest in controlling sexual orientation has not altogether disappeared, it is little wonder that other commentators are less optimistic than Pillard about the impact of sexual orientation research. These commentators worry that far from dissolving the appeal of sexual orientation therapy, bio-genetic research will in fact enable and deliver a mechanism of therapy. Even if research showed that sexual orientation were involuntary in its origin, therapy might still try to undo a given sexual orientation. The undoing of involuntary conditions is, after all, the governing premise and goal of all contemporary medical efforts involving genetic and congenital disorders. People opposed on moral grounds to homoeroticism were not slow to note that biological studies may open rather than close the door to sexual orientation therapy. One syndi-cated media commentator on religious and political affairs, for example, rightly pointed out that a better understanding of the relationship between the brain and behavior might well produce therapies capable of altering a person's erotic interests.[4] Because of worry about the uses of sexual orientation science, Dean Hamer and his colleagues closed their 1993 report with this advisory: "We believe that it would be fundamentally unethical to use such information to try to assess or alter a person's current or future sexual orientation, or other nor-mal attributes of human behavior."[5]

While researchers like Simon LeVay maintain that a biogenetic explanation of sexual orientation offers a moral shield for gay people, it is to be remembered that there is no automatic correlation of social beneficence toward people with "offensive" traits simply because those traits have an involuntary origin. Manifestly involuntary traits like race and gender have to this day elicited some of the most virulent hostility the world has ever known. This sort of hostility is not a museum piece; in the time of the most sophisticated genetic knowledge the world has ever known, there continues to be well-documented discrimina-tion based on genetic status.[6] There is, therefore, no a priori reason to think that a biogenetic explanation of sexual orientation—even one that showed that erotic interests were involuntary—would quench the desire for change in peo-ple who find a trait offensive for one reason or another, and neither does it fol-low that if a trait is somehow "in the genes" or otherwise biologically involun-tary that it lies beyond attempts at intervention.

Biogenetic explanations can, furthermore, be altogether irrelevant to the dis-cussion of attempts to manipulate sexual orientation, since many sexual orien-tation therapists have abandoned the language in which therapy was once jus-tified as the rectification of pathological or disordered states. Many therapists speak now about obligations to serve patient preferences and values, thus alto-gether bypassing contentious questions of its origins. As two therapists once put it: "The decision concerning the modification of sexual orientation should be based on the life circumstances and values of the individual rather than the value systems of the therapists."[7] Therapists and their clients could easily absorb any and all biogenetic accounts of sexual orientation and continue efforts at sexual reorientation without missing a moral beat. For them the origins of homoeroticism, whether strictly caused by genes or something else, would be altogether *irrelevant* to the ethical question of offering a therapy to patients who were unhappy about their sexual orientation.

To be sure, Richard Pillard may be exactly right that some psychiatrists will believe that a biological causal account of sexual orientation would be reason to foreswear sexual orientation therapy, but this is merely a psychological argument, not a morally compelling one. What persuades people on a psychological level does not necessarily have the force of a convincing moral argument about what should or should not prevail as a matter of professional advisories or public policy. To the extent the ambitions of sexual orientation science are realized—the ability to predict, induce, prevent, or reverse psychosexual traits—sexual orientation science may very well hold out more, not fewer, means therapists might use to control sexual orientation. At the very least sexual orientation science will open up new possibilities for research and experimentation. In this chapter I will examine whether and to what extent it would be immoral to undertake sexual orientation therapy using research that uncovered the causal determinants of erotic interests. I will be guided by the assumption that autonomy is the chief fulcrum of analysis in determining the moral legitimacy of sexual orientation therapy. Objections to the use of sexual orientation therapy will be convincing, therefore, to the extent that they show the pursuit of such therapy to be the consequence of compromised autonomy.[8]

There are many social forces that influence people in their decisions involving the kinds of traits they desire and the therapies they pursue. For example, cosmetic surgery and liposuction are much driven by influential social ideals of slender and shapely people, ideals that are influential by reason of their sheer pervasiveness and the rewards socially linked to them. Even if there are influential social forces that shape people's views of what is desirable, I do not accept any strong version of paternalism that would forbid people from pursuing therapies of these kinds. In the first place, raising barriers to liposuction or cosmetic surgery would be to punish the victim of these social ideals not the perpetrators. Second, barring procedures while society continues to promote the ideals obtainable by those procedures is not solution either. Last, the real problem is not that people want to be slender or better looking; the social problem that should be addressed is how society induces people to have these desires all out of proportion to their significance for a rewarding life. The same set of problematics exists in regard to sexual orientation therapy.

Even if I think that people should be respected in pursuing sexual orientation therapies, it does not follow that one may do anything in the name of modifying existing sexual orientations. There are fairly clear guidelines that ought to govern the practice of experimental methods of sexual orientation therapy, and I will try to describe these below. The observance of these principles would rule out some but certainly not all experimental treatments. The discussion in this chapter applies only to adults. Questions of prenatal interventions or interventions in the sexual orientation of children are taken up in chapter 4.

THE STATUS OF SEXUAL ORIENTATION THERAPY

There has hardly been a school of biomedical or psychic science that has not been plumbed for its capacity to control sexual orientation. Many of these attempts at therapy followed the development of scientific innovations of their times in psychology, endocrinology, and neurology, for example, rather than being pioneered independently of movements in these disciplines.[9] The availability of electricity, for example, brought with it an interest in biomedical applications, and it was not long before homoeroticism was treated with "Farradic therapy"—electroshock aversion. Most typically therapeutic efforts were investigated in emerging scientific fields by practitioners with a distinct interest in sexual orientation therapy rather than the originators of medical advances who thought sexual orientation important as an object of inquiry in its own right. Or sexual orientation therapy has been raised in regard to identifying the significance of a particular biomedical theory for the entire range of human disorders and/or complaints. It is in this latter regard that the question of sexual orientation therapy has even been considered by acupuncturists who report that they are not hopeful about the prospects for success.[10]

Regardless of the biomedical or psychological theory underlying the effort, the goal of virtually all this science has been to produce heteroerotic interests in men and women and to suppress their homoerotic interests. Instances of efforts to *develop* homoerotic interests in men and women are rare in the extreme. Psychologists Mark F. Schwartz and William H. Masters mention that they encountered some men with this kind of therapeutic interest, indicating that their primary motive was impotence with women.[11] One other case mentioned in the literature involves a "college-age satyr" with an exceptional sex drive who felt limited by his heterosexuality; he thought he would achieve greater sexual satisfaction with males. Even though he could take "passive/non-ejaculatory roles as a 'call boy' " with men, he remained turned on by women. Try as he might, he could not become homosexual.[12] In theory, of course, a complete sexual orientation science could very well inaugurate homoerotic interests in straight people. Of course, given the historical difference in the social standing between gay people and straight people and the difference in their power over biomedical research, it has been control over homoeroticism that has been the goal of research. That it is almost *always* gay people who seek therapy is by itself

very telling about the social caste system that exists in regard to sexual orientation. This asymmetry ought to be a red flag that there are questions not merely
of therapy but of social standing at stake.

Attempts to extinguish homoerotic interests and replace them with heteroerotic interests have ranged widely: from moral exhortation to surgery, from
religious counsel to pharmaceutical remedy. Aversive therapies have involved
efforts at psychological conditioning and chemical interventions.[13] One British
therapist injected a man with nausea-inducing drugs, played audiotapes of
homoerotic sex, surrounded him with glasses of urine, all to the point of inducing hallucinations in the man.[14] Figure 3.1 shows an electroshock device invented
in the 1960s by British researchers for people to use in the privacy of their own
homes to punish themselves when having unwanted thoughts and behaviors,
homoerotic thoughts and behaviors included. In one particularly gruesome
"therapy," one therapist paired homoerotic images with images of a subject's
mutilated mother.[15] Other interventions against homoeroticism have involved
surgery such as testicle transplants, pharmaceutical treatments provoking con-
vulsions, and an uncountable number of psychodynamic techniques, of which
psychoanalysis is the best known.[16]

To be sure, not all sexual therapy techniques have been risky and injurious;
some have been as benign as they have been ludicrous. In the late nineteenth
century, for example, one U.S. neurologist prescribed fatiguing bicycle rides for
a man who wanted to avoid homosexual "acts which were naturally abhorrent
to him."[17] That physician praised the bicycle's properties not only in regard to
its powers over sexual orientation but more generally: "If physicians would
study the bicycle as a remedy and prescribe it intelligently, they would find it
exerting a beneficial influence far in excess of their expectations." Therapy was
hardly, though, always as mild as this naive adventure in cycling. In extreme
cases some people died as a result of therapy techniques, especially when these
techniques opened people to the possibility of drug overdoses or infection, as
happened with castration and other surgical interventions.[18] Because there is
very little comprehensive research on the effects of sexual orientation therapy,
it is difficult if not impossible to know how many people left therapy with
greater difficulties than they took to it.[19]

Because there has never been a well-established body of knowledge in the
area, sexual orientation therapy has proceeded in a number of ways, reflecting
the views of a particular therapist or the governing assumptions of the disci-
pline involved. Sometimes therapy could proceed without a well-developed
theoretical account of the origins of homoeroticism, as in the case of therapies
that emphasized not the origins but the mutability of sexual orientation. Covert
sensitization therapies, for example, did not worry much about the causes of

FIGURE 3.1
An electroshock device offered by British physicians for the home treatment of
homoerotic impulses. R. J. McGuire, M. Vallance, "Aversion Therapy by Electric
Shock," *British Medical Journal*, Jan. 18, 1964, p. 151. Reprinted by permission of the
BMJ Publishing Group.

homoerotic interests so much as the extent to which they could be modified.
Aversive therapies in general did not dwell overlong on theories of homoerotic
development.[20] Thus are to be explained their emphasis on *reconditioning*
rather than on the reasons homoerotic interests exist in the first place.[21] One
behavioral therapy based on these presumptions counseled homosexual men to
masturbate according to their usual erotic practices but to shift suddenly when
highly aroused to fantasies of women, in the expectation that they would be
reconditioned away from men toward women by linking orgasm with those

fantasies.[22] The Masters and Johnson program for the reorientation of "dissatisfied homosexual men" also depended on the assumption that sexual orientation was mutable regardless of its origin. These researchers claimed that "even if the proportion of genetic or biochemical influences contributing to homosexuality for any individual is equal to or greater than postnatal influences, there is no reason to believe that this fact would specifically deny the possibility of altering the individual's sexual preference."[23] This claim is not overstated. It may very well prove true that traits with an undeniable genetic basis are susceptible to intervention and control.[24] For many theorists, therefore, the origins of homoeroticism, if not altogether irrelevant, are at least moot in regard to the prospect for a sexual orientation therapy.

Other approaches, by contrast, have emphasized the importance of identifying any psychodevelopmental mechanisms by which people have homoerotic interests, which emphasis remains true in psychoanalytic and other psychodynamic traditions today. Because these kinds of therapies are often tied to specific claims about the psychological origins of sexual orientation, it is not surprising that many therapists in the analytic tradition denied outright that homoeroticism had any significant biological or constitutional causes. Such was the view, for example, of psychologist Edmund Bergler, a redoubtable advocate of sexual orientation therapy.[25] Even where analysts admit the potential influence of biological factors, a great deal of psychoanalytic thought today holds that the only way to diminish homoerotic erotic interests is to identify the developmental pathways followed by any given individual and, cognizant of this history, use various psychological and behavioral interventions to pursue other sexual interests. The specific mechanism of the development of homoerotic interest remains theoretically important to the prospect of reorientation. It should be noted, too, that some researchers in the biological traditions have also emphasized the importance of ascertaining the origins of homoeroticism in order to offer a mechanism of control. For example, researchers have attempted to cure homoeroticism by manipulating levels of hormones, on the assumption that men and women have homoerotic interests because they lack gender-typical hormone levels. These sorts of "imbalances" in men were treated to no avail in regard to sexual orientation, though in some cases the intensity of homoerotic interests was, ironically, *increased*.

In spite of the claims of success sometimes made by proponents of sexual orientation therapy, there are reasons to be skeptical that these accounts and treatments have delivered what was expected of them. In the last century British psychologist Havelock Ellis was among the earliest skeptics of sexual orientation therapy, observing that while many homosexual males can be brought to perform heterosexual coitus, this accomplishment failed to extinguish homoerotic interests and amounted to little more than what he called masturbation per vaginam.[26] More than a half century later the British Medical Association echoed his skepticism and declared, "It must be admitted with regret that some of the advice given to homosexuals in the name of treatment is often useless, simply defeatist, or grossly unethical."[27] Three decades ago a review in the *British Medical Journal* concluded: "We have yet to find any evidence, in our experience or in literature, that the direction of intensely homosexual drives can be successfully altered."[28] Psychologist C. A. Tripp says that psychiatrist and psychoanalyst Irving Bieber, whose 1962 report is to this day probably the most often cited on the possibility of sexual reorientation, was unable to offer a single subject for independent evaluation.[29] Even the most ardent supporters of sexual orientation therapy are hard pressed to show that their methods effect significant and durable shifts in erotic interests.

Even with the most generous and sympathetic reading of the literature of sexual orientation therapy, it is hard to avoid the conclusion that there is no confirmed method of altering the sexual orientation of people from the fundamental sexual interests, fantasy structures, and patterns of interpersonal affection that they have as adults. This is not to say that sexual orientation is monolithically uniform in any given person, for there will be in any person fluctuations in the nature and intensity of erotic interests; no one's sexual orientation—considered as the totality of erotic interests—is the same at the ages of fourteen, thirty-one, and sixty-seven. It is to say, however, that there is no confirmed method of therapy that will fundamentally alter the sexual orientation of randomly selected men or women with effects that are confirmably durable in regard to their erotic gender interests.[30] What therapy does sometimes appear to offer is an expanded repertoire of sexual capacities and social skills. The Masters and Johnson program for dissatisfied adult homosexual men, for example, set as its goal increasing the ability of subjects to socialize with women, engage in conversation, ask for dates, and ultimately to interact sexually with women. This kind of therapy may expand the social and sexual capacities of a man, but it does not thereby suppress existing social and erotic interests any more than learning a new language suppresses one's native tongue. If there is a method that can reliably redirect a person's sexual orientation, it has yet to be discovered.

It is interesting to note that virtually every sexual orientation therapy ever formulated has typically passed into history along with its originators. The methods of, for example, chemical aversive therapy and countless psychological treatments have not survived their originators. The McGuire and Vallance home-electrical shock mechanisms may be found, if they can be found at all, in a medical museum, and probably on a dusty and obscure shelf even there.

Whatever these therapy efforts did for individual clients, they did not serve as the foundation for future research and therapy. Many of these therapies have proved, that is, self-limited efforts without significant empirical base or conceptual power.

Psychoanalysis has proved one exception to this rule of obsolescence, and in the United States that school of psychology has been the conceptual foundation of a great deal of sexual orientation therapy. It is, however, a matter of debate whether Sigmund Freud intended psychoanalysis to be used as Irving Bieber and many other psychoanalysts have used it. Literature professor Henry Abelove has argued that Freud did not intend the use of psychoanalysis as a treatment for homosexuality; on the contrary, he says Freud was openly critical of American analysts for their inclinations to "cure" gay people.[31] My own reading is, by sharp contrast, that Freud did not deny the legitimacy of sexual orientation therapy per se or the role psychoanalysis might play in it. In his published remarks and recorded statements, there is nothing to suggest that Freud ruled out sexual orientation therapy as a logical possibility even if he was dubious about the success of such therapy or the need for such therapy.[32] Yet whatever Freud might have concluded about the role of psychoanalysis in sexual orientation therapy, especially when put to use against *all* homoeroticism, psychoanalysis has proved especially durable in its interest in the origins and manipulation of erotic interests.

Despite the fact that sexual orientation therapy has gone down so many blind alleys and proceeded with risk and injury to uncounted people, there has been only limited discussion of the ethics of its practices.[33] In large measure the roiling debate about the psychological status of homoeroticism—pathological or not or only sometimes—eclipsed finer-grained questions about the practices of sexual orientation therapy. For example, Ronald Bayer's account of the A.P.A.'s declassification of homosexuality focuses not on the ethics of the practices of sexual orientation therapy but on the question of whether or not homosexuality is disordered in itself.[34] This is not to say that there was no discussion of the practices (as against the theory) of sexual reorientation therapy, for there was some. One of the earliest public gay protests against medical practitioners involved psychologist Nathaniel McConaghy's methods of chemical aversive treatment, but this sort of protest was possible only following the political organization of gay people.[35] It is only in the calm afforded by settling the question of pathology in the negative and by the emergence of people publicly and politically interested in the matter that the practices of therapy emerged clearly in their own right as objects of analysis and assessment.

In general, the greater an evil therapists and their patients and/or clients thought homoeroticism to be, the greater were the excesses committed against it.[36] Though no other efforts at reorientation were as collectively systematic and objectionable as those of Nazi Germany,[37] condemnable reorientation efforts have transpired individually within the confines of private health care relationships around the world and in public institutions, sometimes at judicial order. The efforts to redirect sexual orientation may be in their historical totality just as objectionable as the historically transient but convulsive excesses of the Nazis. Many of the practices historically offered would today be summarily judged unethical not only because they violate ethical precepts in favor of informed consent and autonomous choice but because they do not "fit" the "problem" of homoeroticism.

There has been accumulating evidence for decades that the psychological problems of gay people are primarily the function of social hostility rather than problems derivative from homoeroticism properly speaking. Such was, for example, the contention of a U.S. National Institute of Mental Health report in 1972.[38] In revising its diagnostic nomenclature, the A.P.A. also attended to the question of the adventitious origin of the psychological suffering of gay people.[39] A 1994 American Medical Association (A.M.A.) report on the health care needs of gay people noted that "most of the emotional disturbance experienced by gay men and lesbians around their sexual identity is not based on physiological causes but rather is due more to a sense of alienation in an unaccepting environment."[40] In light of this emerging consensus it hardly seems just to respond to emotional disturbances in the lives of gay people by trying to eradicate homoeroticism, to treat the victims of social depredations while leaving the source of the burdens untouched. Seen from this point of view, the appropriate response to the problems of gay people should not be treatment of the individual but efforts to abolish the social ills that are the ultimate cause of any emotional disturbances.

For all the attention that should be given to the social origin of the psychic suffering of gay people, the question of therapy nevertheless remains open, if contested. It is to be noted that while the 1994 A.M.A. health care report counsels physicians against the use of aversion therapy as a method of treatment, it does not universally condemn therapy efforts. It leaves open the question of nonaversive therapy even as it notes the social origins of the motives for which most people seek reorientation. Given the medical profession's general view that individual patients and physicians are best served if they enter voluntarily into mutually defined relationships, the A.M.A. does not foreclose health care relationships in which both patient and physician jointly agree on the value of sexual orientation therapy. By retaining in its diagnostic nomenclature the category of "sexual orientation distress" for those with unwanted sexual orientations, the A.P.A. has functionally reached the same conclusion: while there should be no general presumption of the need for therapy for gay people—and they should not in any case be treated with aversive therapies if they desire to be rid of their homoerotic interests—those who suffer from unwanted homoerotic interests may still legitimately pursue treatment. Because it remains a theoretical possibility and because there is nothing in the diagnostic nomenclature or the ethics of the health professions that rules it out universally, there continue to be champions of sexual orientation therapy.

Religious groups also continue to offer ministries to bring men and women back into the heterosexual fold,[41] though these groups have sometimes ironically served as sexual recruiting stations rather than as mechanisms of deliverance from gay sex.[42] One 1980 journal report claimed a significant success rate for a sexual reorientation program that relied on social interactions, religious study, and efforts at spiritual growth.[43] Unfortunately for its authors, backsliding is not uncommon following such "successes," with some of the subjects in this study later confirming their homoerotic interests. Richard Green has also described how other people reported as therapy successes in the professional literature have, in time, been uncovered as undeniable "failures," that is, as people whose homoerotic interests remained intact.[44] Panels of "changed" men and women nevertheless appear in the news and entertainment media from time to time to proclaim the possibility and value of sexual reorientation. The venues in which these people appear hardly permit close assessment of the claims of change being made. Given the lack of confirming data in the scientific literature, claims of change should be treated skeptically. Expectations of greater happiness and the suasions of religious belief and social currents may nevertheless be expected to produce and sustain a market for sexual orientation therapy even if the gains of gay advocacy diminish its appeal generally among women and men who find ways to embrace open and rewarding lesbian and gay identities.

CURRENT RESEARCH AND SEXUAL ORIENTATION THERAPY

Those looking for techniques of sexual orientation therapy in the research reports of LeVay, Bailey, and colleagues, Hamer and colleagues, or Hall and Kimura will be disappointed. There is nothing in these reports that by itself offers a mechanism of controlling the sexual orientation of an adult or manipulating a child or fetus in a way that would permit control over sexual orientation. Joseph Nicolosi's work does describe a therapy, but it is a therapy that is hardly different in kind (theoretically or practically) from the many other therapies that have previously tried and failed to redirect sexual orientation. In fact, Nicolosi does not claim in his book that his therapy has changed anyone's sexual orientation in the sense of extinguishing homoeroticism and leaving only heteroeroticism in its stead. In this section I will describe the implications for therapy of each of these research reports and suggest that while they offer no clear method of sexual reorientation some of them do suggest research pathways that might be explored for the prospect of some measure of control over sexual orientation. At the present time, though, there is no reason to think that a successful therapy is imminent, Nicolosi's enthusiasm for his therapy notwithstanding.

The INAH3 Study   Simon LeVay did not claim that his study of the comparative size of INAH3 in gay and straight men identifies "the cause" of homoeroticism. As LeVay himself notes, it is unclear whether the INAH3 plays an exclusive role in the determination of sexual orientation. It may be, for example, that INAH3 volume is epiphenomenal to the more decisive determinants of sexual orientation or that it is but one element in a cluster of such determinants. He therefore cautiously confined his interpretation of the results to the modest claim that his study suggests a biological basis for sexual orientation. That interpretation, by itself, cannot serve as the theoretical foundation for therapy. In his *Queer Science* LeVay does however speculate that modifications in the INAH3 might effect sexual orientation.[45] This speculation opens the prospect of experiments intended to redirect sexual orientation by manipulating the INAH3 in one way or another.

Let us assume for the moment that the volume of the INAH3 is the single determinant of sexual orientation in a human being and that we had secured through all the ethically appropriate channels gay men willing to submit themselves to experiments on their INAH3 in order to shift their erotic interests from men to women. Gay volunteers interested in this kind of experiment would have been the kind of clients who sought out the Masters and Johnson clinic when it was in operation and who continue to seek out therapists around the country to this day. One could just as easily imagine that the experiment involves the development of homoerotic interests in straight men, though volunteers for such an experiment would be much harder to come by. In any case, a number of hypothetical interventions are imaginable. A neurosurgeon might attempt to increase the size of small INAH3 volumes by, for example, stimulating new cell growth in the area or attempting to increase the size of existing cells. The neurosurgeon might even attempt a kind of sexual orientation brain transplant and introduce exogenous INAH3 cells into a gay man, INAH3 cells taken for transplant from a straight man. At the farthest reaches of the scientific imagination, one might even hypothesize that a genetic intervention could increase the total number of INAH3 cells or their existing size. It would be a matter of experiment to determine whether in fact interventions of this kind could modify the existing sexual interests of adults.

The limitation of these efforts is, of course, that their governing assumptions may prove unfounded. It is to be remembered that the second largest INAH3 structure in LeVay's study belonged to a gay man, and that several INAH3 from straight men were dwarfed by INAH3 from gay men. There is no invariant correlation between INAH3 size and sexual orientation. It does not follow that merely increasing the volume or cell number of the INAH3—were that possible in live adults—would necessarily ensure a straight sexual orientation any more than a reduction in the volume of the INAH3 would deliver a gay sexual orientation in a previously straight man. From the available evidence damage to this cell region seems not to turn straight men into gay men but to eliminate or vastly reduce sexual interest.[46] Moreover, it is unclear that interventions in INAH3 volume or cell density would necessarily reorder the erotic interests of adults, which may be firmly entrenched by reason of developmental experiences and behavior. This is merely speculation, of course, but an increase in cell volume might merely increase an adult's sexual interest, not change its nature. Finally, LeVay himself concedes it is a theoretical possibility that INAH3 size is not a cause of sexual orientation but an effect of other biogenetic and perhaps even developmental determinants of sexual orientation.[47] If this were so, any alterations would be meaningless in regard to sexual orientation.

By itself, then, LeVay's comparative INAH3 study does not offer the basis of an effective sexual orientation therapy, since the role of the INAH3 in sexual orientation is unclear and since there is no known intervention or manipulation that can control its size. Both these matters, could, as LeVay himself notes, be researched further. By all accounts, INAH3 interventions for the purposes of manipulating sexual orientation belong in the speculative future rather than in the health care present.

The Sibling Studies Michael Bailey and his colleagues describe a familial correlation with sexual orientation—namely, probabilities about the likelihood of the sexual orientation of one's brothers and sisters given one gay or lesbian sibling. Theirs is a circumstantial case for genetic contributions to sexual orientation, though a suggestive one, and their methods do not permit any identification of the specific genes or genetic mechanisms that might be involved in the development of sexual orientation. Consequently, there is no method of sexual orientation intervention for either adults, children, or fetuses implied in their reports. At most, one might use these studies as the basis for a study of sexual orientation in one's familial lineage and attempt to calculate the odds of having gay or straight siblings or perhaps offspring. On the basis of these calculations one might wish to forgo having children if one feared a child of an objectionable sexual orientation. Even so, it is unclear that calculations of this kind would be especially useful to parents. Not only would the calculations take probabilistic form—and therefore be unable to offer any definitive predictions—they would also be subject to the accuracy of data about sexual orientation in one's family, data that is often absent or incomplete. Basing decisions about children on expectations of their sexual orientation is not, in any case, a therapy. Sibling studies might contribute nevertheless to the scientific culture in which the search for gay genes is an acceptable research goal, and a therapy might conceivably emerge from future genetic study, but it would still remain to be settled whether and to what extent the sexual orientation of adults is mutable if it has a genetic component.

Pedigree and DNA Linkage Studies   The quest for a "gay gene," seriously hypothesized at least since sociobiological explanations of homosexuality,[48] took a leap forward with the work of Hamer and his colleagues. They not only hypothesized the existence of genetic determinants, they attempted to locate them. Using family pedigree studies that suggested a matrilineal heritability of homoerotic sexual orientation in males, Hamer and his colleagues conducted DNA linkage studies and described a region on the X chromosome of a common genetic region shared by gay brothers. As mentioned in chapter 1, it remains to be determined whether this correlation can be replicated by researchers other than Hamer and whether it is meaningful relative to sexual orientation. If so, further studies might attempt to identify a gene or set of genes within that region that do predict and perhaps determine homoerotic sexual orientation in some males.

If we assume the Xq28 will yield a gene or genes that are responsible for a homoerotic interests in at least some men, it is still highly problematic whether that discovery would also yield any simple mechanism of control over the sexual orientation of adults. At present there is no therapy method implied in Hamer's research, not only because there are no specific gene(s) identified as causally involved in sexual orientation but also because the mechanism by which they could effect erotic interests is entirely unknown. What genes do is effect the production of proteins, and the causal pathway between the production of those proteins and erotic interests would remain to be elucidated. Yet, like LeVay's research, this line of inquiry does open a broad range of research possibilities, some of which might end in some sort of genetic intervention or manipulation capable of controlling sexual orientation. That possibility of intervention would itself likely be a long theoretical way off. It is unclear, first of all, that a genetic intervention in adulthood could undo a habituated sexual orientation. It may be that the window of opportunity to control sexual orientation occurs very early on in development and could not be undone by even aggressive genetic manipulations later on. It is unclear that the cognitive components of sexual orientation—conscious knowledge of and habituation in one's erotic interests—would be easily undermined by a genetic manipulation in adult life. Second, for all the vaunted rhetoric in which genetic therapy is discussed, there is at present very little success in the field. A great gulf divides the rhetoric of genetic therapy and its actual accomplishments, which could at best be called modest and suggestive.[49] Even on the most optimistic interpretations a great deal of research remains to be done before the significance of Hamer's work can be established, and even more work remains in establishing genetic therapies generally, let alone one that could influence a complex and multiply determined trait like sexual orientation.

Dermatoglyphics Studies   J. A. Y. Hall and Doreen Kimura's dermatoglyphics study is similar to the Bailey studies in that it does not imply any intervention that would prove useful as a therapy for adult sexual orientation. In their descriptions of a correlation of finger skin ridge density with sexual orientation, they do not suggest—nor should they—that any intervention in regard to finger ridge density is capable of altering sexual orientation; changing adult finger skin patterns simply will not affect sexual orientation. Hall and Kimura do describe some fetal influences on dermatoglyphic patterns, and they note that there are maternal events that seem to affect dermal ridges. Given a correlation between dermal ridges and sexual orientation, there may be a commonality of maternal-fetal events that influence the determinants of sexual orientation at the same time they influence dermal ridge patterns, but this matter would require considerable investigation. Though future research might discover some correlation in fetal development between determinants of sexual orientation and finger skin ridges, and thereby open the possibility of an prenatal intervention for sexual orientation, there is at present nothing in dermatoglyphic research that lays the foundations for a therapy for adults.

Paternal Harm to Male Children   Unlike the previous researchers, Joseph Nicolosi does describe a therapy that aims to inaugurate or restore a heteroerotic sexual orientation lost to a male child because of psychic trauma suffered at the hands of his father. As Nicolosi offers virtually no evidence on behalf of his claims either in regard to the origins of homoeroticism or the efficacy of his therapy, it is impossible to assess the merits of the therapy he describes, which consists of a program of therapy designed to reconstruct past relationships with a man's father and to assume more gender-typical traits. Join a gym, Nicolosi advises men with unwanted homoerotic interests, despite the fact that gyms are a key nexus in gay social and sexual life. The advantages of pumping iron might yield to the temptations of the shower room.

Nicolosi says his therapy is not a cure in the sense of erasing all homosexual feelings: "However, it can do much to improve a man's way of relating to other men and to strengthen masculine identification. As a result of their treatment, many men have been supported in their desired commitment to celibacy, while others have been able to progress to the goal of heterosexual marriage."[50] This therapy is as scientifically deficient as most therapies that came before it. There is no data offered regarding the number and demographics of the people on whom this therapy has been attempted. There is no baseline description of an individual's sexual interests and practices before and after the therapy, and there is no follow-up assessment made about the durability of any changes toward heteroeroticism. In fact, in describing celibacy as an outcome, Nicolosi describes neither change in homoerotic interest or gender identity. Celibacy—understood not as the ecclesiastical promise never to marry but as abstinence from sex—may be achieved with any gender role, with any gender identity, and with any sexual orientation. Celibacy does not change sexual orientation, only sexual practice. Nicolosi is wise to state the outcomes of his therapy in a guarded fashion. If no promises are made, none can be broken.

It is not difficult, however, to stipulate under what conditions Nicolosi's therapy should have been tested before being offered to the public as a legitimate treatment. At the very least, people entering his therapy should be described objectively in regard to the full complement of their existing erotic interests and behaviors. This assessment should also be conducted again after therapy. Control groups should be identified not only in regard to reports about childhood psychic injury and their influence on sexual orientation but also in regard to similarly situated people who undergo another form of sexual orientation therapy or who undergo no therapy whatsoever. As Nicolosi has met none of these minimal standards of scientific assessment, it is unclear that his account or therapy is anything more than speculation driven by the force of personality, anything more than the latest chapter in the dismal history of unsubstantiated sexual orientation therapies.

EXPERIMENTAL ETHICS

There is nothing illogical about thinking that human erotic interests might be subject to some degree of control, whatever their ultimate causality. If we keep John Money's view of the goals of research in mind, a complete sexological account of human beings will be able to predict, induce, prevent, or reverse any psychosexual trait. While science is nowhere near this sort of functional ideal and there will probably be natural limits to this sort of power, it remains true that the test of the adequacy of a complete account of sexual orientation would be exactly its abilities along these lines. By discussing ways in which erotic interests may be amenable to biological control, it is important to reiterate that I do not deny the influence of cultural and personal factors as determinants of erotic interests. Not only do I fully accept the view that erotic interests are shaped by culture, I welcome this view for its contribution to scientific inquiry in explaining the multiplicity of erotic identities and interests. The right question to ask is not whether biology or culture determines sexual orientation. The right question to ask is, "What is the interplay between developmental experience and biology in shaping erotic interests in a given individual or population?" This matter may be studied empirically, and without scientific study of exactly this question the issue of the social construction of sexual orientation and erotic interests remains contentless and merely an unfounded and otherwise uninformative assumption. It may well be that erotic interests are not more biologically caused than habits of reading text from left to right or right to left. But there is no way to know this in advance of conducting sexual orientation research, part of which will involve an examination of the mutability of erotic interests and the interdependent relationship between social forces, biological processes, and personal choices.

It is also worth mentioning that it is not only biological science that grounds the conceptual possibility of sexual orientation therapy. Social constructionist accounts of erotic interests—accounts in which people are scripted into various psychosexual roles—hold out at least as much hope, insofar as they assume that human erotic desire is a sort of tabula rasa on which social forms are printed. That sort of passivity and mutability of erotic desire is fertile ground for advocates of sexual orientation therapy. There is nothing in a doctrine of social constructionism that rules out the possibility that given erotic interests can be changed.

As I have noted most efforts at sexual orientation therapy are products of their scientific times, reflecting theories and practices of the day. Most therapies followed the development of discoveries in the fields of psychology, endocrinology, pharmacy, and so on. In many ways these fields have been mined out with regard to their potentials for control over sexual orientation insofar as no definitive technique has appeared. It is in the newly emerging sciences, or in the sciences now better equipped with sophisticated technology, that sexual orientation research is likely to raise anew the question of therapy, genetics, for example. There have been to date no therapeutic interventions of a specifically genetic kind for homosexuality, such as interventions to modify a person's genomic endowment or to conduct germ line therapy for the purposes of eliminating gay and lesbian progeny. The principal expositors of eugenics were by and large silent on the topic of homoeroticism despite their interest in cataloguing and eradicating all sorts of socially objectionable traits.[51] By contrast, contemporary geneticists almost routinely mention that the question of genetic influences in sexual orientation deserves sustained debate and deliberation.[52] Given that there is continued interest in the biogenetic foundations of sexual orientation and antipathy toward gay people, efforts to translate the gains of genetic research into therapy may be hard to resist despite the declassification of homosexuality and the political viability of gay people as a social group in many countries around the world. In some ways the question is not whether this sort of genetic experimentation will go forward but how.

Sexual orientation therapy in the past has often violated even minimal standards of research ethics that are today accepted as axiomatic. Men and women were subjected to compulsory treatments, sometimes at court order.[53] Informed consent protocols were simply not observed in regard to spelling out to patients and clients the likelihood of success, the risks to be incurred, and alternative means of dealing with troublesome sexual interests. People captive in one or another way to their situation were selected for treatment: prisoners, the institutionalized, children being treated at the wishes of their parents, and desperate people from all stations in life.[54] The efforts to redirect sexual orientation in gay people are sufficiently egregious to deserve a place of prominence in any history of the moral mistakes of the health professions.

In spite of all the historical ills committed in the name of rescuing gay people from their erotic interests and despite compelling reasons to recognize homoerotic interests as legitimate in their own right, it is still possible to design experiments in sexual orientation therapy that would survive moral scrutiny. Some people might find such research offensive, but the same principles that protect gay people from unwanted biomedical intrusion in their lives also permit others to pursue sexual orientation therapy. That is, the *option* of sexual orientation therapy can be defended in some instances even if its ultimate merits remain in doubt. As sexual orientation research takes many forms, it will be useful to consider the kinds of issues that would be relevant to each.

Research that takes the form of pencil and paper questionnaires or interviews, administered with appropriate consent, ordinarily involves no risk that would justify cessation or censure of research that had therapy as its goal. Such interviews might have as their goal, for example, a determination of the total number of gay people in a family across several generations. The quality of the questionnaire or interview is not definitive in an assessment of its ethics because both researchers and subjects are free to waste their time on bad research. Whether they are theoretically well substantiated or merely hobby projects carried out in ignorance of the counsels of the best developed science in the area, researchers should be free to conduct this kind of research simply by obtaining the subjects' consent, so long as the subjects know what they are getting into and that they may walk away from the project without any penalty.

For the same reasons that apply to pencil-and-paper questionnaires, researchers should also be free to conduct and subjects should be free to enter research protocols that attempt to differentiate people by sexual orientation according to finger ridge density, fat distribution, brain structure, forms of intelligence, or any other trait that captures a researcher's interest. The primary consideration in research of this kind is, again, informed consent: the willingness of a subject to undergo any proposed examinations after having been apprised of the purpose and risks involved in those examinations. This observation applies, again, only to the procedural aspects of the research and does not pass judgment on the merit or quality of such research efforts. So long as consent to participate is voluntarily given, it is hard to object to survey research whether it has as its object erotic histories or somatic traits. Certainly agencies charged with funding research—and especially public funding agencies— would need to pay attention to the scientific merit of research, since it would surely be wasteful and possibly unethical to expend money on poorly designed research projects. It is not, however, inherently unethical for people to engage in poor research as either researcher or subject.

Sexual orientation science that actively seeks to produce a therapy—to produce a change in the erotic interests of a given individual—requires rather more ethical scrutiny than does research that merely wants to describe erotic interests and behaviors or observe morphological or psychological differences between gay people and straight. Experimental psychological therapy especially should hew to standards of respect for informed consent and autonomy better than has been done in the past. For example, given the absence of convincing evidence that sexual orientation therapy is effective, therapists who undertake this kind of effort with a patient or client should unconditionally represent it as experimental in nature. As a matter of course therapists should also disclose their views about homoeroticism, whether they think it pathological, psychologically disordered, morally repugnant, or otherwise inimical to human well-being. They should also apprise their patients/clients that there are competing views more accepting of homoeroticism. Unless therapists do this, patients may unwittingly absorb the therapists' views on sexual orientation without due reflection. Therapists should also disclose their own personal experience in efforts at reorientation, revealing in a general way their successes, failures, and all outcomes in-between, as well as alternative methods of dealing with problems attributed to sexual orientation: how a given individual might, for example, come to accept a gay or lesbian identity and forge a meaningful and rewarding social life. In other words, the therapist should not presume that the only recourse to complaints about sexual orientation involves suppression of the "offending" trait. It almost goes without saying, too, that therapists ought to disclose the likely course of treatment: what it will entail, how long it will last, and what it will cost.

None of these caveats rules out psychological efforts at sexual orientation therapy even if they do raise questions about the standards by which it is practiced. Even the years-long experiments of psychodynamic therapies can be conducted ethically through proper informed consent procedures. In the course of long therapies it would be highly desirable to reconsider the goals and prospects of the therapy from time to time so as to accommodate changing expectations from the patient/client. A patient/client should also be recognized as having the right to abandon therapy at any time. This counsel may not seem especially problematic, since people can abandon voluntary therapy simply by walking away from it. In psychiatric and psychological therapies, however, "contracts" are often formulated by patient/client and therapist and often include a statement of willingness to agree to undergo therapy for a certain time. A therapist can also induce a great deal of emotional dissonance in someone who wants to leave therapy contrary to the therapist's wishes. If contracts about the duration of treatment are to be formulated, they should always include a mechanism for leaving therapy in a way that is not burdensome.

What ethical guidelines ought to guide therapeutic efforts that involve more than "talking cures"? Because of principles of respect for individual choice and informed consent, experimental therapies of even an aggressive kind would not be altogether ruled out. At this point it is unclear that professionals ought to avail themselves of aggressive efforts given the absence of evidence that they will have the desired effect. Should there emerge some scientifically sound reason to attempt therapy anew, with modifications that represent a significant theoretical advance on past failures, they should go forward only after warning subjects about the nature and risks of the intervention to be faced. One might expect that therapists would prudently take several occasions to discuss with their subjects the value of pursuing, for example, behavioral therapy, in order to give subjects the opportunity to change their minds.

The sort of experimentation described above in regard to Simon LeVay or Dean Hamer's work could also be constructed in such a way as to pass moral scrutiny by an institutional review board charged with monitoring the ethics of research, though there would have to be substantial scientific reason for thinking that an intervention could have the intended result, reasons more substantial than currently exist. In the case of LeVay's work there might eventually emerge possible ways to visualize and manipulate the INAH3 in living adults. If manipulations of the INAH3 could be carried out safely, it would remain to science to establish whether they offered any benefit in altering sexual orienta-tion. The same holds true in regard to Hamer's genetic work. If a gene were identified that seemed—by reason of a convincing theoretical account of its effects—to dispose men toward homoeroticism, some men might seek manip-ulation of their genetic endowment in order to modify their sexual orientation. So long as standards of informed consent and protection from undue risk were scrupulously observed, so long as these men clearly understood that the manip-ulations are highly experimental and might prove injurious or be of no avail whatsoever, it does not seem that this sort of experimentation could be ruled out as immoral on its face. Even if the therapist could hold out *no* certainty of hope that a subject's sexual orientation could be altered, experimentation of this kind might be defensible as a project in basic research. As a morally accepted matter of fact many people currently enroll in clinical trials that offer them *no* therapeutic benefit; they enroll knowing that they are contributing only to a general advancement of knowledge and should not expect any partic-ular benefit in regard to an unwanted condition. The same sort of experimen-tation might go forward with regard to sexual orientation.

Certainly sexual orientation therapy could spawn unethical practitioners who fraudulently promise results they cannot hope to deliver or who expose patients to unacceptable risk, but, in general, experiments might be designed by practi-tioners that meet every relevant standard for disclosure and patient safety, and the remedies that prevail against health care fraud elsewhere should apply to practi-tioners of unethical sexual orientation therapy. There is nothing about experi-mentation with the sexual orientation of adults that is inherently objectionable, and it cannot be ruled out in kind, though some experiments might be ruled out if they were predictably doomed to failure, involved unacceptable levels of risk, which are of course the same standards that apply to experimentation elsewhere.

In no instances should any legislative statute or judicial decision impose sex-ual orientation therapy—extinguishing homoerotic interests and inaugurating heteroerotic interests—as a penal sanction. British mathematician Allan Turing is the most famous person to have undergone court-ordered therapy following a conviction for gross indecency.[55] That "indecency" was, in fact, nothing more than consensual sex with an adult male. As part of his sentence Turing was required to accept estrogen injections, thought at the time to have the effect of redirecting erotic interests. No such effect occurred. Turing seems to have looked on the injections as a nuisance to be waited out more than anything else, but his subsequent suicide has complicated a clear understanding of his response to the court-ordered treatment.

Not only does the experimental and unproved nature of these therapies mil-itate against their adoption as legal sanction, it is also far from clear that courts should involve themselves with the extinction of *a disposition to commit* crime as against merely punishing violations whatever their origin or likelihood of recurrence. After the conviction of the accused, prison systems may wish to make modes of therapy available to prisoners for rehabilitative purposes, but this provision of elective services should be very different from requiring therapy. One would in any case have to attend very cautiously to the circumstances of any prisoner volunteering for sexual orientation therapy, for captive populations often suffer morally relevant limitations on the exercise of free choice. Ethical counsel now cautions against imposing the risks of research on populations merely because they are convenient and pliant. Judicial imposition of sexual orientation therapy seems in any case never to have been widely practiced and may in fact be altogether extinct in developed countries. It is nevertheless worth mentioning legal sanctions of this kind because public and judicial rage over sexual crimes can from time to time make therapies attractive as penalties. Going down that road, however, raises more questions than it answers since imposed therapy diminishes personal responsibility, represents an inequitable distribution of research risks, conflates individual well-being with legal behavior, and undermine's medicine's traditional commitment to the individual rather than to the ambitions of society or state.

After this kind of defense of sexual orientation therapy, the one residual question worth examining involves the question of coercion and its damaging influence on the ability of people to give informed consent. Ethical examinations are not complete if they do not attend to the context in which decisions about experimentation are made. A cultural hostility toward homoeroticism may induce some gay people to seek reorientation just as it may spur practitioners to enter the field. Concerns of this kind have been raised with regard to the pursuit of all manner of facial reconstructive surgeries, to heavy people seeking out liposuction, to black people seeking to lighten their skin or modify the appearance of their hair, and there is every reason to attend to cultural coercion in regard to sexual orientation therapy. Can it be that sexual orientation therapy is desired—even conceived as a biomedical goal—because of social hostility toward homoeroticism? I have no doubt that social hostility, transpiring in families and social institutions of every size and scope, contributes to the abjection experienced by many people with homoerotic interests. I also have no doubt that it is that kind of hostility and lack of social accommodation that leads some people to despair of their sexual orientations and seek change. The relevant question is not whether there are some coercive aspects at work in this pursuit but whether this coercion is of a magnitude that sexual orientation therapy should be ruled out in kind in the name of protecting people from decisions that are adverse preferences, preferences that would not be made except for social hostility. I do not think this question can be answered in the affirmative any more than the medical profession or society should rule out liposuction because there prevail oppressive social ideals about the desirable body weight of men and women.

While it is true that people do need to be protected from damaging social ideals, ideals that suggest that the only valuable people are straight, white, thin, and twenty-something, it does not follow that all liposuction, skin bleaching, or sexual orientation therapy should be ruled out on paternalistic grounds. Given the importance of respecting individual autonomy, it is best to respect people who make even unwise decisions, though just as certainly it is also imperative to object to and try to reduce the social influences that artifactually produce interest in therapies in the first place. It is just as important to point out that an implicit function of the therapy is to conform people to pervasive cultural ideals rather than to shape society to accommodate people in the lives and erotic interests they in fact have. For my part, I would rather see sexual orientation distress dealt with by dismantling the pervasive heteronormativity in family life, education, religion, politics, and entertainment than by raising moral objections to sexual orientation therapy. For those adults who do not see it that way, however, I can reluctantly respect experimentation with sexual orientation provided that it goes forward in a scientifically meaningful way and is ethically circumspect. A not incidental effect of failed sexual orientation therapy is that it gauges what does *not* work. Sometimes, that is no small accomplishment.

If we achieve the degree of causal knowledge imagined by John Money as the goal of sexological research, we will have achieved the conceptual foundations for further research into methods by which sexual orientation could be controlled—to the extent it is controllable. This is to say little more than that in its imperative to know everything relevant to a general theory of human erotic development sexological science can be as a matter of course expected to produce theoretical pathways for controlling erotic interests, again, to the extent they can be controlled. If science set out to map the function of every part of the human brain, that project would *necessarily* produce information about any and all roles played by the brain in erotic interests. If science set out to identify behavioral effects of the entire human genome, that project would *necessarily* produce information about any and all genetic components of erotic interests. Both these kinds of projects would, thereby, imply methods by which some degree of therapy for unwanted erotic interests could be pursued, whether that took the form of eliminating homoeroticism, heteroeroticism, or any of the paraphilias. Research does not have to be tightly focused on sexual orientation per se to produce information that might be useful to a theory of sexual orientation control, whether that research involves psychological, neuroanatomical, or genetic investigation.

Even if science does produce a well-confirmed account of psychosexual development on the scale I have imagined here, it does not follow as a matter of course that sexual orientation may be manipulated and controlled at any stage of life. It may prove, for example, that a woman or man who comes to a therapist at thirty years of age for sexual reorientation has waited too long for control over traits that are only manipulable during fetal development or perhaps adolescence. I suppose one could argue that a *genuinely complete* sexological science should be able to alter the erotic interests of anyone at any age—even of the most senescent person on his or her deathbed—but this threshold of success can be only fallibly approached by mortal researchers toiling amid the vagaries of human finitude and erotic desire. Theoretically we should be able to induce, prevent, cure, and reverse such conditions as diabetes and AIDS, but we cannot do all these things either. There will always be a therapeutic promised land into which we cannot enter. If a method of reorienting entrenched and abiding erotic interests does emerge, it may be effective only in a short window of opportunity. If that window of opportunity occurs in adult life, ethical concerns about sexual orientation therapy—for those interested in going forward in this area—involve proper informed consent and protection from undue risk, including protection from fraud, unrealistic expectations, and impediments to autonomous choice. I discuss the ethics of controlling the sexual orientation of nonadults in the next chapter.

To say that some kind of control over erotic interests is possible is very different from saying that this therapy *should* be pursued by either a given individual or the biomedical profession as a whole. Although sexual orientation therapy seems to me conceptually plausible and ethically possible, I do not believe that it should be ordinarily pursued by either individuals or the health professions. I am unconvinced that homoeroticism is any significant obstacle to important human objectives, to the states and accomplishments that confer value on life. On the contrary, homoeroticism holds in my view a singular and important place in the constellation of human value, and therapy implicitly rejects that significance. C. A. Tripp once observed that therapy invites the therapist and the subject to construct the notion of the subject's abnormality against the normalcy of the masses at large.[56] He therefore wondered whether and to what extent the difference and the problems of gay people were artifactually constructed around their homoeroticism, while taking the "normalcy" of heteroeroticism for granted, as coextensive with human erotic nature itself. The pursuit of sexual orientation therapy does seem to me to suggest that the primary value for human beings belongs in their conformity to majoritarian norms, in this case, heteroerotic interests and values.

Moreover, the moral gulf between heteroeroticism and homoeroticism may not be especially wide. Homoeroticism is more like than unlike heteroeroticism insofar as both sexual projects share mutual purposes and meanings; the differences in sexual practices between gay and straight becoming vanishingly small against the background of mutually shared meanings in gay and straight relations. Both sexualities may be put to purposes good and evil. Moreover, the alleged narcissism of homoeroticism is paralleled in degree if not in kind in the many commonalities shared by partners in straight relationships. For all these reasons I conclude that homoeroticism is valuable in its own right as a pathway to human meaning.[57] I do not therefore attach special importance to the goal of achieving an effective sexual orientation therapy that would extinguish an important moral perspective. When it comes to public funding of research, there are plenty of good causes that go begging for funds, including research programs aimed at disabling health crises, that ought to have priority over funds expended to find a way to turn gay people into straight people.[58]

Sexual orientation therapy *will* remain morally problematic insofar as it considers homoeroticism as an isolable, treatable problem of the individual rather than as a systemic social question about the treatment of gay people generally, as if the sole relevant imperative is to help the suffering individual and not to confront the society that makes him or her suffer. While there are no absolute moral barriers to the pursuit of sexual orientation therapy by individual persons and therapists, it is morally irresponsible not to question the heteronormativity that permeates moral and social expectations and sustains the value of therapy as a personal and professional goal. Fortunately, there has been increasing recognition of the social origins of the emotional disturbances that surface in the lives of gay people, though it is clear there is still a great distance to go in articulating the depth and degree of deprivation suffered by gay people. In describing the conditions under which gay people come to maturity, philosopher Joseph Sartorelli has given an extremely sensitive and informed portrait of the enduring ways in which homoeroticism and gay people are abjectly treated.[59] He has described the hardship and abuse of gay people that are abetted by acts of commission and omission by virtually every major social institution. These are no mere inequities to be shrugged off as nuisances; on the contrary, these inequities do profound damage to the self-esteem of gay people, even enslaving them in a servility of temperament. It is perhaps a measure of social and moral gains made against this systemic inequality and of the resilience of human beings generally that the question of therapy for sexual orientation does not arise for most gay people. It is even an ironic side effect of sexual orientation therapy that its failures confirm some people in their acceptance and affirmation of gay identities.

In their 1978 study Bell and Weinberg documented efforts by self-identified gay men and lesbians to redirect their sexual orientation. Depending on their sex and race, between 11 and 23 percent of the subjects had consulted a professional with the idea of trying to give up their homosexuality.[60] Bell and Weinberg studied people who came of age before anything like the revolutionary social and political advocacy the gay movement of the 1970s brought into being and that thrives to this day. Given these gains, it is fair to suspect that far fewer gay people now express dissatisfaction with their sexual orientation and that far fewer people think that homoeroticism is a psychological disorder, that modification of homoerotic interests is desirable, and that they should pursue therapy. Nevertheless, because of the far reach of moral and religious condemnations of homoeroticism and because of the social deprivations that still attach to homoeroticism, the number of people who would see homoeroticism as disordered and/or objectionable—and therefore want therapy—would not be zero. Given a culture in which people can increasingly live openly and rewardingly with a gay identity, however, the lure of therapy will never be as seductive and as misleading as it has proved in the past, however effective it were to become. In any case, if research were to offer an effective sexual orientation therapy, it need not take unwilling victims. The existence of a sexual orientation therapy need not pose a threat to individual adult gay people since anyone would have the right to refuse it. It may well be offered by therapists hostile to homoeroticism and sought by people unhappy about the nature of their homoerotic desires, but such would be their right. There is no state interest that justifies a governmental or professional ban against the use of a treatment of this kind even if that treatment is still in the experimental phase.[61] By the same token there is no state interest that could justify the involuntary use of a therapy of this kind with adults, especially one that is experimental.

Because sexual orientation therapy has been mostly a cause in search of a theoretical justification and an effective practice, not even the rejection of judgments of pathology or disorder by professional associations in medicine and psychology will sweep it permanently into the dustbin of history.[62] Neither would the prospect of sexual orientation therapy be foreclosed by failing to show that erotic desires have causal components in anatomy or genetics. The sheer ambition of sexological science keeps the prospect of therapy alive. For its moral justification sexual orientation therapy may appeal to its conceptual plausibility—that is, it might be possible—as well as the right of therapists to develop and offer therapies to those who think them worthwhile. All this amounts to a prima facie case for noninterference with sexual orientation therapy research. By the same token the search for treatment should be recognized as morally problematic. Historically speaking, sexual orientation therapy is problematic because it has typically and utterly failed to deliver what it has promised. Morally speaking, if sexual orientation therapy is to be taken seriously it must show that it is not imbued with baseless claims about disorder, that it is freely sought, that it is not a displacement of social ills onto the individual, and that there is some scientifically credible reason to believe that a new effort will succeed where other therapies have only failed. Meeting these conditions would raise the threshold of morally acceptable sexual orientation therapy much higher than has been the case in the past. Meeting these conditions would also probably rule out most of what passes for sexual orientation therapy in the present.

4 |||||||||||||||||||||||||||||||||||||||||||||||||||||||||||||||||||||||||||||||||||

CONTROLLING THE SEXUAL ORIENTATION

OF CHILDREN

As the origins of erotic interests are poorly understood, there are no means of ensuring that a child will have a given sexual orientation, though there seems to be considerable folk advice on the subject. Parents of all cultures are imbued with notions of how to influence a child's sexual orientation; these notions often involve conforming a child's behavior to cultural expectations about what it is to be a girl, to be a boy, in the belief that conformity to gender roles produces heteroeroticism in children. These notions also involve the kind of relationships children should experience. For example, as a way of preventing homoeroticism in children, Sigmund Freud cautioned against the rearing of boys by males and the emotional absorption of male or female children by a parent of either sex.[1] There is no evidence, however, that this folk wisdom offers parents unfailing control over the sexual orientation of their children. Unwanted homoerotic and paraphiliac interests—such as necrophilia and raptophilia—emerge in children and families of all kinds, contrary to all efforts at gender conformity and ideal family dynamics.

There has been no shortage of commentary linking the latest findings in sexual orientation research with techniques by which parents might control the erotic lives of their own children. Extrapolating from his hormone studies with rats, Gunter Dörner once suggested that neuroendocrine-conditioned male homoeroticism can, in his words, "be prevented once and for all by a single androgen injection administered during critical [fetal] brain development."[2] As Dörner believes that homoeroticism is a tragedy ending in millions of suicides, it is not surprising that he believes fetuses at risk for homosexuality should be identified through amniocentesis and that abortion would be desirable for those fetuses unable to benefit from androgen therapy. Suppose some parents were convinced by Dörner's work that hormone treatments should be administered during the fetal development of male children to ensure their heterosexual orientation. Should doctors accept parents' requests to carry out such an intervention? Or suppose a genetic probe were commercially available that could identify the genetic traits thought to be highly predictive of homoerotic sexual orientation. Should parents be able to obtain that test and then go on to use its results in their decisions about prenatal interventions, even abortion, in order to avoid having a child they think will be gay? Simon LeVay has said that parents should absolutely not subject their children to genetic or neurosurgical treatment in order to control their sexual orientation, but that neither should legislation be adopted to prevent women from using prenatal diagnostics in order to ascertain the likely sexual orientation of their child or to abort any unwanted child.[3] Other commentators have been less willing to accept the aborting of pregnancies likely to end in gay children.

While these sorts of issues can seem highly speculative, they are nevertheless engaging, if only because so many people think we are headed toward some kind of sexual orientations tests. LeVay, for example, thinks that a test and possible interventions for sexual orientation are neither theoretically nor temporally far off.[4] What moral conclusion may be drawn about the right to use tests and interventions for sexual orientation were they in fact available to the average parent? In order to answer this question, it will be necessary to consider in a general way the extent to which parents are entitled to control the sexual orientation of their children; the specifics of possible kinds of tests or intervention may then be discussed. A caution to be kept in mind throughout the discussion is that there are at present no interventions of any kind that are confirmably known as identifying or controling the sexual orientation of any child one way or the other, whether these interventions involve hormones, genes, anatomy, or rearing practices. As John Money has made clear in his survey of the biological factors involved in psychosexual development, no single aspect of anatomy, hormones, genetics, or rearing is sexual orientation destiny.[5] This does not mean, however, that moral issues cannot be illuminated by considering the nature and extent of parental control over the erotic lives of their children.

I will discuss here only the morality of attempts to extinguish *homoerotic* inclinations, behaviors, and predispositions in order to replace them with *heteroerotic* interests. I will not discuss other aspects of sexual orientation, including transvestism, transsexualism, and the paraphilias, though the control by parents of these forms of sexuality in their children is certainly worth discussion in its own right. The question thus construed, I will try to show that interventions designed to control the sexual orientation of children are morally problematic because children are not entitled to or obliged to have a sexual orientation of a specific kind, because parents have no right to a child of a specific sexual orientation, and because parents have no duty to secure a specific sexual orientation for their children except one that affords them a measure of personal value and satisfaction—and homoeroticism is well within the range of sexual orientations that do exactly that. These conclusions do not amount, however, to an argument that parents should be forbidden to use sexual orientation controls that are safe and efficacious prenatally and that violate no moral interest of a child. Although there is very little to be said in favor of trying to control the sexual orientation of children, there is just as little to be said in favor of restricting parents should they want to use safe and efficacious sexual orientation diagnostics or interventions so long as that use does not conflict with a child's interests. This is not to say that children have no rights to be protected from sexual orientation controls, but it is to say that a political presumption in favor of parents' rights gives them the right to make even morally problematic judgments so long as the abiding interests of their children are not compromised in the ways I will discuss.

CONTROLLING THE SEXUAL ORIENTATION OF CHILDREN

Historically, experimental efforts to replace or suppress homoeroticism have been overwhelmingly directed toward adults. This therapeutic focus has shaped not only public debate but also the historical record. For example, Ronald Bayer's account of the A.P.A.'s change in judgment about the "pathology" of homosexuality offers no discussion of children except to note that psychodynamic theories often locate the origins of adult sexual orientation in childhood events.[6] This sustained focus on adults might appear surprising given the presumption that the lives of children are more plastic and susceptible to intervention than those of adults entrenched in their habits and identities. It is the conventional wisdom of psychology, after all, that sexual orientation is more or less "fixed" during childhood. A small number of researchers have proposed that intervention and prevention in "the potentially homosexual child" is a more promising course of action than interventions in adulthood.[7] One might therefore expect to find efforts to eliminate homoeroticism focused in a more sustained way on children, especially among those theorists who favored "nurture" when that explanatory category of sexual orientation was favored against its wrongly supposed opposite, "nature." In fact, however, it is and has been adults at the center of most sexual orientation therapy.

There are a number of reasons psychiatry and psychology have focused on the homoeroticism of adults this way. Parents, psychologists, and psychiatrists have sometimes seen the homoerotic behaviors of children as transient experiments and therefore not worth sustained theoretical analysis or therapeutic intervention. It may be, for example, that some degree of homoerotic behavior among children is simply a mechanism of learning the body's sexual mechanics in a nonthreatening way. Given that early sexual behavior does not predict adult behavior necessarily, childhood homoeroticism has also been ignored in the hope that it will simply go away. Homoeroticism is also more typically a stronger disvalue in adults than in children; it therefore draws more attention in adults, interfering as it can with issues without exact parallel in the lives of children, including erotic relationships, marriage, and employment. Homoeroticism can also be hard to detect in children who conceal their sexual interests in the face of perceived hostility, thus evading close scrutiny by parents or researchers. In fact, it appears that gay children will often conceal their sexual orientation from their siblings, even twin siblings, and even gay twin siblings.[8] Inattention to children may also be rooted in recent shifts in major medical and psychological organizations away from pathological interpretations of homoeroticism. If homoeroticism is not a disorder, there is little theoretical warrant for defining therapies that would prevent its emergence in children. Had some clear and effective therapy for adults been identified in fact, therapists might have well looked to extend their pool of patients by extending the therapy to children feared likely to become gay. The limitations of existing interventions may have swayed therapists away from extending their practice to children.[9]

Whatever the full complement of reasons, there has always been a more acute interest in the theory and therapy of homoeroticism in adults than in children.[10] To observe a lopsided interest in the homoeroticism of adults is not to say, however, that there has been no interest in the homoeroticism of children. The debate about sexual orientation therapy with children reached a peak in the 1970s, with George A. Rekers squaring off as the champion of therapy and Stephen F. Morin and Stephen J. Schultz its chief opponents.[11] Even now some parents send their children to therapists in the hopes of altering their sexual orientation, even if that hope is expressed in terms of worries about gender roles rather than erotic desires properly speaking.[12] Some parents worry about a child's gender nonconformity—for example, a young male's sustained preference for playing with dolls or a girl's tomboy behavior—rather than sexual orientation per se, although they may believe that unconventional behavior will lead to homoeroticism as an adult. For the most part, though, the vast majority of children with gender atypical behavior (including homoerotic behaviors) have not faced any kind of formal therapy to influence their sexual orientation. It would be a matter of speculation to guess how many parents would find such interventions attractive, though it is reasonable to assume that some would. There would be a market of unknown size for therapies that could bring children's sexual orientation and behaviors into line with their parents' expectations.

Moral philosophy has traditionally extended broad latitude to parents (and surrogates as relevant) over their children, and parents do profoundly influence the lives of their children in regard to language, education, psychological traits, ambitions, manners, religious beliefs, and values. Is it an ethically defensible extension of those rights to pursue interventions that have as their goal the control of sexual orientation in children? One way, though not the only way, to frame an answer to this question is to ask whether children have a duty to have a particular trait and more specifically whether they have a duty to have a particular sexual orientation. It turns out that it is far from clear that a child has the duty to exhibit any particular trait, especially a complex behavioral trait of unknown causality. For what reason could a child be said to have a duty to be intelligent, gregarious, patriotic, disposed toward the study of engineering, or, for that matter, straight? Although most parents might wish their children to be straight, it is unclear that children are required to be straight any more than they are required as a matter of duty to be cultured or refined in a manner that suits parental tastes. Parental desires to see a particular trait in their children do not for that reason alone create a duty on the part of children to have that trait, however beneficial those traits might be for both children and parents alike.

It may be true that parents will find homoeroticism evidence of moral failure in their children, but it is not true that parental definitions of moral failure create duties on the part of children to avoid those perceived failures because children have no necessary duty to replicate their parents' moral values and standard, and this exemption should include sexual values and standards. With respect to the broad and variable patterns of human development and the moral defensibility of differences, it is not clear that there is some more or less absolute pattern of achievement a child must observe as a matter of duty. This becomes all the more true when it is unclear how traits emerge, because one of the first conditions of an observable duty is that it must be within an agent's power to achieve. As it is unclear in general how psychodevelopmental processes lead to one particular sexual orientation rather than another, it is unclear how children could have a duty to observe an unknown psychodevelopmental standard. Consider for the sake of the argument—and only for the sake of the argument—the proposition that relevant causal events governing sexual orientation occur at age two, and that these causes have to do with the quality of family relationships. Under such circumstances there can be no meaningful attribution of duty to the child because the conditions of choice that make the notion of duty relevant are not in place: a two-year-old child cannot be held responsible for the quality of his or her family relationships. In this speculative example sexual orientation would be involuntary because the life circumstances that induce one set of erotic desires rather than another are literally beyond the child's choice. It becomes impossible, therefore, to maintain that children have an observable duty to exhibit a specific sexual orientation under such circumstances.[13] These same limitations would also impede parents' surrogate exercise of a duty on behalf of their children in regard to sexual orientation. If they were no better situated than children to identify or impose a course of psychosexual development certain to end in one sexual orientation or another, they would not have the responsibility to foster a particular sexual orientation as a matter of duty.

Even if one wanted to argue that there was some sort of attenuated duty on the part of a child to achieve a particular sexual orientation, because a child ought to be striving toward a moral ideal, it does not follow that one's duty would *always* require heteroeroticism. Relative to the variable circumstances of a child's life, there might conceivably be a duty to be gay if that sexual orientation proved of greater benefit to a child or served some social obligation incumbent on the child. Some psychologists have argued, for example, that homoeroticism represents a developmental *success* in negotiating particularly troublesome family dynamics. If so, children in such familial contexts might have a duty *to themselves* to be gay if the only alternative were a profoundly stunted heteroeroticism. If sexual orientation has a social component, one might follow the sociobiologist's lead here and suggest that some children ought, as a matter of kinship duty, follow pathways of homoerotic interests in order to free up their time for altruistic care of their siblings' children.[14] I am not suggesting that the sociobiological account of the genetic durability of homoeroticism is true or that homoeroticism has social value only insofar as it serves kin reproductive interests; I am suggesting that it is unclear that there is any relevant moral standard that would require heteroeroticism of all children as a prima facie duty. To the extent that homoeroticism is compatible with a broad range of human accomplishments and happiness, there can be no general expectation that all children ought to be straight as a matter of a generalized duty. No such narrow focus of outcome is acknowledged with respect to children in regard to goals of health, intelligence, occupational interests, or patterns of sociality; why should it prevail in regard to sexual orientation? If parents want to control the sexual orientation of children, they will have to look for their rationale to something other than the notion of a child's duty.

For many of the reasons just mentioned, a child could not claim the *right* to a heterosexual orientation. The right of a child could not be meaningfully asserted against parents as a duty to provide since there is no well-confirmed method of securing heteroeroticism in a child. Should parents look for help in controlling their child's sexual orientation, they will find none that is well validated. Little work has been reported about sexual orientation therapy with children regardless of the fact that the literature on the subject identifies the predictors of success in sexual orientation interventions to be youth itself, lack of habituation in sexual practices, and minimal homoerotic experience.[15] Claims of success can be found in the history of adult sexual orientation therapy, but even the most sympathetic reading of that literature reveals that only a fortunate few have demonstrably achieved heteroerotic capacities and that this achievement by itself does not extinguish homoerotic interest.[16] Research is even more ambiguous in regard to children. Some parents and researchers have attempted to correct gender atypical behavior in children and thereby obviate homoeroticism in later life, but these efforts have not necessarily achieved the latter goal even where they do minimize gender atypical behavior.[17] In one of the very few long-term studies to date, Richard Green found that most boys treated for marked atypical gender behaviors do eventually exhibit some degree of homoerotic interest and behavior, even if they do come to exhibit some degree of gender typical behavior.[18] The conclusion seems unavoidable: there is no successful sexual orientation therapy that works on randomly selected adults, and there is even less evidence that a therapy exists for assuring the heteroeroticism of children. For this reason children cannot be said to have the right to be straight for there simply is no mechanism parents can use with confidence to achieve exactly that goal. One cannot have a right to that which is impossible to provide.

Moreover, even if children did have rights in regard to sexual orientation, it does not follow that they would always have the right to be straight. If, in the totality of things, a child would be better served by a homoerotic orientation—because it offered a surer pathway to happiness or because there was some social obligation incumbent on him or her that would be better served by being gay—a child might be said to have the right to be gay, not straight. If, as I will stipulate, homoeroticism is no inherent deprivation but fully compatible with important human achievements and happiness both individually and socially, it does not follow that failure to achieve heteroeroticism in one's erotic dispositions would count as a deprivation or failure such that a child's rights would be abrogated if he or she were gay.[19] Even if one concedes the point that society does not much value the lives of its lesbian and gay members,[20] it does not follow that a child's rights would require that parents do everything possible to make them straight. A child's rights in regard to sexual orientation could be met, for example, by parents who helped their children resist any hostilities that do in fact attach to gay and lesbian lives, whether or not their children end up gay or straight. Observing children's putative rights in regard to sexual orientation need not therefore take the form of avoiding homoeroticism when other beneficent measures would seem to satisfy any duties a parent might have because of those rights or because of parental duties to protect a child.

So far this discussion has proceeded without reference to any specific method by which the sexual orientation of children might be treated. The exact nature of a treatment would, however, be relevant in making a determination of any rights and duties. A simple extension of the methods that have been used with adults to adolescents would, for example, be ethically problematic. It is unclear that it would be desirable, for example, to enroll a fourteen-year-old boy in a program modeled on the Masters and Johnson reorientation program, a program that involved extended sexual exploration and experimentation with a supportive female.[21] Covert sensitization techniques have been used in therapy to produce a psychic link between homoerotic behavior and repugnant associations. Should a thirteen-year-old girl really undertake a sensitization process that requires imagining repulsive sexual couplings between women until she can no longer endure to engage in those acts herself?[22] Would it really be desirable to subject adolescents to the prospect of costly years-long therapy that is the hallmark of psychoanalysis? Past efforts at sexual orientation therapy have included hormonal therapy, chemical convulsive therapy, electrical convulsive therapy, chemical and electrical aversive therapy, and even brain surgery. To the extent these measures are unproved, it is not clear that anyone could claim that parents had a duty to try them on children or that children had a right to them. Parents and children might have the right of access to these therapies, to use them if they think fit, but that is very different from saying that parents meet their responsibilities as parents *only* if they enroll their children in therapies of these kinds.

What, though, if control over sexual orientation were as easy as administering a single pill? Would that change anything in regard to the rights and duties of parent and child alike? Philosopher Lawrence Crocker has argued that should a "magic pill" become available for ensuring a heterosexual orientation in children, it should be made available and used as parents see fit. For the sake of his argument, Crocker assumes that (1) heterosexuality in children leads to a greater good for the child, the family, and society, (2) that homosexuals are significantly less happy than heterosexuals, and (3) that no social transformation can alter these previous two conditions.[23] Crocker uses these assumptions to come to the conclusion that parents should have the option of using such a sexual orientation pill. In fact, the conclusion here must be much stronger than Crocker allows. If the governing assumptions he proposes are accepted as true, then parents would hardly be responsible if they did not use the pill with their children. Indeed, if the fate of homoerotic identity were as desperate as Crocker describes it, parents acting in the best interest of their children would seem to have a prima facie *duty* to use the pill: parental beneficence would seem to *require* the use of the pills because it would be negligent to let one's children grow up in ways that caused individual and social detriment and less overall happiness, under conditions that were intractable to change.[24] Given the assumptions of his argument, only significant extenuating circumstances would seem to absolve parents from charges of outright neglect if they did not administer the pill. In fact, given Crocker's assumptions, pills of the kind he imagines should probably be routinely administered at birth if not dumped into the water supply along with fluoride as a matter of routine public health.

The more damning problem with Crocker's position is not in the conclusions he draws from his assumptions but the governing assumptions themselves, assumptions so untenable as to render them useless. Crocker himself calls them "far-fetched" and "implausible."[25] If they are far-fetched, there is no reason to respect them as forming a legitimate basis for discussions about informed choices. That point is ironically made by Crocker himself when he postulates the existence of sexual amnesiacs, people who have forgotten their own sexual orientation. Crocker imagines that such people would choose to become heterosexual, since by hypothesis the governing assumptions could under no circumstances permit homoeroticism to be construed as a rational choice.[26] There is no choice at all in the matter since there are no other live, morally defensible options.

In fact, the life circumstances of men and women with homoerotic interests do not preclude personal, familial, and social well-being, individual gay people are not inherently less happy than their straight counterparts, and social transformations can and do certainly improve the lot of gay people. Less contentious characterizations of homoeroticism than Crocker's would take these facts into consideration. While homoeroticism does carry certain social disadvantages, it is nevertheless compatible with human happiness and achievements, and most self-identified gay men and lesbians do not wish for some intervention, magic pills included, that would have spared them their sexual orientation. When polled by Alan P. Bell and Martin S. Weinberg, the largest majority of gay men and women rejected (72–89 percent, depending on sex and race) the prospect of a magic pill given at birth that would have guaranteed their being straight. By even larger majorities (86–95 percent, depending on sex and race), they rejected a pill that would *today* (at the time of the survey) change their sexual orientation to heterosexual.[27] Given this evidence about the acceptability of lesbian and gay orientations to the people most directly affected by them, it is not unreasonable to think that a sexual orientation amnesiac might choose homoeroticism as a legitimate pathway to erotic fulfillment. At the very least, an amnesiac pondering that choice should know that for the most part gay people *do not* regret their sexual orientation. A choice by a sexual amnesiac in favor of a gay or lesbian orientation could be made in the confidence that homoeroticism is not so disabling as Crocker represents its. Such a choice might even be buttressed by considerations of social justice: a sexual orientation amnesiac might want to cast his or her lot with an oppressed people and fight for their liberation.

To be sure, the choice sexual orientation amnesiacs would make would be highly dependent on the sorts of information that was available to them. If it were possible that people could lose their race and choose to be restored in one race or another, those decisions too would be highly conditioned on what sort of information was available and whether that information skewed the decision in one way or another. It is nevertheless unfair at the outset to discuss homoeroticism in terms that would, in the abstract, force people to choose against it uniformly and universally—even if most sexual orientation amnesiacs would choose to be restored to a straight sexuality rather than any other after being advised of the options available to them.

This conclusion should inform parental choices about using a magic pill or any other intervention designed to control the sexual orientation of their children. If we approach the question of sexual orientation in children as one of substituted judgment, trying to judge what is in their best interests, one cannot assume that favoring heteroeroticism over homoeroticism is the only defensible course of action open to parents. At the very least, there can be no universal assumption that respecting children's best interests would lead only and in every instance to heteroeroticism or that parents were acting irresponsibly if they tried to bring their children up gay. This is not to say that a magic pill should not be made available to parents, but it is to say that most of the motives for wanting to use it seem to rest on indefensible assumptions about the nature of gay and lesbian life.

In spite of the majority opinion in the Bell and Weinberg study, there were small percentages of women and men who regretted their homosexuality a great deal, whose occupational lives were disrupted by their homosexuality, who thought themselves afflicted with an emotional disorder, and who would deliver themselves from their fate if only some magical pill were available.[28] Some gay people, too, would be much disturbed if their own sexual orientation were visited upon their children.[29] That there is no monolithic opinion among gay men and lesbians on whether their children should be spared homoerotic destinies certainly suggests that there should be no reason to expect uniformity of opinion among prospective heterosexual parents faced with the same issue. In fact, many people might well agree with the view of one sexual orientation therapist that "a young child's natural instinct might be to just eat salty or sugary food. But every parent knows that is bad for them. They'll have a healthier life if they have a balanced diet. And emotionally they'll have an easier life if they are heterosexual."[30] That they would agree with this statement is not to say that most heterosexual parents would fail to accept and love their homosexual children, but it is to say that if a measure were available to ensure heterosexual children it is reasonable to believe that many parents would want to use it, asserting the need to protect the well-being of their children and, perhaps, themselves as well.

I think parents who wanted to use a magic pill governing the sexual orientation of their children should have the political right to do so because parents have the right to be left alone in certain kinds of decisions. This is a political right of noninterference asserted against all individuals and society, a right that is ultimately grounded in the recognition of the plurality of moral goals if not also in the recognition of the evils that attend socially enforced moral visions. Even if parents are ultimately wrong about the best interests of their children, they should nevertheless have this kind of political right of noninterference as they try to promote the moral outlook, religious beliefs, and political interests and values of their children. With young children who have no interest in what kinds of erotic desires they have, in the sense that deprivation of one sexual orientation and the imposition of another would not cause them any harm as they could express it, parents should have the right to promote certain erotic interests and values of a kind consonant with their own values so long as those efforts do not harm abiding interests of the children. Certainly no harmful therapy should be morally tolerated, and there will come a point in each child's life when a parent's right to control sexual orientation evaporates just as that right evaporates in regard to political and religious interests.

Let me make this latter point through an example: on returning home unannounced, parents might discover their fifteen-year-old son in sweaty sexual play with his male wrestling teammate. Outraged because his behavior violates not only their moral precepts but also disrupts their sense of his identity, they might wish to send the boy to a therapist in order to "change" him. The boy himself, however, might have no appreciable conflict about his homoerotic interests; he might be well on his way to embracing a gay identity without apology. He might express more concern over his parents' moral censure than his sexual orientation per se: what *he* wants to change is his parents' attitudes. He would like to bring his boyfriend home to the welcome his parents would have shown a girlfriend. On the assumption that moral philosophy has the duty to protect people in their legitimate interests, it is hard to see that parents' wishes regarding their son's sexual orientation should have precedence over their maturing adolescent's interest in his gay identity. This right of a child to noninterference in sexual orientation grows stronger as a child matures and increasingly evinces a durable interest in the sexual identity he or she has and wants. Even though a son or daughter remains a child at fifteen, a parent's rights of control are not uniform across the entire period of minority.

For parallel reasons parents might have the duty to help a child change an unwanted sexual orientation. The current nomenclature of the A.P.A. recognizes sexual orientation distress, characterized by "persistent and marked distress about sexual orientation."[31] It might be argued that a parent sometimes has the responsibility to help a maturing child reject homoeroticism in order to control this kind of distress. For example, a fourteen-year-old girl raised in a religious home might find herself repulsed by her own sexual interests in the lithe cheerleader next door yet find herself unable to control those feelings. If discovered spying on the showering cheerleader, the girl might confess to her parents that she has long suffered from interests in females and that she wants desperately to "go straight" in order to fulfill her dream of a married life with children of her own. If the fifteen-year-old boy above is to be respected in retaining his homoerotic interests, consistency requires that a child equivalently situated should be respected in dealing with unwanted homoerotic interests. A parent would be justified in trying to relieve a child's distress in either case. In the latter case, however, it does not follow that distress can or should be relieved only by attempting to redirect sexual orientation. The distress might be managed equally well by showing the child how to cope with stress and how to incorporate her actual erotic interests into a vision of a rewarding life. Given how little success has been reported in effecting fundamental shifts in people's erotic lives, raising expectations about the prospects for change can do more harm than good.

Certain stresses and distresses, moreover, seem to be a developmental feature of men and women with homoerotic interests. That is, for the vast number of people there is necessarily some degree of psychic distress attached to maturation as a gay man or lesbian. This developmental hardship should not be seen as ipso facto justification for sexual orientation therapy. That is, not all distress is sexual orientation distress of the kind or degree that should be identified as a pathological effect. To the extent, moreover, that stress and distress are tied to social devaluations of homoeroticism, sexual orientation therapy seems under the circumstances too much like treating the victims for the ills visited upon them by society. Nonetheless, there may be some children for whom a magic pill or some other form of treatment could be morally justified, and a parent might have the responsibility to help in those instances. I should say that I am not advocating this therapy as routinely desirable; my point here is only that maturing adolescents have rights in regard to the nature of their erotic lives. Equal protection of all those erotic lives will require respect for differing viewpoints on the value of homoeroticism.

I fully acknowledge that morally indefensible views may undergird parental efforts to control their children's sexual orientation. In fact, the vast majority of them may be morally defective, especially when they seem more protective of a parents' interests than a child's. A parent's duty to protect is worth further consideration because it might, at first blush, suggest that parents act responsibly only insofar as they act on their knowledge about the relative fate of straight and gay people. Parents could say, for example, that it seems to them that heteroeroticism is a superior pathway to social goods such as prestige, jobs, sexual and romantic partners, and grandchildren. It is, therefore, morally prudent to try and raise straight children. In many ways, though, this position embodies untenable or objectionable assumptions that gay men and lesbians are embarrassments to their families, that they cannot find rewarding personal and familial arrangements for themselves, that they will of necessity be excluded from rewarding jobs and social prestige, and that they do not have children. It is heterosexist to believe that as a class lesbians and gay men must necessarily suffer an inferior personal and social fate. In fact, many gay men and lesbians do achieve fulfilling relationships, important jobs and social prominence, good relations with their parents, and more and more single and coupled gay men and lesbians are having children.[32] It is heterosexist to assume that social deprivations that attach to homoeroticism (such as feared loneliness in old age, risk of sexually communicable diseases, etc.) are necessary features of gay life and not merely artifacts sustained by heteronormative standards of culture and, it must be admitted, the culpable and nonculpable failure of gay people themselves to resist their political and social mistreatment.

Whether or not parents' beliefs about the fate of gay children are ill-founded or not, the morally relevant question here is whether any error in their beliefs would justify constraint on their use of magic pills or other means of control over the erotic lives of their children. Not all evils are of a magnitude that they ought to be barred by law or professional consensus.[33] It strikes me that parental wishes in regard to sexual orientation controls should not be formally sanctioned so long as those controls do not jeopardize the health of children or work against their self-identified interests. As I have said, were there a magic pill available that, administered at birth, could give a child a specified sexual orientation, I think parents would be within their rights to use it so long as it was entirely without side effect. Moral philosophy already rightly accepts parental influence over a great many traits of children, even influence ultimately damaging to children, e.g., raising children as racist, failing to develop children's intellectual capacities, blunting artistic capacities, and so on. It does not seem to me that the administration of a magic pill guaranteeing heterosexuality can be construed as damaging to a newborn child even if it is done for heterosexist reasons. If, however, the mechanisms of control involved harm to a child or involved conflict with a child's interests in having a gay or lesbian identity, it becomes much harder to argue that a parent's rights to control sexual orientation should prevail as a matter of ethics or law. If children may be emancipated from their families in regard to work and residence, they should also be eligible for emancipation in regard to sexual orientation.

The logic of this position would protect parents who might want to bring their children up gay. So long as we are in the business of speculating about magic pills, these pills could just as easily make children gay as make them straight. Were they given identifiable mechanisms of sexual orientation control, some gay and lesbian parents—and maybe other parents as well—might choose gay and lesbian children just as others would choose straight children. The largest percentage of lesbian and gay respondents in Bell and Weinberg studies said they would not be at all upset or only very little upset if a child of theirs became homosexual.[34] They were not asked if they would actively want gay children, but it is not unreasonable to think that some would. The same moral entitlement that permits parents to try and raise straight kids would help parents who wanted to do so to raise gay kids, no matter if other parents objected, so long as the means involved were safe, efficacious, and did not interfere with a maturing child's self-identified interest in having a straight sexual orientation.

It belongs to speculation, of course, to entertain the notion that parents will be able to choose a child's sexual orientation in any simple way by using a magic pill or its biopsychological equivalent, but there are moral lessons to be drawn from this discussion. If we know as a matter of fact that many children have homoerotic interests, it is hypocritical to pretend that they do not, and it is damaging to subject them to uncompromisingly heteronormative standards of behavior and expectation. It may be therefore that parental control of sexual orientation should not even be taken as the central feature of a discussion about protecting and promoting the interests of children. Perhaps one should begin discussion of this kind with a question about what parents and society should do to raise potentially gay and potentially straight children together in an environment that does not promote antagonistic prejudice. It may be that parents have more responsibilities in that regard than in trying to ensure that a child has one particular sexual orientation or another. At the very least, there ought to be a rejection in familial, educational, and social settings of the presumption that heteroeroticism is the nature and destiny of all children.

PRENATAL INTERVENTIONS

Whereas the previous discussion focused on interventions with children, in this section I will consider the ethics of prenatal interventions intended to control sexual orientation. There will be nothing in this discussion that alters the main frame of the argument I have been advancing so far, but a consideration of particular interventions will give an indication of the contours and limits of that argument. I will therefore consider possibilities involving gamete selection, parthenogenesis, hormone interventions, anatomical and genetic manipulations, all in order to tease out the way in which these prenatal interventions can elucidate the ethics of control over the sexual orientation of children. I will also consider the way in which certain Christian objections to these kind of prenatal interventions would figure in the debate, as these are illustrative of religious concerns generally. As will become clear, there are certain religions objections to prenatal control of sexual orientation that do not have an exact parallel in moral philosophy.

Gamete Selection and Parthenogenesis   At one conceptual end of the continuum of possible prenatal interventions for controlling sexual orientation lies gamete selection. On the highly speculative assumption that identifiable genetic endowments, discernable in ova and sperm, determine sexual orientation in the children conceived with them, prospective parents might wish to select gametes in order to do exactly that. This is, as I say, a highly speculative scenario, since it is not known whether or to what extent sexual orientation could be manipulable by gametic selection or how effectively gametes might be screened for genetic traits likely to control sexual orientation, whether those gametes come from people who themselves intend to raise the children born from them or from donors. Parthenogenesis, the practice of inducing unfertilized eggs to develop into mature—and always female—adults, is also an extremely remote consideration since no adult organisms have been produced by this method in mammals let alone humans. Even if such a practice were possible for human beings, there is at present no way to discern how the genetic endowment of an egg is related to adult sexual orientation. I mention these examples not to fan intemperate ways of thinking about the control of sexual orientation but as a way of introducing the morality of their use if they were, contrary to fact, available to parents.

If gamete selection *did* offer control over sexual orientation of children, it is hard to see why parents should not have the right to use it for that purpose. Gamete selection is presently carried out for a wide variety of reasons involving heritable disease and the desire to have a certain genetic parentage. Women seek sperm from, for example, the Repository for Germinal Choice, which banks sperm from "outstanding" men, and ova are now nationally marketed by infertility clinics. It is unclear that sexual orientation control is different in moral degree from the goals that otherwise spur scrutiny of gametes involved in conceiving children, that is, trying to influence traits especially important to parents and to avoid traits parents think objectionable in children. Trying to control sexual orientation is not so markedly different in degree from the kinds of goals parents have in selecting gametes for other reasons that it ought to be forbidden by policy or law.

This is not to say that heterosexist impulses would never be involved in gamete selection, but it is to say that the "harms" of gamete selection would not justify overriding the choices of adult men and women in this regard. Gametes are not, after all, "harmed" by being selected for use in conception or by not being selected. Children conceived with selected gametes would not be harmed simply because they were selected *as* heterosexual or *as* homosexual. If there are to be designer babies, there seems to be no reason to exclude sexual orientation from the elements that parents may legitimately design. The same conclusion would apply to parthenogenesis if gametes could be stimulated to produce adult human females,[35] though I rather suspect that if science ever produces mechanisms by which to achieve adult human beings parthenogenetically we will be preoccupied by worries eminently more serious than the sexual orientation of those single-parented beings.

Hormonal and Genetic Interventions   One might also try to control sexual orientation by fetal interventions consonant with the views of Dörner, who has said that if his findings were confirmed it might become possible to manipulate sex hormone levels during sexual brain differentiation in order to prevent the development of homoeroticism. If hormonal interventions carried significant risk of disorders to women or their children, they would be unethical on their face. Subjecting a child to the risk of, for example, permanent behavioral disorders in order to avoid an unwanted sexual orientation would be a morally unacceptable experiment. Nevertheless, I do not see that a convincing case could be made against hormonal interventions if they were safe for woman and child and if science had theoretically sound reasons to expect success from them. In fact, parents consciously and unconsciously attempt to control the sexual orientation of their children through thousands upon thousands of acts. It is unclear that the totality of these measures during a child's development is morally more significant than, say, a single and safe hormone injection carried out during pregnancy. This latter event has *less* potential for coercion and damage than a childhood of exposure to a sexual education whose overriding goal is to bring about heteroeroticism. A single injection, if it were effective in bringing about its aim, would decide the matter of sexual orientation once and for all, affording less opportunity for the damage that can occur during a childhood constantly monitored and disciplined to achieve that same result.

Interventions attempting to manipulate a child's genetic endowment would raise parallel issues and have similar conclusions. So long as a prenatal therapy was safe, efficacious, and likely to succeed, it should be within the rights of parents to use. At present science is a long way off from proposing, let alone conducting, any justifiable genetic experiments of this kind. Once again the formidable obstacles in the way of genetic experimentation have not proved a barrier to discussion of its possibility. Extrapolating the significance of his neuroanatomical research, Simon LeVay has said of efforts to genetically manipulate the size of the hypothalamus: "Reversing an adult's sexual orientation would be farfetched, because the genetic system is all set up. But in utero it is much more realistic. Developing a prenatal test that will give some indication as to whether a child will be gay as an adult could come about in a few years. But such a test would never be 100% informative because sexual orientation is not 100% genetic."[36] LeVay speculates that it would nevertheless be interesting to study children's brains at birth for hypothalamus size and, twenty-five years later, correlate that size with adult sexual orientation. There is, at present, no way to do this since the size of the INAH3 can only be measured in postmortem examination.[37]

If there were a way to determine the INAH3 size of fetuses or newborns, would hormonal or genetic experimentation be ethical to manipulate a size found wanting? The answer would depend on whether the method of measurement were safe and whether parents consented to the measurement. If, for example, some method of positron emission tomography—which images electron distribution in tissues—could be used, it might be entirely safe to subject fetuses or newborns to such study. If parents were persuaded that no harm could come to their children, they might agree to let researchers measure the size of their children's INAH3 at birth and at various points thereafter.[38] One could, that is, plausibly construct such an experiment within guidelines that protect subjects from risk and that respect informed consent. There is nothing inherently objectionable about this sort of longitudinal study simply because its object is sexual orientation. If a theoretically sound way to alter the size of the INAH3 during fetal or neonatal development were to come out of such a study, whether by genetic or other means, its morality would be gauged by its expected safety and efficacy. I continue to assume here, as in the preceding section, that an embryo, fetus, or newborn has no interest in one sexual orientation or another, and that safe and efficacious interventions do not jeopardize any rights they have in regard to their sexual orientations as adults.

Religious Views   Some religious analyses will find reproductive interventions to control sexual orientation more objectionable than I have characterized the matter philosophically. The Roman Catholic Church, for example has offered two documents that have significance for questions of reproductive interventions and sexual orientation. These documents are worth consideration because of the objections they raise against linking reproductive interventions with the control of sexual orientation.

The 1986 *Letter to the Bishops of the Catholic Church on the Pastoral Care of Homosexual Persons* characterized exclusive homoeroticism in adults as an involuntary condition, though it did not conclude that homoeroticism is a morally innocent condition, saying it remains an "objective moral disorder."[39] This moral analysis is said to be supported by the findings of the natural sciences, which findings are presumably intended to support an interpretation of homoeroticism as involuntary rather than the judgment that it is an objective moral disorder. Given both the involuntary nature of homoerotic orientation and its status as moral disorder, the document recommends that pastoral care of homosexual people include as far as possible the assistance of the psychological, sociological, and medical sciences. The exact nature of this assistance is not clarified further, but as it stands the claim is broad enough to validate medical or psychological programs of eliminating homoeroticism. This was often the thrust of past Catholic advice on the topic. One 1950s medical ethics text, for example, put the matter this way: "The aim of all pastoral care of the homosexual should be ultimately his [*sic*] reorientation to heterosexuality," and, where this fails, chastity is to be counseled.[40]

Presumably, then, the Catholic Church looks favorably on techniques designed to assist individuals in refraining from homoerotic acts and eliminating homoerotic desire. If the psychological, sociological, and medical sciences offered a treatment for homoeroticism in adults, it would appear to be acceptable to this religious community so long as relevant standards of safety and consent were respected and there were no violations of therapeutic integrity. Yet methods by which homoeroticism might be eliminated in children might nevertheless prove objectionable insofar as they involve certain prenatal interventions. The position of the Catholic Church on reproductive practices can be illustrated by reference to the 1987 *Instruction on Respect for Human Life in Its Origins and on the Dignity of Procreation: Replies to Certain Questions of the Day.*[41] Briefly summarized, the *Instruction* argues that at least the following practices are wrong: abortion, artificial insemination, cloning, embryo transfer, in vitro fertilization, twin fission, and any prenatal diagnosis undertaken with an eye to abortion in consequence of undesirable test results. It follows, therefore, that any attempt to eliminate homoeroticism in children would be forbidden under Catholic morality if it involved any of these techniques. Even if there were a measure *certain* to eliminate homoerotic desire in progeny, a goal compatible with the language of the *Letter*, if that measure involved any of the foregoing reproductive techniques it would have to be rejected as immoral.

If, however, techniques such as hormonal monitoring and adjustment during fetal development that could eliminate homoeroticism were available, these, on first sight, might prove to be morally permissible. Flushing a fetus with hormones at a particular developmental point, after all, involves none of the proscribed techniques mentioned above, but there are other considerations that muddy the water here. The *Instruction* says that "certain attempts to influence chromosomic or genetic inheritance are not therapeutic but are aimed at producing human beings selected according to sex or other predetermined qualities. These manipulations are contrary to the personal dignity of the human being and his or her integrity and dignity." Clearly, the *Instruction* rejects nontherapeutic interventions whose purposes are to conform the child to parents' expectations. If homoeroticism were defined as a pathology, the attempt to eliminate it prenatally would be nonproblematic because it would be a matter of controlling the expression of disease, and hormonal or genetic interventions would be acceptable toward that end. The *Letter* does not, however, directly apply the label of disease to homoeroticism; the *Letter* is altogether silent on the specific origins of homoeroticism and its status with regard to disease. If homoeroticism is *not* a disease (even if ultimately involuntary) and is properly speaking a moral problem, it would not seem to be the legitimate object of medical intervention. It is unclear that the moral problem of homoeroticism, if such it is, should be dealt with by prenatal genetic or hormonal interventions. No one has seriously advocated, for example, that moral problems such as fornication, adultery, and divorce be dealt with by biomedical interventions rather than by religious education and moral suasion.

The limits of parental intervention in fetal development also come up another way. Insofar as God has reasons for people having the traits they have, one wonders whether homoeroticism—as an involuntary trait—should be understood as an essential part of divine intentions for humanity. Perhaps God intends that certain people carry the burden of homoeroticism, that they find their way to salvation *precisely through* the trials associated with homoeroticism, that society benefits from having gay people in it. One Catholic moralist has said that it sometimes happens that once the gravity of this deviation, this love condemned, hopeless, and tragic in its essence is recognized, and once an individual has accepted the painful, endless struggle that it entails, homosexuality can become the occasion of a very exalted spiritual life.[42] It is certainly possible, therefore, that God intends certain people to have homoerotic interests as a condition of their spiritual development. There may therefore be religious reasons to see homoerotic traits in children as a spiritual charism that ought not be interfered with as a matter belonging to divine prerogative and as an occasion of personal growth for both child and parent alike.

To the extent homoeroticism is not a disorder or disease properly speaking, therefore, interference in embryonic or fetal development might properly be understood in some religious viewpoints as an assault on the dignity and integrity of the embryo or fetus.[43]

What is more, the Catholic Church elsewhere rejects eugenic interventions that would conform children to parental or social expectation, even where disability and difference cause suffering to both parent and child, this because it views suffering as integral to the Christian life. Carrying the cross, the *Letter* says, "is the way to eternal life for *all* who follow Christ."[44] Consequently, it seems unlikely that a rationale for the elimination of homoeroticism, based purely on the relief of the suffering of either children or their parents, would be found convincing within the confines of Catholic doctrine. One may conclude that the Catholic Church and others holding similar views must reject reproductive measures designed to eliminate homoeroticism insofar as those measures usurp the prerogatives of divine intention, involve immoral practices, or evade occasions for spiritual growth.

PARENTS AND THEIR CHILDREN

One might argue that prenatal techniques carried out by parents as a guard against children of unwanted sexual orientation are morally objectionable not because they necessarily harm children but because they embody values incompatible with parenthood. Ideal parents, it might be said, should be open to any kind of child they might have: prenatal testing aimed at selecting against gay and lesbian children not only enacts heterosexist values but also erodes unconditional attachment to children. In response to these moral evils, should prenatal testing for sexual orientation be legally barred or at least regulated so that it could not be coupled with abortion? Legal barriers or even consensus among health care practitioners against coupling genetic testing and abortion would appear to have the benefit of keeping in check heterosexist impulses in parents and their abortion providers. While that kind of policy would appear favorable to gay people, it is uncertain that this solution is plausible given the accepted logic of abortion practice in the United States and given that it would only suppress and not eliminate heterosexist practices. In the long run, a barrier against using abortion to control the sexual orientation of children could harm gay people.

In the first place, it would be hard to argue that a policy barring abortion on the basis of unwanted sexual orientation could be anything but a matter of selective enforcement. Current abortion policy in the United States generally allows adult women to choose abortion for reasons of their own without scrutiny or the permission of any public bodies or moral authorities. Adult women may choose abortion without the moral approval of spouses, family, or physicians. It is true that a U.S. Supreme Court decision upheld states' rights to require that information regarding abortion be offered to women (information regarding fetal development, state-sponsored child care programs, and so on),[45] but women may nevertheless choose abortion these informational sessions notwithstanding. At present, then, women would be legally entitled to choose abortion even for heterosexist reasons. And so the situation should remain.[46] Heterosexism is an important social evil, but it does not follow that any social sanction may be brought to bear against it. Limiting access to abortion in order to inhibit heterosexist reproductive choices of women would be an idiosyncratic policy decision and invite social scrutiny of all other abortions as to the quality of their moral rationale. In any case, sanctions against heterosexist uses of abortion would hardly offer any clear victory if they had as their result the imposition of gay and lesbian children on antigay parents who did not want them.

Moral philosophy generally presumes a rule of noninterference in the lives of adults, this on the assumption that they are individually better situated than religious, political, or other authorities to understand which choices best offer life's rewards. In such a view parents should be free to choose among possible traits for their children so long as that choice is not the result of incompetence, is adequately informed, and does not inflict an involuntary harm on a child. There is no evidence in the preference for heterosexually oriented children that parents suffer from diminished capacity. Surely, parents who wish to spare their child the social disapprobation associated with being gay or lesbian cannot be said, on that basis alone, to be suffering from any relevant mental impairment. Such a parent might not even believe homoeroticism to be a moral or psychic disorder; it may simply be the case that parents wish to protect a child in the ways they can from feared social circumstances. Of course, more selfish reasons might exist if the motive for prenatal interventions involved, for example, trying to avoid any stigma attached to having lesbian or gay children. But by themselves failure of nerve or unmitigated selfishness are no warrant for inferring any morally relevant mental incompetence.

The attempt by parents to ensure heterosexual children, if the techniques were safe, would not involve any involuntary harm against those children. It would be odd to think of heteroeroticism as an evil inflicted on a child. A parent might be wrong in thinking that heteroeroticism is the only way to happiness, but it is hard to see how a child is *harmed* by being straight, particularly since the child will not experience any harm from a safe prenatal intervention or suffer any loss of the benefits of homoeroticism that go uncompensated in kind. A child, whether straight or gay, will still have opportunities for a rewarding sexual, social, and civic life. On the contrary, the selection of sexual orientation in a child might even benefit children; if children knew that they were chosen for their traits, they might feel more secure in the relationship with their parents.[47] These points are analogously true for both gay and straight children.

One danger of reproductive controls is their perceived commodification of children, imputing to children the status of possessions desirable only as they conform to parental expectation. Moreover, an insistence on controlling the kind of children to be born might endanger parental preparedness to accept the children they actually do have, children with unwanted traits, that is.[48] The use of prenatal sexual orientation techniques, moreover, might have the effect of a self-fulfilling prophecy: insofar as these techniques are available, it will be thought that they *must* be used, and homosexual children who continue to be born will be seen and condemned as failures of medical technique or public policy.[49] These are serious concerns, but it is hard to see that these issues have more force here than they do wherever parents, as they do directly and indirectly, control the kind of people their children become in the language they learn, the values they express, and the ambitions to which they aspire. There is no reason to think that control of sexual orientation would be any more damaging to children or parents—because somehow unduly influential—than other deeply influential forms of parental influence over children. If there is to be a serious objection to the control of the sexual orientation of children through prenatal diagnostics or interventions, it bears the burden of proof in showing that of all the other ways in which parents mold their children, efforts to make them straight (or gay) are somehow beyond the pale. It is not clear how this argument could succeed if children do not have an a priori right to a particular sexual orientation and if they are left with no morally objectionable harms following what interventions might be used.

It is also worth noting that the use of abortion to eliminate fetuses with defects of one kind or another has not proved incompatible with simultaneous governmental and private efforts to protect the interests of the handicapped who continue to be born. In fact, for both judicial and legislative reasons, the rights of people with disabilities are greater at present than they have been at any time during the period in which nontherapeutic abortion was criminalized in the United States. A social climate increasingly hospitable to gay people is therefore imaginable even if some parents try to abort pregnancies likely to end in gay children. Further consideration of the meaning of abortion practices for gay people will be given in chapter 7, where I try to forecast the effects of advanced sexual orientation science for gay people more specifically.

To acknowledge the right of parents to try and have children of a particular sexual orientation is not to say that parents have a right to be supported in those efforts necessarily. If physicians believed such efforts were immoral, they should be free to decline helping in that regard, though they may have duties of referral to physicians who are willing to assist. If the prenatal intervention necessary to ensure a straight child were unproven or extraordinarily expensive, health care payers (whether government or insurers) might reasonably decline to cover the cost. If the use of prenatal interventions for sexual orientation diverted important social resources away from basic prenatal care elsewhere, society might justifiably intervene to redirect those resources to the places where they assured more important outcomes. Even if there is, then, a political and legal right to try and influence the sexual orientation of one's children, it may be of limited practical effect if one is not in a position to pay the costs of the efforts or if, through just decision making, society chooses to forgo those rights in favor of other important social objectives.

FETAL PRIVACY

Pediatrician Jeffrey R. Botkin has argued that there is a domain of diagnostic privacy that ought to be extended to the embryo and/or fetus.[50] It will be useful to examine this argument to see whether it would generally preclude parents and physicians from using prenatal diagnostics in order to determine and/or influence the sexual orientation of their children. I believe that Botkin's position would tend to favor this conclusion, though I also believe that it is ultimately unwise to adopt the notion of fetal privacy and confidentiality. Nevertheless, to work within the frame of his argument is to see that homoeroticism does not parallel the medical worries that justify prenatal diagnosis in the majority of cases.

Botkin's argument in favor of a domain of fetal privacy is utilitarian in nature and is, therefore, independent of moral and legal questions about the personhood of embryonic and fetal organisms.[51] It is important to notice about such a position that a right is therefore socially conditioned: if there were no objectionable outcomes to even the most aggressive prenatal testing, then there would be no reason to invoke the notion of a fetal right to privacy. But Botkin does see grave consequences to unlimited prenatal testing, especially as that testing is coupled with preparedness to abort if results are unsatisfactory to parents in one way or another. He says there would be serious consequences for fetuses (insofar as they would be aborted), for children (insofar as they believed themselves more or less engineered), for parental-child relationships (insofar as children must increasingly conform to the expectations of their parents), and for physicians (insofar as costs and standards of practice would be adversely affected). Botkin is worried in particular that through prenatal diagnostics parents will start down a slippery slope of wanting and accepting children only as they meet increasingly fine-grained expectations, with physicians being the all-too-willing accomplices of demanding parents. Botkin argues that a presumption of fetal privacy and confidentiality would prevent or at least minimize these sorts of harms. Botkin recognizes that the law permits greater access to prenatal information than he believes morally acceptable, but he suggests that his views be established in physician practices anyway: in their general standard of care physicians should recognize a right to fetal privacy and confidentiality, regardless of what the law permits.

Just as privacy is not absolute for adults, neither does Botkin see it as absolute in prenatal diagnostics. He models the logic of testing for and disclosing prenatal information on breaches of confidentiality justified in the name of preventing harm to third parties.[52] Botkin identifies four general categories of justifiable breach. These involve conditions that (a) are fatal in childhood, (b) are chronic and involve considerable expense and burden to the family, (c) are barriers to independence in adulthood, and (d) are severe disabilities imposing considerable strain on families.[53] If these are the moral criteria for permitting inspection of the fetus through prenatal diagnostics, then a child's disposition toward homoeroticism would not justify routine prenatal diagnosis or the disclosure of that information to parents were it to take place anyway.

Certainly homoeroticism is neither fatal nor akin to disabling diseases requiring repeated hospitalization and significant burdens of caretaking. Neither is homoeroticism a barrier to independence in adulthood, and since many families are entirely unaware of their children's homoeroticism, it can hardly be said that undue medical expenses are involved. If parents *did* want to treat a child with sexual orientation therapy, such costs would parallel those for other psychobehavioral therapy; there would be nothing exceptional about them in that regard.[54] I take it therefore that Botkin's position implies that testing for sexual orientation should not be routine in prenatal examinations and that there should be a presumption against disclosure of test results to parents.

This argument may be extended by considering the instances in which Botkin explicitly says prenatal diagnostics should *not* be made part of routine physician standard of care for pregnant women. He says there should be no prenatal diagnostics for conditions (a) for which there is a cure or effective treatment, neither of which imposes a substantial burden on a family, (b) for which there is a treatment that does not impose unreasonable burdens on the family, (c) that do not affect children but manifest themselves only later in life, and (d) that involve uncertainty about the significance of the test finding for the actual trait or condition in adults, i.e., uncertainty about its penetrance, and (e) that are rare or unlikely to appear in the absence of demonstrated familial susceptibility.

Applying these criteria, fetal privacy should ordinarily be respected with regard to sexual orientation testing. To accept the judgment of major psychiatric and psychological organizations, homoeroticism as a trait unto itself is nonpathological. Consequently, all considerations of cures and treatments justified in treating pathology become moot, as does the question of whether pathological effects of homoeroticism manifest themselves in children. On these grounds there is a prima facie case against testing. Further, if there is some identifiable trait predicting homoeroticism, it will likely be expressed in probabilistic terms because of the various cultural environments that will—as much as the genes themselves—influence the expression of any given individual's erotic interests. A fetus disposed toward homoeroticism may, after all, turn out to be an adult who rejects his or her sexual orientation for religious reasons and lead a sexually abstinent life. Or a fetus thought disposed toward homoeroticism may end up as a functionally bisexual adult. Homoeroticism in adults means many things, and under these circumstances it will remain difficult to know what a prenatal test can meaningfully predict. As homoeroticism is not especially rare, it is unclear how Botkin's last condition should be applied. Perhaps fetuses should be routinely tested, given that many parents might have a strong interest in knowing the likely sexual orientation of their children. If I read Botkin right, however, parental interest alone is not enough to establish a test as justified—if a domain of prenatal privacy is to mean anything at all. Furthermore, all of the examples Botkin offers involve manifest pathology, and homoeroticism is not pathological. I suspect that he would not be willing to extend testing to nonpathological traits even if there were a high index of parental interest in that testing. After all, Botkin wants to define a domain of privacy, and that enterprise will be meaningless if parents may inspect any fetus simply because a majority of parents are inclined to do so.

There are, of course, some commentators who do argue that homoeroticism is pathological. If Botkin's guidelines were accepted, it would still remain unclear that prenatal testing for sexual orientation could be justified as a matter of routine prenatal diagnosis since homoeroticism is not fatal, does not involve considerable medical expense and burden to the family, and is no barrier to independence in adulthood. On a pathological model one might possibly argue that homoeroticism in a child was a disability imposing considerable strain on a family, but, then again, children often conceal their homoeroticism so that this argument cannot be true generally. Moreover, homoeroticism is not amenable to any effective cure or treatment, does not disable children, and is widely variable in its manifestations so that broad characterizations about the extent of its "disabilities" are difficult. Even where homoeroticism is thought to run in families, putting some families at risk of an allegedly pathological trait, it is hardly so widespread that all pregnancies ought to be tested for homoeroticism as a matter of a physician's routine standard of care.

For the sake of the argument I have thus far tried to extend Botkin's argument to the matter of prenatal testing for dispositions toward homoeroticism. To carry out this exercise is not, however, to accept his overall approach, because I think there are many limitations to Botkin's analysis. First, as Botkin himself notes, the law permits a greater range of prenatal diagnosis coupled with abortion than he is prepared to accept as morally justified. In effect, the guidelines he proposes here are completely evadable by parents and physicians who do not accept his views. Indeed, as I read Doe v. Bolton, the U.S. Supreme Court decision that came down with Roe v. Wade in 1973, it is unclear that the law has a substantial interest in limiting abortion practices by limiting the information parents may have in regard to their embryos and fetuses. Doe asserts a broad array of health justifications that serve as a legitimate constitutional reason for securing an abortion: "The medical judgment may be exercised in the light of all factors—physical, emotional, psychological, familial, and the woman's age—relevant to the well-being of the patient. All these factors may relate to health."[55] One can certainly argue that a woman's unwillingness to have a gay child would meet the criteria laid out here, and it is hard to see why she should be denied access to information that would help her make that decision. If a woman has a constitutional right to abort for the broad reasons described in Doe, then it is unclear that states or physicians could impose limitations on access to information that supports those reasons. In effect, then, Botkin may be asserting a right to fetal privacy that is entirely unsupported under the law. Some ethical advisories are in fact at odds with prevailing practices and laws; this is not an inherent objection to the advisories if their intention is to provoke critical scrutiny of existing objectionable practices.[56] Perhaps the better approach here would not be to assert a right of fetal privacy but to resist the objectionable practices themselves, i.e., to condemn the trend of designing and accepting children as if they were just another consumable product manufactured to match parents' expectations about what kind of children they should have.

To assert fetal rights against parental interests and rights is a controversial proposition, even when those former rights are unconnected with the disputatious question of embryonic and fetal personhood. To do so when that right will in no regard be recognized by the law is to offer a dubious solution to the eugenics practices that Botkin thinks objectionable. Moreover, one effect of recognizing Botkin's proposal regarding fetal rights would be that some parents would have gay children who did not want them. Whatever the detrimental consequences of broad-scale eugenics might be, it cannot be a solution to impose gay children on parents who find them repugnant. This observation forces a hard question: which is better for gay children, abortion as fetuses or a familial life utterly hostile to them? Reluctantly, because of the damages hostile families can impose on their gay children by direct and indirect means, I cannot say I think it would be better if no such unwanted children were aborted.

Like others worried about the subjugation of children to parental manipulation, Botkin is concerned about increasing control over their genetic endowment:

> Parents have significant control over the social and physical environment of the child, but no control over their own genetic influences. The question that is emerging is whether it is desirable to permit parents social, environmental, *and* biological control over children. The issue is one of independence and individuality in their deepest senses.[57]

But in response to this suggestion that genetic control is of an order altogether unlike what we have known in the past, we should ask: is there something about extending the domain of parental control over genetic traits that is unparalleled in kind in the social and environmental degree of control that parents already have over children? That is, is there any reason to think that genetic tests and manipulations, although perhaps novel, have more influence over a child than those in social, educational, and environmental domains? It seems that a strong case can be made that genetic controls are not necessarily any more influential in regard to the traits of a child than overall efforts at socialization and education. In trying to choose, for example, a child's eye color via a prenatal intervention, a parent would be exerting far less influence over that child than in the kind of opportunities the parent opens for the child (or closes to the child) in regard to language, religious values, social skills, and so on.

We should not, moreover, assume that extending biological control over children will necessarily and always work to the disadvantage of the child. Botkin seems to assume exactly this: that biological control will undermine the well-being of the child. For example, he says,

> Strong parental expectations based on genetic testing may significantly limit a child's personal freedom. Children who are perceived as "predisposed" to certain health problems or behaviors may be excessively controlled or treated as fragile. A belief in "genetic determinism" by parents may severely limit the child's ability to find and chart his or her own course in life.[58]

But by the same token, parents aware of their child's genetic traits might find ways to *enhance* the lives of the children they have. For example, if parents knew they were likely to have a gay child (and assuming they were not so heterosexist to believe that only straight children were of value, thus ruling out the question of abortion), they could create a more welcoming climate for the child. In this case foreknowledge could be of mutual benefit to parents who could use it to adjust to the idea of having a gay child and to the child who, in consequence, enjoys a family environment open to gay identities.[59] Prenatal foreknowledge of a child's traits is not necessarily damaging or of more significance than existing control over their social environments as newborns and young children.

If, finally, there is a prenatal right to privacy, one must ask how strong it is. My sense is that while Botkin sees it as a prima facie right, it would not be a very strong right. In fact, it might collapse in every instance in which a parent had a reasonable, specific rationale for wanting to know about a child's likely disposition toward a particular trait. For reasons both laudable and lamentable, some parents will want to know whether their child is likely to be gay. Their right to know, their need to prepare their lives for the child they are likely to have, and their desire to avoid children who would be repugnant to them would override an embryonic or fetal interest in privacy. A presumption of fetal privacy turns out to be hardly a right at all, then, because it cannot be meaningfully asserted against parents' morally stronger rights to conduct prenatal tests that will reveal information important to their reproductive choices and family integrity. For all these reasons I believe one should resist recognizing a fetal right to privacy even as I recognize that heterosexist motives may be at work in efforts to predict traits of children through prenatal testing.

I do very much agree with Botkin's observation that "the most important individual and social problems are not secondary to flawed human biology."[60] People should not be misled into thinking that more rigorous efforts at prenatal diagnostics will offset the need to pay critical attention to personal values and social institutions alike. In his advocacy of a fetal right to privacy Botkin is mistrustful of parents, suspicious they will approach child rearing with a laundry list of desirable traits, all to ill personal and social effect. Many gay and lesbian commentators also worry about this same sort of problem. I do not believe, however, that closing down options in reproductive choices will do very much by itself to work against heterosexism. On the contrary, this course of action might aggravate rather than improve the standing of gay people in social opinion because it might appear that gay people continue to exist only because people are barred from the information they could use to eliminate them altogether. The rights that will protect gay people are not those that might be extended to fetuses but those privacy and liberty rights that protect human adults in their sexual behavior and identities.

RIGHTS AND DUTIES REVISITED

Thus far I have relied primarily on the language of rights and duties to analyze the question of parental control over children's sexual orientation. Even as this language is useful in setting out many of the issues at stake, it does not tell the whole story. For example, if moral analysis focuses exclusively on the rights of particular individuals to the exclusion of all else, it may obscure the overall social treatment of gay people or the social effect of parents trying to control more and more traits of their children. It is worth, therefore, trying to look at the issue as if it were something other than one of rights and duties.

One can try to assess, for example, the morality of parental control over children in terms of the moral development of children, of fostering important virtues and values. Along these lines, parental interest in sexual orientation can be compared with fostering the religious beliefs or the musical talents of children. Most parents hope that their children will share the same sort of religious values they themselves have, and they often taken powerful steps in religious training to inculcate those beliefs, steps that include socialization into private and public observances as well as formal instruction in religiously sponsored schools. Some parents do everything they can to foster the musical abilities of their children, finding special schools for them as well. If asked, most parents would deny that they take these measures because they have an explicit moral right to children with specific religious beliefs or that children are duty-bound to have those beliefs. Most parents would likely tie their motives to the value of the religion itself: as an important source of values in its metaphysical view of the world and in its social institutions, as full of rewarding experiences in its observances, as offering a commonality with others across history and even across eternity, as a bedrock of personal and social identity. Parents might similarly identify important values to be obtained through efforts to instill musical ability and appreciation in their children. Parents raise children in a particular religion because they believe that religion is good for them, and they foster practices in music, reading, and the rest, questions of rights and duties apart.

One could make a similar case for parents trying to influence their children's sexual orientation. Parents wanting straight children could say that heteroeroticism offers important values for personal identity, interpersonal relationships, and social community. Such a view can even be offered without deprecating homoeroticism: all things considered among competing erotic interests, parents might choose to promote heteroeroticism not because homoeroticism is wrong but because they believe heteroeroticism to be a little easier pathway to human happiness and value, just as they believe one religion to be a better pathway than others. Parental fostering of heteroeroticism is important, moreover, because it assures a commonality of ideals and values between parents and children: differences in something as important as sexual orientation could estrange parent and child. Parents want children whose sexual interests are intelligible and familiar to them. In all these ways parents can believe that heteroeroticism is good for their children and themselves.

None of the foregoing argumentation need resort to the language of rights and duties, yet such language will necessarily emerge, for even if parents should be respected in the motives they have for trying to ensure, for example, straight children, it does not follow that they may do anything they choose in that regard. This is to say that parents have, for example, a duty not to inflict harms on their children even as they take measures to instill in them values and identities they believe are important and rewarding. Parents should not take measures to control the sexual orientation of their children if those measures involuntarily suppress a legitimate interest of a child or the measures would have deforming effects on the child. A comparison with religious beliefs can make this point plainly. Parents should be respected in their desires to raise their children to hold, for example, Islamic or Jewish beliefs. This respect is based on the moral principle of respecting the conscious and chosen views of adults, a principle that recognizes that adults can and should be able to disagree in fundamental ways about matters of religion. A newborn is entitled to no such respect because that child lacks altogether the sorts of capacities and interests that make respect for differences of views meaningful. As children mature, however, they develop exactly these sorts of capacities and interests; their maturation entitles them to principled moral respect. As children mature they acquire more and more entitlement to moral respect in regard to their own interests, whether these be religious or sexual. Insofar as young children have no capacity to sort out competing religious views, they may properly be guided in them by their parents.[61] Parents would not, however, be entitled to force religious views involuntarily on maturing adolescents who reject them, by using therapies or biomedical interventions. In any case, that kind of imposition hardly ever achieves its goals. Roughly the same conclusion holds for parental control over sexual orientation.

This view means that parents should not drag unwilling adolescents into sexual orientation therapy just as parents should not drag adolescents into religious brainwashing programs. If an adolescent espouses religious beliefs about polytheism, polygamy, or polyandry that are repugnant to parents, parents should be free to reason with their children, discuss the theological pros and cons of competing views, and even ask the children to consult with priests and rabbis, but because the adolescent has views, the very holding of which establishes the need for their being respected, the child should not be subject to involuntary treatments whether those treatments would be successful in altering the view in question or not. Similarly, parents unhappy with their fifteen-year-old daughter's announcement that she "likes girls and that's not going to change" may discuss their assessment of lesbianism with her, but they should not submit the child unwillingly to therapy for purposes of redirecting her sexual orientation. If there were a magic pill that could change her sexual orientation, they would be in the wrong if they slipped the ground-up pill into the soup she eats for lunch. They would be in the wrong even if the drug did its job, even if the daughter experienced no subsequent regret about what the drug had done to her erotic interests. The parents would have wronged her because they would have treated her more like furniture to be arranged according to their interests than like a person deserving respect by reason of being able to have and to express moral views.

In the absence of magic pills, parents will try to influence the sexual orientation of their children through what means they can. The moral limits of these efforts should be recognized clearly. For example, it would be intolerable to use a prenatal technique that ensured straight children but left those same children harmed in some way, for example, if the techniques made them blind. Second, even if we grant parents the right to control the sexual orientation of their children, there should be some escape hatch for those children who will not be straight. That is, parents should not raise children under an expectation of heteroeroticism so strong that the children will feel guilty or inferior or ashamed should they turn out otherwise. Certainly parents should not raise children to feel that they need separate from the family irrevocably if they are in fact gay; that threat can only work against the family. Efforts to ensure straight children should not be damaging to straight children either. Straight children may be damaged if they grow up with the belief that their sexual orientation is always in question, is always in need of being proved. It is exactly this sort of attitude that can lead to objectionable harm against gay people as straight people in crisis about their identities struggle to prove themselves and their worth through an endless series of "hypermasculine" or "hyperfeminine" acts that are antagonistic to gay people. I will also observe here that stringent expectations of straight children can be deforming to parents, too, who may lose in their insistence on straight sons and daughters certain virtues of tolerance and sympathy. Such parents too may focus on the question of sexual identity all out of proportion to its significance and to the exclusion of a child's other developmental needs and interests.

Philosopher Mary Warnock has said that "it seems to me to be a fundamental moral principle that we ought to love and cherish our children as beings separate from ourselves and with their own distinct characteristics."[62] But, she goes on to observe, this principle does not lend itself easily to the clarification of rights and duties. If I have dwelled overlong on rights and duties in this chapter, it is because I think this approach clarifies many of the important issues at stake. Parents should be respected in efforts to control the sexual orientation of their children so long as those efforts do not adversely affect the interests of a child. For all that, the hard question to be asked here is whether a preparedness to control the sexual orientation of children is in keeping with a principle of love for children as beings separate from their parents, with their own distinct characteristics. There are ways to harm children that do not violate their rights, and there are ways to help children that do not fulfill their rights properly speaking. It is worth keeping alive the question whether or not willful and sustained efforts to thwart homoeroticism in a child could engender harm that is not, properly speaking, the violation of parental duties or children's rights but that is nevertheless real and pernicious to both parents and children alike.

Worrying about the future of children is a stock rhetorical tack used by commentators on virtually every social topic, despite the fact that people of the future have very little moral authority for requiring that we shape the human community to their imagined needs, despite the fact that it is unclear that the best future is one that mimics the present as much as possible. It is not surprising that the fate and protection of children would arise as a topic for discussion in an age of highly publicized sexual orientation research. It is also not surprising that two issues that are already lightning rods for moral debate, abortion and homosexuality, would draw even more attention when joined with one another by the implications of that research. It is unclear, however, that the joining of these two issues has thus far done much to clarify the ethics of abortion, the ethics of homoeroticism, or the future of children. Matters are certainly confused if one assumes that there will be some simple prenatal intervention or campaign of abortion that could wipe away all homoeroticism. No sexual behavior emerges in a cultural vacuum, and as neither neuroanatomy, hormone levels, or genetic endowment dictate sexual behavior in any inalterable way, homoeroticism will survive even the most aggressive biological search-and-destroy missions. I say more about these issues in chapter 7.

To observe that effects at controlling the sexual orientation of children will have limits is not to say that parents will not use prenatal interventions, abortion included, to avoid having gay children. I think that the reasons that could be offered as a justification for trying to do so fail utterly to be convincing. I nevertheless want to uphold parents' rights to use prenatal techniques, including abortion, to avoid having gay children, presuming these techniques are safe and efficacious and violate no interest of a child, because it is unclear that these interventions are morally different in kind than tests and interventions that are rightly accepted elsewhere in reproductive decisions. I also believe it would be a social policy mistake to begin inspecting the quality of motives for which parents make decisions about the use of prenatal diagnostics. Adults should be free from government oversight in regard to diagnostic tests, safe biomedical interventions, and abortion not only because the canons of biomedical ethics ordain that conclusion but also because gay children should not be forced on parents reluctant to have them.

The moral counterballast of this position for gay people is that if it permits parents to select against gay children it also shields the right of parents who *want* gay children to use any safe and effective techniques to that very purpose. It is to be noted, of course, that many of the reasons that might be offered on behalf of having gay children could be just as morally implausible as those offered for wanting only straight children. No one is, however, more centrally affected by the lives and traits of children than their parents, and both that effect and the investment of parents in their care justifies a presumption of parental prerogative when it comes to questions of controlling sexual orientation. At the level of political rights parents should be equally entitled to have gay or straight children according to their own lights, and if safe and efficacious techniques could assist them in that pursuit they should be free to use them. It is a separate question whether society treats gay people fairly, and in examining this question one will find a better preparation for a just future for gay people than in trying to close down sexual orientation science or to forbid the use of its findings in reproductive decisions.

5 ||||||||||||||||||||||||||||||||||||||||||||||||||||||||||||||||||||||||||||||||

THE USE OF SEXUAL ORIENTATION TESTS

It has sometimes been the goal of sexological science to identify not the causes of sexual orientation properly speaking but an objective way of distinguishing people according to traits they have in virtue of their sexual orientation, whether these traits are anatomical, behavioral, or psychological in kind and whether or not they play a causal role in a person's erotic interests. Distinctive traits in brain structure or finger skin ridges would be of interest not only to researchers wanting to know merely for the sake of knowing whether such differences exist, they would also be of considerable interest to those people and institutions who want an objective mechanism for identifying gay people. Since the 1940s, for example, the U.S. military has worked assiduously to find an effective way of excluding gay people from its ranks. In *Coming Out Under Fire: The History of Gay Men and Women in World War Two* historian Allan Bérubé describes a number of efforts by which military psychiatrists and administrators tried to distinguish straight people from those tainted to various degrees with homoeroticism.[1] In this chapter I will describe how the military might use a sexual orientation test were one available. I will then describe the extent to which current research offers the prospect of a sexual orientation test. No definitive sexual orientation test is to be found in the current research data, but it may nevertheless come to pass that some more or less objective indicator of erotic interests might be found that could be used in testing military personnel, job applicants, and even marriage partners.

While prejudicial uses of any such test are the usual topic of discussion in this area, it should not be assumed that a test must always and only work to the disadvantage of gay people. To make this latter point I will describe some hypothetical scenarios to show how sexual orientation testing might work to the advantage of gay people. It will be nevertheless important to protect gay people from predictable prejudicial uses of testing, whether that testing is actually meaningful or only perceived to be meaningful. In fact, the protection needed by gay people is the same as the protection needed by all people in regard to ill-treatment that might be linked to biomedical test results. At the close of the chapter I describe some of the principles that ought to prevail in making this sort of protection possible. That protection consists, first of all, in observing informed consent, in protecting confidentiality, in ensuring opportunities for correction of false test results, and in mechanisms for redress of any prejudicial use of test results. If these protections exist for all people across the board in regard to tests to which they are subject, a sexual orientation test need not prove necessarily harmful to gay people.

TESTING FOR SEXUAL ORIENTATION

Like efforts elsewhere in the history of sexual orientation science, techniques used by the U.S. military to identify and exclude gay people reflected both the science and the stereotypes of the times. For example, military physicians in the early 1940s were directed to observe whether potential male draftees and recruits exhibited "degenerate physiques," discomfort while naked during examination, or embarrassment in discussing masturbation, traits thought characteristic of homosexual men. Examiners also attended to any excessive sensitivity in features, manners, or gestures.[2] Candidates found to be homosexual by these measures were excludable from induction.

Depending on the regulations in force at the time, the military also had an interest in distinguishing so-called true homosexuals, who were excludable from service, from straight people who lapsed into homoerotic misadventures due to naïveté, manipulation, or drug-impaired judgment and who might be retained by the military following rehabilitation.[3] To discover who was a true homosexual and who had merely lapsed unwittingly into homosexuality during a drunken spree, the military resorted to various tests of anatomy, urine hormone levels, Rorschach inkblot tests, and recollections of childhood. By testing oral gag reflexes with tongue depressors and by assessing reports of the techniques and satisfactions involved in oral sex, military physicians also tried to ferret out true homosexuals from malingerers wanting to use the pretext of homosexuality to avoid military service.[4]

The greatest part of this testing took place with male draftees and recruits. Because of the lack of history in prosecuting sexual crimes against women and because of their comparatively marginal status in the overwhelmingly male services, for the greater part of World War II women in the military were never under the sort of systematic assessments for homosexuality that men faced, though they were sometimes asked whether they had homosexual feelings or attitudes. For the most part, during World War II, "female masculinity" was not treated as the same kind of disqualifying defect as "male femininity," though there were certainly exceptions to this general rule. In one of the most celebrated instances of resistance to antilesbian efforts during World War II, General Dwight D. Eisenhower's directive to ferret out lesbians was met—and dissolved—by a Women's Army Corps sergeant's response that her name would have to be first on a list of offenders.[5] Always sporadic and uneven in enforcement, the exclusionary policies of the military do now seem exercised against greater and greater numbers of women.[6]

All told, the U.S. military has examined more men and women for homosexuality than has ever occurred elsewhere in human history, and to this day the military continues to discharge gay people on the grounds they are unfit for military service, if not because of their personal failings then because of their allegedly disruptive effects in otherwise presumably straight groups. This threat remains for the most part largely theoretical since the military has *never* been effective in its goal of excluding gay people in any systematic way. From his analysis Bérubé concludes, for example, that the World War II screening of eighteen million U.S. draftees and recruits led to the rejection of only four to five thousand as homosexual.[7] So many gay people evade detection in the U.S. military that it is hardly an overstatement to say that the most ambitious antigay surveillance ever conducted in history has uncovered only a negligible fraction of the gay people it sought, a state of affairs that continues to this day.[8]

Despite the fact that most gay people in the military evade detection, exclusionary standards nevertheless create a great deal of stress for both draftees and volunteers alike; the *threat* of discovery and expulsion are never entirely forgotten even if that discovery and expulsion never come. Most gay people in the military live, as they often live elsewhere, by their wits in avoiding threats of exposure and retribution. Some gay people worry about sexual orientation research because they fear it may offer an instrument of assessment that could eclipse even their most sophisticated abilities to evade discrimination. Of course, some gay activists condemn passing as straight—or not being publicly out as gay—as a form of intellectual dishonesty and/or moral cowardice, but passing—or not being out—has proved a benefit at one time or another in the life of *every* gay person insofar as it has protected against unwanted scrutiny, discrimination, and violence, and this protection is especially important during early sexual awakening and exploration. Sexual orientation science threatens to subvert gay people's capacity to protect themselves from various kinds of social voyeurism, inimical policies, and outright malice. Seen from the perspective of gay people, sexual orientation tests are potentially dangerous instruments of discrimination, no matter their relative value in scientific research. Even though they would not necessarily uncover the causes of erotic interests, sexual orientation markers could offer institutions like the U.S. military an instrument by which to assign people to sexual orientation categories and, thereby, to segregate people according to the value assigned to those sexual orientations.

If it were possible to screen draftees and recruits for sexual orientation, regardless of the *origins* of erotic interests, it should not be doubted that the military—or at least a considerable portion of its leadership, rank-and-file members, and civilian sympathizers—might be tempted to institute such screening. How the screening test would be implemented in regulatory terms would, of course, remain open to debate: whether it should be required at induction, its results entered into medical records as a matter of course, or conducted only during disciplinary actions. However it was conducted, the test would—in revealing the presumptive erotic interests of service members—extend the current controversy about standards governing discharge from the military.

One of the central questions of the debate would be whether test results would be sufficient to bar the enlistment of men and women identified as gay or lesbian. At the present time, for example, standards of exclusion from the U.S. military no longer require psychiatric or medical certification of homoeroticism for an involuntary discharge to go forward. Indeed, discharge proceedings can go forward simply on the basis of one's own verbal reports about one's sexual orientation. That is, as the military currently construes matters, no independent medical or behavioral evidence is necessary to substantiate a statement of homosexuality by a service member. A statement by the service member that she or he is lesbian, gay, or homosexual in orientation is sufficient to commence an investigation and lead to discharge.[9] The military defends this standard of exclusion by asserting that statements of gay identity are prima facie evidence that the person making them is likely to commit prohibited or disruptive sexual acts. An appeals court upholding the exclusion of Joseph Steffan from the U.S. military academy held, for example, that "for purposes of these proceedings, it is virtually impossible to distinguish or separate individuals of a particular *orientation* which predisposes them toward a particular sexual conduct from those who actually *engage* in that particular type of sexual conduct."[10] Though there was no evidence that Steffan had ever committed any offense, sexual or otherwise, his statement that he was gay was taken as equivalent to evidence that he had committed offenses or was so likely to commit those offenses that he could be treated as if he had. In light of this kind of judicial precedent, there is legitimate concern about whether a sexual orientation test would be taken as similarly definitive evidence of erotic interests.

If a genetic marker could, for example, identify someone as disposed to homoerotic interests, military attorneys might well argue that this biological trait was prima facie evidence of the likelihood of prohibited and disruptive sexual behavior and therefore by itself a sufficient ground for exclusion. The military might possibly drum people out of the service not because of disruptive sexual behavior or forbidden statements but because they were presumptively gay by reason of a sexual orientation test. Even though U.S. policy at present does not permit inquiring about a recruit or draftee's sexual orientation as a condition of induction, a test for sexual orientation might prove attractive in that process. It is not hard to imagine a hawkish member of Congress demanding that the military use the test in order to prevent the induction of men and women who could be drummed out of the military if the same test were used on them after induction.

Sexual orientation screening would also appeal to other institutions with an interest in excluding gay people, for example, insurance companies and health maintenance organizations concerned with limiting their expenditures on health care. Given that gay men are disproportionately affected by HIV-related disease, pre-paid health organizations might try to reduce the total number of gay people entering their health plans and thus, by extension, avoid real and imagined HIV-related health costs. In the stereotypical belief that gay teachers pose greater risks to children than straight people some religiously sponsored schools or day care centers might also wish to test job candidates for sexual orientation. Although many religious orders of priests and nuns acknowledge that they take in gay people, there are those in religious life who would just as soon see that practice come to an end.[11] Some religious orders require an HIV test from applicants in order to assess their health, which test also offers a coded method of identifying some of its gay applicants. It is not outside the realm of possibility that those same religious orders might require a sexual orientation test of applicants. The test might be justified in the name of a global health assessment; religious orders could say that they need to know all they could about an applicant in order to offer the best medical care later on, but, in fact, that global assessment might also offer a method of identifying some gay applicants and marking them for exclusion or at least heightened scrutiny. It is also not hard to imagine that some people entering married life would want their partners tested for sexual orientation if they worried about hidden sexual interests. One might even condition prenuptial agreements on certification of one's erotic interests by whatever sexual orientation test were available. In short, there would be an incentive to the use of a sexual orientation test wherever gay people are not welcome.

There is presently, of course, no way to distinguish categorically between straight people and gay people on the basis of any simple and objective anatomical, behavioral, or psychological test. This is not to say that there cannot be tests that will eventually differentiate people according to their likely erotic interests, for there may well be some way to distinguish people either disposed to certain erotic interests or habituated in certain erotic interests. Despite the formidable history of failure in this project, science should simply remain agnostic and wait for the evidence to come in, affirming only what withstands skeptical scrutiny.[12] In the next section I consider whether the research described in chapter 1 withstands that skeptical scrutiny.

SEXUAL ORIENTATION TESTS

At the turn of the century psychologist Havelock Ellis mentions the following traits as common in male "inverts": breast development, psychic "menstrual phenomena," an inability to whistle, limitations in spitting, skill at feminine occupations, a marked disposition toward literature, artistic aptitude, a tendency toward dramatic aptitude, vanity and the love of applause, heightened consciousness of one's physical appearance, and a fondness for the color green.[13] Female inverts were said to be prone to excessive hairiness or hairlessness, an infantilism of the genitals, and, in the context of a tendency toward "masculinism," they showed masculine handwriting, were skillful in the throwing of a ball, and unlike their male homosexual counterparts could whistle quite well. Ellis thought some distinguishing traits were harder to define than others: "A marked characteristic of many inverts, though one not of easy precision, is their youthfulness of appearance, and frequently child-like faces, equally in both sexes."[14] While admitting to difficulty in establishing these differences with certainty, Ellis nevertheless thought them compatible with "all that we are learning to know regarding the important part played by the internal secretions, alike in inversion and the general bodily modifications in an infantile, feminine, and masculine direction."[15]

In fact, none of these traits offers a definitive mechanism for differentiating people according to sexual orientation, but the historical failure to distinguish people by sexual orientation with some anatomical trait has not made researchers since then less confident about the prospect of a biological marker even if they have had to shift to physiological traits to find one. A 1984 study of estrogen responses in gay men, for example, led one team of researchers to conclude that "biological markers for sexual orientation may exist."[16] Despite the fact that these estrogen responses were not confirmed by subsequent research,[17] the expectation of such markers has continued to drive research in the area.

The conceptual foundations of this research have often undermined achieving their very goal. A great deal of the effort to differentiate people according to sexual orientation has been driven by an unsophisticated expectation that stereotypes about who was gay and straight provided important clues as to the markers that might be found. Thus were men and women examined in relation to their conformity to expected gender roles, without consideration of the extent to which those roles were artifacts of culture rather than objective traits rooted in human biology. The fondness for the color green, for example, is certainly a social artifact rather than a trait derivative of or predictive of homoerotic interests. At present gay people do not necessarily favor the color lavender *because of* their homoeroticism even if they use it in many contexts as a way of identifying themselves to others. Moreover, it does not follow that nonconformity with prevailing gender roles predicts the existence of objective markers differentiating people along the lines of sexual orientation because nonconformity can be learned. There is no a priori reason to think, therefore, that there will be anatomical or genetic markers for learned traits. The likelihood of a sexual orientation marker is also complicated by the fact that erotic interests can take variegated form in any person, depending on the life experience of that individual. Neither is it necessarily true that sexual orientation traits would endure across a given individual's life. Some trait indicative of entrenched erotic interests at age thirty might be altogether absent in a teenager or fetus. Nevertheless, with all these caveats in mind, it is not implausible to believe that there may be observable differences between gay people and straight people just as there probably are observable differences between people who speak English and people who speak Swahili, even if these differences are remote and hard to describe.

If subsequent research confirmed his 1991 findings, Simon LeVay's work in INAH3 brain structures might offer a rough guide in distinguishing adult males according to their sexual orientation, but it would be only a very rough guide and useful, at present, only posthumously. Even if it were possible to discern INAH3 size in living males, the distributional range of the INAH3 in both straight and gay males would work against establishing an exact sexual orientation in a given test result. It is to be remembered that according to his own data LeVay has not identified necessary or sufficient sizes inextricably linked to one sexual orientation or another. At most, LeVay's work would offer only a probabilistic guide to sexual orientation. Errors in the attribution of sexual orientation to particular people would necessarily occur, as the test would fail to identify gay men with large INAH3 structures, straight men with small INAH3 structures, and would *completely* fail to identify bisexual males.[18]

As LeVay's work does not report the comparative size of INAH3 structures in straight, bisexual, and straight women, the research could not be used as the basis for any test of sexual orientation in women, though it might be used speculatively on the assumption that INAH3 sizes in lesbians were comparable in size to those of straight men. Further study might show that the INAH3 structure in lesbians was in fact likely to be larger than that in straight women, but this data would be probabilistic in nature as well and not a necessary indicator of the sexual orientation of a particular individual. The certainty of the test results for a particular individual would be, again, only as good as the probabilities reported. Until there are confirming accounts of LeVay's work in regard to males and his speculations in regard to women, we simply do not know how good or how limited those probabilities could be. In the interests of fairness, therefore, it is unclear that the military, insurance companies, or religious orders should use an INAH3 test—were it possible for living persons—as a guide to the erotic interests of any given individual, even though probabilistically speaking they would likely be right some of the time.

The work by J. Michael Bailey and colleagues on the prevalence of homoeroticism among twins and their siblings does not offer any method by which to identify individual people as gay or lesbian. It might offer a probabilistic prediction of whether or not a given brother or sister would be gay, but it would do so simply by extrapolation from its general findings rather than by the examination of any trait of a given individual. The work might also have some power for predicting whether or not gay children would be more likely in one family or another, but one would have to know a great deal of familial history in order to make these sorts of determinations, and this knowledge would not, in any case, identify specific pregnancies likely to end in gay or lesbian children, for example, first-born sons or middle daughters. By themselves the Bailey studies do not, therefore, offer any theoretical basis for the development of a sexual orientation test, though by suggesting that genetics plays a role in sexual orientation they do add conceptual fuel to the genetic fire of sexual orientation markers.

The research by Dean Hamer and colleagues on Xq28 genetics does identify a particular chromosomal region that can be analyzed for individual males, but results of any test based on this research would, again, offer only probabilistic tools by which to estimate the likely sexual orientation of some men. The research does open up the prospect that there may be a specific gene or genes at work disposing some men to homoeroticism. Further research might, therefore, offer a more precise mechanism for identifying a genetic trait associated with adult male homoeroticism, but any such genetic trait would be inconclusive about the nature and propensities in a given adult male's erotic life. It is to be remembered that some gay men in the Hamer studies did not exhibit the Xq28 genetic commonality highly correlated with homoerotic sexual orientation. As in the case of LeVay's research, the work of Hamer and colleagues would be completely unuseful in testing for sexual orientation in women because evidence that the Xq28 genetic region is correlated with homoerotic interests in women is altogether lacking.

J. A. Y Hall and Doreen Kimura's work on the leftward asymmetry of finger-print ridges would also fail as a uniformly correct test of sexual orientation. The researchers themselves were at pains to point out that their test would indicate very little about the sexual orientation of a particular individual since leftward dermatoglyphic asymmetry—indicated by the research to be disproportion-ately prevalent in the sample of gay men they studied—occurs in both gay and straight men and women. Further research would be necessary to confirm whether the pattern of reported asymmetry held up in larger population stud-ies. Even if it did, one would be still hard-pressed to look at fingerprints left by, for example, the murderer of a gay man and to judge definitively whether the killer was himself gay on the basis of a leftward asymmetry in the finger skin ridges. Men of all erotic persuasions can have a leftward asymmetry, so it would be inappropriate for authorities to narrow the search for the killer to gay men alone. If used as a way to test the sexual orientation of men, this research could offer only probabilistic clues rather than any sort of definitive conclusions.

I should also note that at least as Joseph Nicolosi has thus far described it his claim that male children who go on to be gay have suffered some kind of injury would also provide no benchmark by which to judge the erotic interests of adult men. Nicolosi has not described with any precision the kind of injury that, in kind or by reason of its context, allegedly produces a gender deficit in some male children who eroticize men as a result. Because the nature of the injury is unspecified, someone looking to determine the sexual orientation of adult men could not definitively do so by identifying certain memories of childhood.

There is room for a great deal more research in the determinants of sexual orientation, though this research may complicate rather than advance the quest for a holy grail of sexual orientation if it discovers, for example, that homoeroti-cism is compatible with all manner of anatomical, genetic, and psychological endowments. Human behavior is enlarged by behavioral and cognitive capaci-ties so that in their sexual interests people are not puppets tugged unwillingly through life on genetic or hormonal strings. At the very least, in order to make better headway in sexual orientation research, it would be profitable to conduct large-scale studies in preference to the small studies that dominate current research. Larger studies could more decisively establish the significance of INAH3 size, sibling patterns of sexual orientation, the commonality of matrilineally shared genes at Xq28, and leftward dermatoglyphic asymmetry. This is not to say that larger studies will necessarily make the discovery of traits dividing people by sexual orientation easier. Larger studies might even complicate matters by dilut-ing the significance of specific traits as accurate predictors of sexual orientation.

The Hamer team noted, for example, that their research subjects could be treated dimorphically as either gay or straight. A broader pool of subjects might not cleave so evenly, in which case a genetic test (or any test depending on the presence or absence of a certain trait) might not prove as useful among people whose erotic interests and behaviors are more complex than categories of gay or straight. In any case, a key scientific question to be resolved is whether some of the correlations asserted between sexual orientation and traits reported in contemporary research are not artifacts of testing small numbers of people.

It is also important to attend to the fact that none of the research mentioned here—by LeVay, the Bailey team, or Hall and Kimura—offers any hope of typologizing lesbians and straight women, for their research did not study any putative anatomical, genetic traits, or skin ridge traits of lesbians. The Bailey team did report a significant indication of the familial occurrence of lesbianism, but this report only suggests a genetic link, it does not identify any specific genetic endowment that might be made the subject of a test. The Hamer studies do not do for women what they do for males: identify a chromosomal region correlated with erotic interests. On the contrary, they noted that the Xq28 locus seemingly involved with male homoeroticism did not seem to be correlated with homoerotic interests in women at a rate any more frequent than might be predicted by chance. Hamer and colleagues rightly note, then, that even if there are biological markers for sexual orientation, they will not necessarily be the same in both men and women alike. It is therefore an entirely open question whether and how women might be differentiated by sexual orientation on the basis of INAH3 structures, chromosomal traits, or finger skin ridges—and with what degree of accuracy.

While I have noted that none of the research described so far would offer a definitive test of sexual orientation, it might very well be that one could make a pretty good guess regarding sexual orientation if one had, for example, information about a given male's INAH3 size, his Xq28 gene map, information about the sexual orientation of his siblings, and information about his finger skin ridge asymmetry. All this information together might well predict a given male's sexual orientation with a high degree of probability even if each individual test were less certain. All this depends, of course, on whether the initial reports in this area hold up to confirmatory scrutiny, and none of these reports either singly or in tandem would be useful in predicting the likely sexual orientation of a woman.

SOCIAL USES OF SEXUAL ORIENTATION TESTS

Rather than seeing the future as an uninterrupted continuation of the past, one can try to understand future implications of sexual orientation research by imagining the kinds of circumstances that could arise given the identification of a marker that could identify the likely erotic gender interests of an adult with some high degree of precision, interests either homoerotic or heteroerotic. The following case scenarios raise some of the issues that could ensue in the wake of a test capable of identifying sexual orientation in a highly effective way. For the sake of the discussion the following scenarios presuppose that there exists a clear genetic difference between people with substantial homoerotic interests and those without. The scenarios also presuppose the existence of a genetic probe for sexual orientation, a probe that is easy to administer, widely available, inexpensive, and can pose no health risks whatsoever to the person tested. The following discussions also presuppose that the probe is generally useful in identifying a person's sexual orientation for the majority of his or her adult life. The time in which the scenarios are set need not be the remote future but only so far ahead as might be required to achieve the level of biotechnological sophistication capable of producing a fairly accurate genetic probe for sexual orientation. The scenarios are intended to show the way in which the impact of a genetic probe or other sexual orientation test might be felt rather than to argue how they should or should not be used. Following each scenario, I offer some commentary on the significance of a test in the circumstances described.

Case 1. Criminal Evidence   An obscure member of the U.S. House of Representatives is found bludgeoned to death in his northeast Washington townhouse just blocks from the Capitol. Jeb Slainey was widely rumored to be gay, but he had distanced himself from gay political causes and had focused his legislative efforts on agricultural policies important to his home state. A young man who had been seen entering and leaving the congressman's home on the night of the murder was eventually identified by the police and brought in for questioning. The young man, Ty Maclean, had just moved from the congressman's district to Washington in the hope of finding a job as a legislative assistant. Arriving at the congressman's office, he asked about such a job. Mr. Maclean said Congressman Slainey had no job available but, much to his surprise, offered to let him stay at his home while looking for employment. After long hours of questioning, Ty Maclean eventually confessed that he had killed the congressman, saying he had done so unintentionally in defending himself against the congressman's forceful sexual advances. The suspect denied ever having had sex with men, saying he was repulsed by the whole notion. Striking the congressman with a fireplace iron, he said, was the only way he could protect himself against the man's aggressive advances.

When the police questioned the congressman's secretary, Dorrie Sanchez, she told them she knew the congressman was gay and that he socialized with a small circle of discreet friends. She found it unthinkable that the mannerly congressman could be sexually aggressive with an unwilling partner. Mrs. Sanchez remembered Ty Maclean coming to the office to meet with the congressman. His appearance in the office was surprising because even though he said he was looking for a job he brought no résumé with him. Because of his mannerisms and speech patterns, she thought that the young man was gay. Mrs. Sanchez suggested that the police seek a genetic test in order to establish the assailant's sexual orientation. She believed a gene probe for the suspect's sexual orientation would help build a murder case against the man by dismantling his self-defense argument. She suggested that he was a gay hustler who tricked his way into the congressman's home and then killed the congressman during the course of attempted extortion or burglary.

COMMENTS   Invoking the privilege of self-defense against unwanted sexual advances is a standard legal strategy for people accused of harming and even killing gay people.[19] Defenses of this kind sometimes succeed in convincing juries that battery is acceptable against unwanted sexual advances even if it ends in death. Indeed, there is something of a cultural presumption that violence is somehow a "natural" and justified reaction to gay people, and the notion of self-defense takes advantage of that presumption. In this particular scenario the congressman's secretary suggests a way to assess the assailant's self-defense argument. If Ty Maclean were shown to have a genetic marker for homoerotic interests, one would have reason to interrogate him aggressively about his actual sexual behavior and practices, about whether in fact he could have been as unprepared for the congressman's alleged sexual advances as he says he was. This is not to say that evidence of this kind would be decisive in establishing the guilt of someone under suspicion of murder. Neither is it to say that police ought to have automatic access to such tests or to say that attorneys for the defense should have no right to contest the accuracy and significance of the test. It is to say, however, that if there were a statistically significant sexual orientation test it might well serve a role in criminal investigations and prosecutions. In the scenario described above such a test might help lead police to the killer of a gay man or, by the same token, help exculpate a man under wrongful suspicion.

Case 2. Civil Litigation   While in hypnotherapy a thirty-six-year-old man with AIDS, Jason Roberts, suddenly remembers being sexually molested at age fourteen at an Ohio Catholic seminary for high school students. He recalls that one priest initiated him into oral sex during weekend retreats at an isolated country shrine. That same priest often kept the boy late in the locker rooms or kitchens on one pretext or another and directed other priests to him for sexual encounters. Mr. Roberts says he now recalls that he was eventually led into the office of a visiting priest for sexual intercourse. Mr. Roberts now says that he was too much in awe of his religious elders and too confused about sexuality in general to report these incidents to anyone. His emotional distress about the encounters, he now alleges, confused him about his sexual identity and kept him from pursuing sexual relationships with women. Mr. Roberts says he therefore pursued a "gay lifestyle" and that psychologically compelled life put him at risk of AIDS. Only now, after long sessions with his hypnotherapist, did he recall clearly the repressed memory of events that he says set him on the path of a gay life, events he had repressed from consciousness for over twenty years. In that period the priest who had intercourse with him had gone on to become one of the most prominent bishops in the United States. Mr. Roberts sought fourteen million dollars in damages from the Roman Catholic Church, alleging that the molestation he endured with the priests channeled him into an immoral lifestyle that put him at risk of AIDS. The bishop denied any memory of this former seminarian and denied any sexual contact with any man. The courtly bishop declared, moreover, that not only had he remained true to his vow of celibacy and never married but that he was at sixty-seven years of age still a virgin. He was, moreover, wholly heterosexual and was prepared to undergo a genetic sexual orientation test in order to substantiate that claim. Mr. Roberts says that he will also undergo a sexual orientation test to show that he is "by nature" straight and that only the wrongdoing of priests forced him into gay sex.

COMMENTS   In civil court cases it is individual parties rather than the state that bring a claim of wrongful action. One can well imagine that both plaintiffs and defendants in this case would try to introduce the results of sexual orientation tests as part of their efforts to convince judges or juries about claims of wrongdoing. In the case here the test might show, for example, that the bishop had the genetic trait characteristic of straight men, thereby bolstering his claims of innocence. By the same token, though, a sexual orientation test could not prove that the bishop never had sex with a male; no test could. Or the test might show that the bishop had the trait characteristic of gay men, thus perhaps undermining the credibility of his defense, though, again, no test of this kind could show that a person had ever had sex with another person, let alone with a specific person. The same ambiguity would obtain for Mr. Robert's results: they might show that he is genotypically straight, but that does not mean that he would never have had sex with men except for the alleged molestation of the priests. Or the results might show that he was genotypically disposed toward being gay, which result might work against the credibility of the claim that he was channeled into being gay solely by the alleged molestation of the priests. While the test results could not therefore prove decisive in regard to all the claims being made, they might be introduced as part of the total evidence presented. Their ultimate significance would be for the judge or jury to decide on a case-to-case basis.

Case 3. Hidden Pasts   While growing up in a troubled family in Philadelphia, adolescent Jim Randall fell into a life of prostitution. In fact, when he was fifteen, his mother said to him, "You've got a nice body. Why don't you make some money with it?" Jim had sex with large numbers of men for monetary gain, but not only for that reason, since it turned out that he enjoyed the sex. He retained, though, an idealized image of himself as straight, as eventually having a wife and children. In practice, his social circumstances as a prostitute ensured that most of his sexual contacts would be men. After many years Jim began to tire of hustling and enlisted a therapist who assured him that he could direct Jim's sexual attraction toward women through a variety of psychological techniques and religious counseling. Jim found that the therapy did seem to reduce his social interest in men and to increase his sexual interest in women. When he was twenty-five Jim's therapist advised him to move to a location that did not have the temptations of an established gay culture.

Jim moved to Wilkes-Barre, found employment, met Sharlene, with whom he became romantically involved, and married. When Sharlene became pregnant Jim feared that he might pass homosexuality on to his child, so he asked his wife's doctor to conduct a prenatal test to see whether the child was likely to become homosexual. He asked the doctor to keep both the test and its result secret from his wife. He said that if the test showed the child likely to become homosexual—whether a boy or a girl—he would ask his wife to abort, telling her he did not feel emotionally or financially prepared to rear a child at this time. In fact, he told the doctor, he could not live with the guilt of passing on to any child of his a trait he now despised. He thought, moreover, his wife would uncover his past sexual life and prostitution. One of the things that had attracted him to her was her intolerance of homosexuals. Jim's therapist had advised him to seek out a woman who would not tolerate homosexuality lest she reinforce his sexual interests in men. Now he feared a gay child might destroy the new life he was trying to make for himself.

COMMENTS   If their child were shown by the test as disposed toward being gay, Jim and Sharlene might wrestle with the question of their genetic responsibility for that trait and Jim's hidden past might come to light as would any lies he told Sharlene. Whatever one thinks about the ethics of abortion, it is by ethical and legal consensus unacceptable for physicians to conduct secret prenatal tests on unwitting pregnant women at their husbands' behest. I would hope that a physician would never conduct a test under the circumstances described here. Nevertheless, a sexual orientation test might be jointly requested by both parents, especially if Sharlene openly shared Jim's disinclination to have a gay child. At the present time there would be no legal barrier to conducting such a test or having an abortion on the basis of unwanted results. In any case, the point to be made here is that a sexual orientation test need not mean the same thing to both parents, and, where it does not, it can raise serious conflict within a family.

Case 4. Media Use of the Test   At a news conference a publicist announces that her client, the internationally famous supermodel Raimondo, has entered a private Los Angeles hospital, that he is seriously ill with AIDS and is near death. During the previous year the model had said that he was suffering from anemia, but rumors had been widespread in Hollywood that the model was in fact searching out AIDS therapies all around the world and that he had just recently returned from Switzerland where he had been treated with exotic herbal infusions. In her statement the publicist says that Raimondo was neither homosexual nor an intravenous drug user and that, therefore, no one was certain how he had developed AIDS. She suggests in vague language that he may have received blood transfusions in the late 1980s in the course of medical treatment for injuries he sustained falling off a horse during the filming of the cologne ad that first made him famous. Citing the model's right to medical privacy, she declines to offer any details about the nature or time of such injuries and treatment. Citing the American Medical Association code of ethics, Raimondo's doctors also decline to discuss his condition.[20] A *National Evening Tabloid* reporter has been long familiar with rumors about the model's all-male poolside sex parties but has never found anyone willing to go on record with confirmation. The reporter knows, however, that samples of the model's long black hair, his trademark, are in the hands of a number of fans. He therefore attempts to purchase some of these snippets so that he can have them genetically profiled in order to prove the Raimondo's homosexuality. The *Tabloid* offers fifty thousand dollars for a usable sample of the model's hair. On learning of this offer, the model's attorney threatens to sue the *Tabloid* for invasion of medical privacy and threatens to seek prior restraint if the newspaper does obtain and test the hair samples. The *Tabloid* responds by saying that there are no laws against obtaining privately held hair samples and noting that Raimondo routinely auctioned locks of his famous tresses for charity. The newspaper also cites journalistic privilege in reporting information it uncovers about a public figure.

COMMENTS   If the results of a genetic test of Raimondo's hair were consistent with the results typically found in gay men, the newspaper would seemingly be free to publish that information and "out" the prominent model, though people who are not public figures could probably not be treated this way. Whether people should be outed about their sexual orientation is, of course, a matter of debate, with opponents arguing that outing can have prejudicial results.[21] Raimondo's estate might lose its value if it were known publicly that he was gay or perceived as gay. By contrast, some advocates of outing point out that the prejudicial effects of being gay are less important than the evil of complicity with the gag order society imposes on gay people about their erotic interests and identities. They also point out that some people have been energized to the task of gay activism by being outed.[22] The use by news media of sexual orientation tests would fall squarely within the established confines of this debate. If a sexual orientation test substantiated rumors of the gay life of a public figure, a newspaper might well choose to go forward with them. If, by the same token, a sexual orientation test did not substantiate rumors of a gay life, and a paper chose not to run a story, the test might protect a public figure against unwanted intrusion and speculation.

Case 5. Civic Benefits   At a time when Canada is enjoying significant budget surpluses and wishes to assert its national identity through its envied health care system, the political party of Chief Health Commissioner Patricia Illingworth is able to shepherd legislation through Parliament that will compensate gay men with AIDS ten thousand dollars each. Commissioner Illingworth had long argued that such compensation was owed by reason of the social repression of homosexuality, which repression forced gay men into "fast lane" sexual behaviors and put them at risk of HIV infection.[23] To receive this compensation, men must document a diagnosis of AIDS and provide a certified genetic profile establishing that they do indeed carry the genetic marker for male homoeroticism—in order to support the presumption that they acquired an HIV infection through sex with men and not another way. Some AIDS activists, however, protest this standard, saying that homosexual behavior is not reducible to genetic causes and, therefore, many gay PWAs will fail to meet the eligibility standard for compensation. The activists find the distinction between compensable and noncompensable PWAs objectionable in any case. Commissioner Illingworth does not, however, believe that all PWAs should be compensated since some PWAs are not as socially compromised as gay men in their ability to protect themselves against HIV. She insists that genetic profiling is the only standard Parliament would accept as identifying legitimate recipients of the compensation and is unwilling to accept other forms of documentation regarding sexual orientation, else every male person with AIDS would pose as a gay man in order to achieve the health entitlement.

COMMENTS   Should there ever emerge civic benefits, such as those described here, that attach to lesbian and gay sexual orientations, governments would immediately confront the problem of certification of eligibility for the benefits. A genetic sexual orientation test would be one objective way to make that determination. Any such test would be open to the charge that it does not by itself establish a person's sexual behavior in any authoritative way. Some people may come to homoerotic interests for reasons independent of the testable facts of their genetic endowments; these people would lack genetic markers implying homoerotic interests. In order to be fair, there probably should be an alternate mechanism by which men and women alike could demonstrate their gay identities before the law. Nevertheless, a genetic sexual orientation test could provide at least a prima facie basis for determining eligibility for any civic benefits that attach to gay or lesbian sexual orientation. The question of eligibility for benefits is altogether separate, of course, from the question of the likelihood and wisdom of benefits along these lines. Giving benefits to gay people—however certified as gay before the law—could engender a kind of social backlash if those benefits were actually or perceived as political favoritism. This problem obtains with many civic benefits, of course, so that a benefit to gay people cannot be ruled out simply because there is some social objection to it. That the benefit survived a legislative review, sure to be stormy, would be a procedural presumption of its fairness. The same might be said of any affirmative action programs that have been advanced in favor of gay people, whether those programs are designed to redress past evils or to achieve a more equitable future.[24] In any case, it is not inconceivable that some civic benefit might be due gay people, and, if such benefits emerge, then there will have to be some standard for deciding who is and who is not gay. A sexual orientation test could help in this regard.

Case 7. Military Service   Because of the expanding capacities of genetic medicine the military proposes that the genetic sample required of all new personnel be tested with all easily accessible, reliable, and inexpensive genetic tests, especially all genetic tests linked to disease or susceptibility to disease. Included in this battery of tests will be the genetic test for sexual orientation. To this point the genetic test for sexual orientation had been carried out only after allegations of misconduct. Now, the military says, the test is necessary as a matter of complete medical records. Military scholars also want to conduct the test on all available banked genetic samples of past personnel in order to determine the extent to which gay people were in fact in the military. Gay leaders are divided about the value of this proposal. On the one hand, some leaders object to the testing of all service members, arguing that the testing will be used prejudicially against gay people even though a pledge of medical confidentiality has been offered. In keeping with the policy of the current administration, a sexual orientation test would be ordered only following an allegation of misconduct and from a sample taken specifically in that event. On the other hand, some gay leaders think that it would be useful to know the extent to which gay people have in fact served in all the branches of the military, at what ranks, and with what degree of accomplishment. They believe that in the long run the results could help erode resistance to the ban on openly gay men and lesbians in uniform. They also argue that it certainly would be useful for health care workers to know if someone they were treating was in fact gay or lesbian. Knowing that a service member was lesbian or gay could help, for example, military psychiatrists formulate better treatment plans for their patients troubled about adjustment in the military or at risk of violence or sexually communicable diseases.

COMMENTS   The prospect of testing for sexual orientation will arise wherever there are banked genetic samples, regardless of the original purpose of the samples, whether they involve historically significant people or ordinary folk. In this instance the question is whether routine sexual orientation screening should go forward in an institution that has policies excluding gay people. If tests revealing a gay sexual orientation were not used as prima facie evidence in favor of discharge from the military, and if test results were kept confidential and made available only on a medical need-to-know basis, it is unclear that testing of this kind would significantly alter military practices of discharging people only if evidence of homoerotic behavior came to light independent of rustling through medical records. If universal testing showed that gay men and lesbians were prevalent in the military in significant ways throughout the period for which genetic samples were available, there might well be something to the argument that this knowledge could help activists working against the exclusion of gay people. Nevertheless, there are serious questions about the confidentiality of medical information held by the same institution responsible for carrying out discharge proceedings. It would be hard, that is, to erect an impermeable barrier between medical records and those who could put that information to use in discharge proceedings. Researchers interested in the historical prevalence of gay people in the military could conduct that research independently of military oversight as a way of ensuring confidentiality and the protection of any people still in the service. The research might be conducted, for example, by university researchers who could withhold individual test results from the military. The argument that the military needs information about an individual's sexual orientation in order to maintain complete medical records is a compelling argument since there are many instances in which the adequacy of health care services depends on knowledge about patients' sexual lives. It is unclear, however, that the military needs to obtain this information from a genetic test. If the military had no ban on openly gay service members, it could simply ask its members about their sexual orientation in much the same way its medical records rely on answers to questions about childhood diseases. Except for the prejudicial effects of its exclusionary ban on openly gay people, it appears that military health care workers could get the information they wanted simply by asking and without having to institute a program of universal genetic testing.

Case 8. Lesbian Identity   The Womyn's Ranch in Nevada conducts an annual week-long festival that offers hiking, camping, political sessions, support groups, health care and self-defense seminars, and entertainment. Approximately ten thousand women from around the world attend the festival. Because the organizers believe that a women-only policy best serves the interests of the mostly lesbian attendees, they have adopted strict standards of admission. Male-to-female transsexuals are not permitted to attend the festival,[25] and certification of one's birth as female may be required at the time of admission. No male children over the age of eight are permitted on the ranch. A few lesbian attendees believe that the festival's purpose is being diluted by the admission of nonlesbian women and male children of any age. They therefore propose that a certain section and certain events of the festival be limited to those women who can prove their lesbianism through a genetic test. They see this proposal as ensuring the women-centered purity of the events and social interaction. Others claim that the proposal establishes a hierarchy that will be used invidiously against nonlesbian-identified women or women who come to be lesbians for, as they see the matter, political reasons, that is, reasons of their own choosing. Critics say the "biological-lesbian-only" proposal is profoundly antiegalitarian and threatens to fracture the women's movement generally. They say that anyone willing to identify as a woman or as a lesbian should be welcome in any part of the festival.

COMMENTS   This scenario highlights the way in which a sexual orientation test might be used to define the boundaries of the lesbian/gay/queer community for reasons that suit that community—or a part of it. Some gay men and lesbians have called for separatist communities on ideological grounds, and many more live in such communities as a matter of practice. It might well prove that these same people would find their interests served by having some objective standard by which to *include and exclude* members of self-defined groups. Some lesbians and/or gay men might have an interest in using a sexual orientation test to outline a genetically unified community. Other lesbians and/or gay men might object to such uses, as would many straight people, but so long as the purposes of gay men and/or lesbians are being served, it would not be immediately evident that this use of a sexual orientation marker served heterosexist purposes or that it would be inherently immoral to use it in this way. On the contrary, such testing might be said to offer a community a clear principle of identification and thus a more secure social and political commonality, which, as some would see, is all to the good.

Case 9. The New Baby   Married couple Jon and Joan have expectantly awaited Joan's first pregnancy, as they are eager to have children. Early during Joan's pregnancy her doctor offered and she accepted certain prenatal tests aimed at identifying fetal disorders, both genetic and developmental. None were found through ultrasound, fiberoptic fetoscopy, and selected genetic tests carried out through chorionic villus sampling. When Joan delivers her newborn daughter, the doctor asks permission to take new samples from the child for a genome profile; he says this is a standard procedure at this particular hospital and that the samples will help doctors to, among other things, predict genetic susceptibility to certain diseases and disorders in the baby, especially cancer and disorders associated with aging. While other hospitals do not offer this service, the doctor is happy to tell Jon and Joan that their child is getting the very best medicine has to offer and that this information will be useful to doctors treating the child across her entire life. He says that the information may even make her eligible for enrollment in clinical trials if she should prove to be at risk of genetic disorders. He also mentions in an offhand way that the profiling will reveal the child's likely sexual orientation. The vast majority of time, he says, children will be heterosexual, but he says if parents know now that their child will be homosexual, it can give them time to adjust to the news and help raise the child in a secure environment. Jon and Joan both agree that while they think a genome profile will be useful to their daughter regarding her susceptibility to disease, they do not think information on her sexual orientation should be part of the medical record. First of all, they are not sure they are prepared to receive information like this, partly because they had not foreseen the possibility of a lesbian daughter. Second, they are not sure the record can be kept confidential and fear that their daughter might be discriminated against in the future when she applies for jobs if she is in fact lesbian. The doctor tells them that the genetic samples he takes will contain this information and there is no way he can take samples for everything but sexual orientation. The parents therefore tell the doctor no genetic samples should be taken at all. He will comply with their wish, he says, but notes that their decision will leave a huge gap in the child's medical record.

COMMENTS   The banking of genetic samples or the data banking of genetic information is likely to prove less and less resistible to medical practitioners, epidemiologists, and others with an interest in the genetic traits of both specific individuals and populations. Whether a genetic sample will be banked for each newborn remains to be seen, though it is likely that some institutions may adopt exactly such a program. The questions that emerge from taking and storing a genetic sample at birth include not only the control parents ought to have over the testing of their children but also what standard ought to govern access to these samples and the information they contain. At present hospitals routinely conduct various epidemiological tests on children, including, for example, HIV testing.[26] Should a similar sort of program go forward with respect to the epidemiology of genetic traits, genetic markers for sexual orientation among them? Epidemiological studies, producing a great deal of useful information about the incidence and prevalence of any given trait, may be conducted anonymously in the sense that the samples are not linked to identifiable people. Or these studies may be carried out in full knowledge of the identify of the person from whom the sample is taken. Anonymous studies have the benefit of protecting people from any invidious uses of the test information, but they also do not return to parents information that the parents might in fact find useful. Testing newborns at birth for sexual orientation could be conducted anonymously for strictly epidemiologic purposes or it could be part of a package of testing done routinely for parents. Because of the significance of sexual orientation tests for both newborns and their parents and because of the significance of banked genetic samples in general, there should be a great deal of public discussion and education before standards in either regard were adopted.

Case 10. False Positive   James Hoy, twenty-seven, applies for a job with a computer company that makes virtually every computer the federal government uses in its most advanced military and intelligence operations. The company has, therefore, a special interest in whether employees pose security risks to the nation. As a condition of employment, the company requires each prospective employee to submit a genetic sample, ostensibly to confirm his or her identity, but also to test for known traits, including sexual orientation. The company does not discriminate on the basis of sexual orientation, but they do want to know whether their employees are gay so that they are not vulnerable to blackmail. Mr. Hoy willingly supplies the blood sample but is alarmed to learn from company officials that he has been identified as having a genetic region associated with gay men. When he denies that he is gay, the company thinks he may be lying and therefore open to blackmail in regard to his true sexual interests. They therefore decline to hire him. As the state in which Mr. Hoy lives has no laws that forbid discrimination on the basis of sexual orientation, Mr. Hoy is unable to sue the company for redress. He does, however, sue the company that carried out the sexual orientation test, alleging that its practices wronged him by imputing a false sexual orientation, which imputation harmed him in job prospects and in the mental anguish it caused.

COMMENTS   In all previous cases in this chapter I have presumed that the hypothetical test for sexual orientation is more or less definitive about an adult's sexual orientation, a presumption I vary here to reflect the realities of biomedical testing. Testing may yet leave much to be desired since in practice there is plenty of room for error even if the test is theoretically well designed. Some of the test results will be wrong because of the inherent limitations of any test and because the test will sometimes be poorly conducted. It may be that Mr. Hoy has a legitimate complaint against the company conducting the test if its personnel were negligent in the way it conducted the test. Or it may be simply that the test will predictably, because of its inherent limitations, give false results from time to time, whether it falsely identifies someone as gay or falsely identifies someone as straight. Because of these limitations, the kind of complaint offered by Mr. Hoy here will appear in courts from time to time, and judges and juries will decide whether and to what extent companies have been negligent, what damages occurred, and what compensation is deserved, if any.

Cases like the foregoing could be multiplied without much difficulty. For example, were a sexual orientation test available, parents might wish a physician to carry out a test on a recalcitrant teenage daughter who refuses to discuss her sexual orientation with them.[27] A wealthy and eccentric uncle might divide his considerable estate according to the sexual orientation of his male heirs. He might, for example, want to favor gay male scions of the family in the hopes that his largesse will help them overcome any adversities they might face because of their sexual orientation. He could therefore stipulate that his estate be divided among those nephews who are gay by a confirmed sexual orientation test. Historical researchers might wish to exhume the body of President James Buchanan in order to substantiate claims of his homosexuality. Or divorcing parents might wish to have their child tested in order to obtain custody in a dispute pitting a bisexual father against an antigay mother. If the child were disposed toward being gay, the father might argue that he would be a better parent, understanding as he does the nature of same-sex eroticism and its social meaning.

There would certainly be important ramifications of the uses of a genetic or any biological test for sexual orientation, but as is evident from this assortment of case studies it does not follow that the test would only work to the disadvantage of gay people. I have, of course, presumed that the test would offer more or less definitive conclusions about sexual orientation. In real life it is clear that any such test would be much more ambiguous and limited than I have presumed thus far. Consequently, scenarios about the use of tests with ambiguous and fallible results would be considerably more complicated than those I have presented above.

PROTECTING AGAINST WRONGFUL USES OF SEXUAL ORIENTATION TESTING

It may come to pass that some sort of marker for sexual orientation will emerge or, what comes to nearly the same thing, this testing will be believed to exist. I am convinced by the unequal social treatment of gay people that there are many social institutions that would be tempted to use a sexual orientation test were one available, the U.S. military being among the most likely candidates. I am equally convinced that these exclusions are ordinarily unfounded. If markers for sexual orientation are found, those wanting to use them for exclusionary purposes should bear the burden of showing why the exclusion of gay people is justified in the first place and why a biological test is the least burdensome way to achieve that exclusion. It does not seem to me that these justifications can ordinarily be convincing in a moral sense, which is different from saying that these justifications will be found wanting in a political sense. A little antigay argument often goes a long political way.

I believe, for example, that it would be wrong to extend the powers of surveillance over sexual orientation in the military through the use of a sexual orientation test because the rationale currently offered by the military for the exclusion of openly gay people is not defensible as a matter of hard evidence. First of all, not only is this exclusion of extremely recent vintage, it is simply not true that homosexuality is incompatible with military service in any clear or monolithic way. Of all the many wars that have been fought in human history, no battle, no war has been won or lost because a military organization has failed to examine the sexual orientation of its generals or grunts. At the present time a good number of the people who do this nation's military work are gay men and lesbians, including gay men and lesbians in some of the most important positions to be had in the military.[28] Second, the military policy is incoherent because it functions randomly. As a matter of fact, gay people are *not* uniformly excluded from the military even when they are known by military officials to be gay, as the retention of self-identified gay troops during the Persian Gulf War showed. For all intents and purposes, the military keeps gay people in when it needs them and finds ways to evict them when it wants them out.[29] Third, in defending some of the exclusions they have carried out, military lawyers are forced to turn statements of gay identity into the conceptual and moral equivalent of actual sexual behavior; they do this when they take statements of gay identity as coextensive with prohibited sexual behavior. To make this sort of conflation is to treat an accusation as its own evidence. Fourth, if it is real or feared sexual behavior of gay people that is objectionable, the military is not employing the least intrusive mechanism for controlling the behavior. If there are behaviors that disrupt unit cohesiveness, then those behaviors—and not gay people as a class—should be the object of sanction. Tellingly, in *none* of the most publicized litigation involving gay people has the military tried to demonstrate that the particular service member in question—Margarethe Cammemeyer, Tracey Thorne, Keith Meinhold, Miriam ben-Shalom, Perry Watkins—has in fact proved disruptive to his or her unit. On the contrary, their disruptiveness had to be alleged in the face of long histories of documented commendation. In the final analysis the exclusionary policy depends for its credibility on *hypothetical* damages to unit cohesion. For all these reasons I find the exclusionary bar on openly gay people in the military to be morally indefensible.

I have discussed the military case in detail here because it seems to me that virtually every sort of organizational or institutional policy that would discriminate against gay people as a class suffers from the same sort of contradictions and hypocrisies to be found in the military policy. The central question to my mind, then, is not whether a sexual orientation test could be used by the military or other organization but whether the motives for using such a test are defensible in the first place. It may not be possible to sway people from ill-founded or discriminatory motives, but it may be possible to control the effects of those motives and to do so along lines that will be important for all people, regardless of sexual orientation, in an age increasingly dependent on biomedical testing and computer-banked information. I would like, therefore, in the last section of this chapter to outline some of the features that should govern testing.

MORAL STANDARDS IN TESTING

My remarks here are of a general nature, intended to sketch broad principles rather than to describe specific policies governing all imaginable circumstances under which sexual orientation testing might occur. My remarks here are not especially novel; they will be familiar to those who have considered other kinds of testing having the potential to open people to preferential and/or substandard treatment. Again, this discussion is hypothetical since there are no tests for sexual orientation, but the discussion is instructive for what it shows about how such testing should be conducted were it possible.

First of all, tests for sexual orientation in adults should never take place without express and informed consent about the purposes of the testing and the expected use of the results. If the tests are to be conducted on a child or an incompetent adult, a legal guardian or surrogate decision-maker should have standing to make the decision about testing and should receive all the same counsel that would be offered to someone making the decision for him- or herself. Sexual orientation tests should not be conducted on banked genetic samples unless express permission for such testing has been obtained at the time the genetic sample was banked or subsequent permission has been received. Unless a person consents, the results of sexual orientation tests should not be transferred or sold to organizations or institutions such as insurance companies or businesses that bank test records. Unless there is consent otherwise, sexual orientation test results should be kept under a strong presumption of confidentiality. One of the things this would mean is that physicians should not disclose the sexual orientation of a deceased patient or discuss the tests of celebrity clients, again, unless there is specific consent to the contrary. In all cases people should also have the right to have access to data banked about them and the right to make corrections to erroneous information. Any epidemiological surveys for sexual orientation should be conducted to the extent possible through methods that involve the informed consent of the subjects from whom test samples are taken. At the very least, epidemiological studies should not proceed in ways that permit the direct identification of subjects from genetic samples or test results, whether these subjects are living or long dead. Last, I also believe that sexual orientation tests should not be made a condition of employment, including military service.

Most of these safeguards should be fairly noncontroversial as a matter of ethics even if they would require a fair amount of wrangling to enact legislatively.[30] The proposals are entirely consonant with the prevailing medical and legal ethic of autonomy in biomedicine and afford the person who could be tested the broadest range of protection by requiring that she or he consent to any sexual orientation tests and to the disposition of test results. It may be that some researchers would find the standard of consent proposed here burdensome, yet it is hard to see that a test for sexual orientation should be exempted from consent simply for the convenience of researchers. Information about sexual orientation remains highly volatile, and it would be a mistake to open people to the prospect of testing without their full knowledge and consent.

I make the proposal that testing should not be a condition of employment because even if an employer like the U.S. military objects to the presence of gay people in its ranks, it still has less intrusive alternatives available to it for controlling the allegedly objectionable effects of gay people. The military and employers generally could adopt policies against objectionable sexual behavior in the workplace, which policies could be just as effective in achieving the goals of workplace "cohesion" as any program of universal testing of applicants and rejection of gay people. Moreover, some jurisdictions—including states such as Wisconsin and Massachusetts—now have statutory prohibitions against discrimination toward gay people in employment, housing, and the like. In such jurisdictions sexual orientation tests by employers would be unuseful (except for some exceptions provided by statute) if they observed the laws prohibiting discrimination against gay people in employment. Employers should not be testing for information they are forbidden from using in making hiring decisions.

Although I have taken pains in this chapter to outline the ways in which sexual orientation tests might prove beneficial to gay people, and although I have tried to outline the mechanics by which confidentiality ought to prevail in such testing, it might be objected that I am unduly optimistic about the capacity of social institutions to change their heterosexist spots and about the extent to which people can be protected from discrimination based on their sexual orientation. To be sure, the raucous political world is often more complex and unpredictable than the lineaments of a philosophical argument. For example, 1992 presidential candidate Bill Clinton campaigned on a pledge of lifting the Pentagon's ban on gay people in the military. Facing formidable political opposition once in office, he instead became the first president in history to sign federal legislation formalizing a ban against openly gay people.[31] Not only was the Clinton administration responsible for shifting what had been simply an administrative policy of the Pentagon into federal law, that shift may be in some ways more detrimental to gay people than the policy it replaced. Because of that federal legislation, it seems that more gay people have been dismissed annually from the military than were dismissed under the Pentagon's own self-imposed regulations—in spite of the fact that the new law does not permit military authorities to inquire about sexual orientation as a matter of course.[32] In the face of the enormous gap between Clinton's goals as a candidate and his effects as chief executive, I am mindful of the distance between lofty ethical ideals and compromised political realities. For this kind of reason, sexual orientation science should be scrutinized and closely, in keeping with the standards of rigorous science, but the consequences and uses of sexual orientation science should be subjected just as closely to analysis, in keeping with the standards of circumspect moral philosophy. If there are objectionable uses of sexual orientation science, they should be confronted directly and not used to paint all science and politics as morally compromised from the start.

The nature of erotic life and the variability of human beings may well defeat the search for any simple marker for sexual orientation, though the question of its possibility remains open in the sense that people disposed toward or habituated in one erotic life may exhibit a discernible trait that distinguishes them from others with other kinds of erotic interests. Whether or not a definitive test for any such trait will emerge, some people may *believe* that a particular test offers meaningful results and try to use it in ways that extend whatever interest they have in marking people off according to sexual orientation. A sexual orientation test would well serve social institutions having formal and informal reasons for excluding gay people. As the scenarios presented above show, however, it is simply not true that a sexual orientation marker would necessarily and always work to the disadvantage of gay people. Without wanting to overstate their merit, I would like to suggest that sexual orientation tests may sometimes be of positive value to gay people wrestling with questions of identity and equality before the law. A marker for sexual orientation, whether it takes the form of an anatomical, genetic, or some other objectively measurable trait, need not be an inherently evil development in the history of science, something irreducibly an instrument of antigay discrimination and eugenics.

It is immediately necessary to add that there are important reasons to attend to the proper use of any markers for sexual orientation that might be discovered. The history of genetic testing affords examples of problems that could reemerge were there some genetic test available for sexual orientation. As attorney Larry Gostin has observed:

> Complex and often pernicious mythologies emerge from public ignorance of genetically-based diagnostic and prognostic tests. The common belief is that genetic technologies generated from scientific assessment are always accurate, highly predictive, and capable of identifying an individual's or offspring's inevitable predestination of future disability. The facts are diametrically opposed to this common belief. The results of genetic-based diagnosis and prognosis are uncertain for many reasons. Predicting the nature, severity, and course of disease based upon a genetic marker is an additional difficulty. For most genetic diseases the onset date, severity of symptoms, and efficacy of treatment and management are highly variable. Some people remain virtually symptom free, while others progress to seriously disabling illness.[33]

What Gostin describes here in regard to genetic disease will be even more true of complex behavioral traits having a genetic basis. There is a moral and social variability to erotic life that no test can ever express even as there are social impulses to make tests more precise in their meaning than they can be.

Even if there were a genetic or some other kind of marker for sexual orientation, employers or religious orders or insurers would be unable to predict from that marker alone the exact nature of people's sexual lives, their social fate, or their value as an employee, priest, or nun. Homoeroticism and heteroeroticism encompass a *vast* range of diversity, and to know that a given child is likely to be gay or straight is to know little about how that sexual orientation will add to or detract from a meaningful life. One could not either conclude anything about the general moral character of an individual simply on the basis of sexual orientation, for there are some gay people who have richer moral lives than some straight people. Yet a marker for sexual orientation will remain attractive for the reason that it appears to offer a simple accounting of erotic difference. If people were definable as gay or straight according to a simple test, parents might absolve themselves of a sense of failure they sometimes have on learning their children are gay. They might think their child's erotic life was part of the natural lottery rather than something they caused through some lapse in their parental duties. People might feel more secure in their own identities if they were, once and for all, marked gay or straight.[34] Straight people might feel more comfortable around gay people, and vice versa, if they thought themselves separated off by some objective trait and did not have to construct their expectations of difference around the shadowy imaginings of sexual behavior unfamiliar to them. They might not therefore have to forge and assert their identities through harmful antagonisms based on those imagined differences. The meaning of sexological research for the social accommodation of gay people is explored in detail in the next chapter. It does appear, though, that a genetic or other kind of marker for sexual orientation could in its own way protect some of the interests of gay people, though certainly that kind of protection is only possible in a society consciously willing to protect gay people. That sort of society need not be especially different from one in which all people are respected in regard to privacy, liberty, and equality before the law.

6 |||||||||||||||||||||||||||||||||||||||||||||||||||||||||||||||||||||||||||||||

SEXUAL ORIENTATION RESEARCH, NATURE, AND

THE LAW

Contemporary biological studies of homoerotic sexual orientation have received an almost schizophrenic social reception. On the one hand, these reports have evoked durable worry that discovery of any biological components of sexual orientation will be used prejudicially against gay men and lesbians in programs of discrimination and diminishment. On the other hand, Simon LeVay, for one, believes that this research works to advance the moral and social prospects of gay people. LeVay says that biological research shows that being gay is a natural behavior and, therefore, something that one can accept in oneself and other people.[1] This kind of enthusiasm about the meaning of biological sexual orientation research is shared by some gay legal advocates who see important implications in the domain of the law, for example, in civil rights that depend on fundamental interests or immutable characteristics.[2]

A bifurcated reception of sexual orientation research is not new to this era. Lillian Faderman has pointed out that biomedical research on gay people in the early part of this century divided opinion in the emerging U.S. lesbian community.[3] Some lesbians of that era embraced that research with enthusiasm, finding in it an explanation for their erotic interests and a locus for themselves in nature. They were at least favorably enough disposed to the science to participate as subjects in research. It was also a gay man who set in motion Evelyn Hooker's psychological study of gay men.[4] At the very least, sexological research had the effect of publicizing the widespread existence of men and women with homoerotic interests, which was to the advantage of gay people looking to learn more about themselves. These interpretations were not universally shared, of course, and many women and men either rejected biomedical characterizations of homoeroticism outright or were at pains to distinguish themselves morally and socially from the biological inverts described all too unflatteringly in the biomedical literature. Both favorable and unfavorable interpretations of biological sexual orientation research in our own time thus have historical antecedents even if some of the particulars of each era are unique in their own right.

For better or worse the idea of nature has carried a great deal of the debate about the morality of homoeroticism, and for this reason it is worth considering whether and to what extent sexual orientation research illuminates this debate. My first main task in this chapter is to show why sexual orientation research of a biological kind is of limited value in rebutting claims that homoeroticism is "unnatural" in the way that term is usually invoked in moral arguments. Sexual orientation research *can* falsify claims about the nature of homoeroticism if they are empirically incorrect but insofar as the "nature" of homosexuality at stake is not the nature composed of empirical facts but the nature of metaphysical ideals, sexual orientation research cannot rescue homoeroticism from claims of unnaturalness. Metaphysical ideals of nature against which homoeroticism appears morally defective must be fought on their own turf, philosophical adequacy, rather than as matters of empirical research.

This is not to say that sexual orientation research is unimportant to social judgments about homoeroticism and the place of gay people in society. There are *many* ways in which sexual orientation science, understood not only as the study of the origins but also of the effects of sexual orientation, are relevant to a complete understanding of eroticism and how it is to be socially and legally accommodated. Richard Green, for example, has sketched many of the ways in which data produced by scientific study would be relevant to the law in making determinations about, for example, custody of children, the rights of the transgendered, sex education, immigration regulations, and so on.[5] Such research can show, for example, that as a matter of course gay teachers do not prey sexually on students. In this sense sexual orientation research is relevant to gay people insofar as it affects the factual view held of them, which in turn certainly affects legal enactments and social attitudes. There is no substitute for empirical research when moral debates turn on matters of fact in, for example, determinations of whether gay people make fit parents or whether sexual age-of-consent laws have any appreciable affect on the emergence of sexual orientation in young adults.

The rights people enjoy sometimes depend on how biological explanations are related to civil standing. In the U.S. constitutional tradition certain social rights belong to people by virtue of their having a fundamental standing in human interests and systems of value. These rights are thought fundamental because they are tied in profound ways to the interests people have by virtue of being human. In this category U.S. law has recognized, for example, the rights of marriage, having children, using contraception, and having abortions under most circumstances.[6] Richard Green has argued that sexual orientation research does show homoeroticism to be fundamental to human life in ways parallel to these other interests.[7] In its 1986 Bowers v. Hardwick decision, however, the U.S. Supreme Court rejected the notion of a fundamental right to sex between members of the same sex, even between consenting adults in private.[8] Unless there are important changes in the makeup of the Supreme Court or some form of constitutional revisitation of that decision, it is unlikely that this line of argumentation will afford meaningful change of laws affecting gay people, advances in sexual orientation science notwithstanding.

Some gay legal advocates therefore turned their attention to another line of defense, the countermajoritarian judicial mechanism designed to protect groups defined by "immutable" characteristics that allegedly provoke and justify discriminatory treatment. My second main task in this chapter is to demonstrate how far it is from settled that science shows homoeroticism to be immutable within the meaning of this legal mechanism. Indeed, sexual orientation research is nowhere near showing that sexual orientation is fixed in the way people's national origin is fixed by reason of the place they are born. In any case, the 1996 U.S. Supreme Court case of Romer v. Evans may have preempted this line of argumentation as the one most useful to the legal advance of gay people. In that case the Supreme Court did not appeal to "the facts" of the origin of sexual orientation or its immutability in order to conclude that no state may adopt laws that strike down existing sexual orientation antidiscrimination laws and forbid all such laws in the future. The majority decision that prevailed in that decision was grounded in the logic that I think should prevail in regard to all judicial review of antigay discrimination, namely, whether laws and policies having a discriminatory effect on gay people have a rational relationship to a legitimate governmental interest. In most instances an account of the causal determinants of sexual orientation would be irrelevant to such analysis, as I will argue below, though certainly reports about the effects of sexual orientation might still be useful in clarifying matters of fact.

READING SEXUAL ORIENTATION INTO NATURE

There is hardly a concept more perennial to debates about the morality of erotic interests than nature, and yet there is hardly a moral concept less uniformly precise in its meaning. Moreover, some of those meanings are manifestly ill-suited to moral determinations about sexual matters. In what follows I will try to show what sexual orientation research can and cannot illuminate about the nature of homoeroticism.

The Meaning of Nature   As there is abundant evidence of human homoerotic behavior, no one disputes that homoeroticism is "in nature" in the sense that it occurs within the realm of observable events. In this sense homoeroticism is as "natural" as laughing, crying, or giving birth. Sexual orientation research can have plenty to say about the observable properties of homoeroticism, and this is not an insignificant task. For example, it has sometimes been wrongly argued that homoeroticism does not occur in nature except among human beings.[9] In fact, the study of nature reveals that homoeroticism exists among many descendants of Noah's ark. Bonobo chimps, for example, routinely and without social fuss have same-sex erotic interactions, males and females alike.[10] The homoeroticism of primates has been of special interest given the biological proximity between human beings and other members of their order, but there is homoerotic behavior in lower orders of animals as well, apparently even in such insects as fruit flies.[11] This is not to say that homoerotic behavior in fruit flies or chimps is wholly analogous to homoerotic behavior in human beings, but it is to say that there is a continuum of homoerotic behavior across the animal kingdom.

Both Simon LeVay and Dean Hamer believe that the study of animal sexual behavior will contribute to the liberalization of social attitudes toward homoeroticism.[12] If it does, it should not be because descriptions of the behavior of animals have normative force in regard to the behavior of human beings. It does not follow, that is, that the behavior of animals, even animals genetically close to human beings, describes a domain of moral permissibility for human beings. Because of the unique cognitive status of human beings, the place of choice in their lives, and their distinct goals, human beings are not simply moral extensions of other animals. For a similar reason it does not follow either that humans have moral dispensation to behave in one way rather than another simply because most other human beings do so or would do so. The classical philosophical principle at stake here is that no assemblage of facts about behavior—human or otherwise—necessarily implies a morally acceptable course of action. This is so because normative claims about the actions of human beings cannot be derived from factual descriptions of animal—even human animal— behavior. In the standard shorthand formulation, "ought" cannot be derived from "is." Even if *every* other animal in nature exhibited some form of homoeroticism, it would not follow that human beings were for that reason entitled to do so as well. Even if every human being exhibited some degree of homoeroticism, it would not follow that it was by that fact alone justified.

I should note that some people *might* be convinced that homoeroticism in human beings is morally acceptable if they learn that the practice is not confined to a small set of human beings but is familiar across the animal kingdom. This is, however, a merely psychological argument inasmuch as the position begs the question of why homoeroticism in human beings is permissible because analogues are to be found in nonhuman species. Animals exhibit all manner of traits that should be counted morally unaccepted in human beings. What would it be about homoeroticism that is somehow privileged by reason of its prevalence in animals to serve as a moral exemplar for human beings? Unless this question is answered, there is no convincing reason to think that human beings should take their moral cues from the behavior of other animals. Moreover, even if most human beings behaved homosexually at one point or another, that behavior would still be subject to the same kind of analysis, namely, justifying it apart from the psychological dispositions that dispose people toward common but nevertheless possibly objectionable behaviors. If homoeroticism is going to be morally defended on the grounds of "being natural," nature must mean something other than merely occurring in the animal kingdom or, more specifically, the human enclave in that kingdom.

Some commentators see the events of nature as having—at least to a point—normative implications about what is morally permissible and valuable and, therefore, protectable from moral sanction. This is the implication in defenses of homoeroticism when the "natural" is used to suggest that sexual orientation has its origins in predictable biological and/or psychological development, whether those origins are particular to specific individuals or characteristic of species development as a whole. This usage of nature suggests that insofar as erotic desires are *developmentally natural* they should be shielded from unfavorable moral judgment. Some commentators go further to suggest that this argument implies an inherent goodness or inviolability to homoerotic desires.[13] Historian D. Michael Quinn has adopted a position along these lines when he says of the relation between nature and morality:

> I accept current research that indicates that (like left-handedness) genetic or pre-birth factors determine whether some persons have primary sexual attractions for their same gender. . . . From the above I conclude that heterosexuality is no more moral than right-handedness and that homosexuality is no less moral than left-handedness. Homosexuality is simply left-handed sexuality, and bisexuality is simply ambidextrous sexuality.[14]

Quinn's inference that the apparent explicability of homoerotic interests by the life sciences, its natural development, establishes a prima facie case of moral respect for homoerotic behavior is not without historical precedent at the very dawn of sexual orientation research.

Late in the last century the pioneer German gay advocate, Karl Heinrich Ulrichs, constantly adverted to scientific studies of sex in order to make the claim that homoeroticism was natural in the sense described here. Not a scientist acting under the banner of disinterested inquiry, Ulrichs offered his views on the origins of homoeroticism in an expressly political context. He wanted to convince the public at large and legislators and jurists in particular that statutes criminalizing "unnatural acts between persons of the male sex" were biologically uninformed and morally unjust.[15] In the main he argued that Urnings, so-called as mythically descended from Uranus, could not act otherwise but on their homoerotic interests and that these interests were rooted in their natures. In so arguing, he explicitly rejected views of what I call the moral dissolution theory, the view that people venture toward homoeroticism for reasons of moral laxity including, for example, the effects of sexual gluttony in straight sex.[16]

The moral dissolution theory has at its core an assumption that human beings choose their erotic interests and are ultimately responsible for them. By contrast, Ulrichs argued that nature forced the issue. Most important, he naturalized men and women with homoerotic interests as categories unto themselves. Speaking of men, he said the Urning was not a true man but a mixture of man and woman, having the appearance of a man and the sex drive of a woman. Thus "is his sexual nature organized. He experiences a constant aversion to sexual contact with a woman, which bears all the marks of a natural horror. He feels sexual love only for male persons. He *cannot* do otherwise. He did not give this sexual drive to himself. Also, he cannot take it from himself."[17] To explain this state of affairs, Ulrichs offered an intricate account of how the female germ for the love of males was present in all embryos but failed to be extinguished in some male bodies for developmental reasons.[18] He ultimately encapsulated his theory this way: a man with homoerotic desires has a female mind enclosed within a male body, and a parallel situation obtains in females with homoerotic interests. Ulrichs did not see these biological types as developmental failures but as developmental variations given by nature itself. Ulrichs thus thought homoerotic interests should be respected as morally defensible not merely by virtue of occurring in nature but occurring in nature for an identifiable developmental reason. As Ulrichs was fond of noting, one of the corollaries of his biometaphysical view of human beings was that it is antihomoerotic behavior that is a crime against nature, not homoerotic behavior itself.[19]

To be sure, Ulrichs did not rest the case for the moral and social advancement of homoeroticism entirely on erotic developmental theory. He also argued from a consequentialist point of view that homoeroticism was not any inherent degradation or social offense. He noted, for example, that homoeroticism was not only eminently compatible with love but that Urnings were to be counted among the era's most noted and estimable citizens. He never strayed from the view that "the Uranian bond of love is legitimate according to the law of nature as well as to the inalienable rights of humankind, and legislators have no right to interfere with the sword of punishment."[20] He therefore defended the right of Urnings to fulfill their sexual interests in same-sex marriage.[21]

On the one hand, Ulrichs's reading homoeroticism into nature does have certain advantages as a moral defense of homoeroticism. Using the prevailing assumption in moral philosophy that only voluntary behavior is morally judgeable behavior, some critics argue that homoeroticism is chosen in the same way objectionable behaviors such as murder and adultery are chosen. There is enough freedom of choice in homoerotic interests and behaviors, so goes the argument, to create the conceptual space necessary for the possibility of moral judgment, specifically moral condemnation. These critics are then free to assess the morality of homosexuality as a matter conceptually independent of biological or psychological causation. It is against exactly this kind of argument that efforts to read homosexuality into nature—via the biological or psychological sciences—have their greatest effect, but *only* to the extent that they show that homoerotic interests develop involuntarily. If, in fact, erotic interests develop for reasons that have more in common with the uncontrollable processes of cell division than with choices about how to spend an evening, scientific evidence *can* work to read gay people into nature. It is for this reason that many people look to sexual orientation science to offer entirely naturalistic accounts of erotic desire, and to, thereby, establish homoeroticism and heteroeroticism as moral equivalents: both are equally products of nature.

This line of defense only goes so far, however, in shielding homoeroticism from moral judgment. As any number of critics of homoeroticism have pointed out, an involuntary inclination to have homoerotic interests is quite different from acting on them.[22] As these critics judge homoeroticism to be objectionable for consequential and other reasons, for example that it has damaging social consequences or that it is inferior emotional pathway to the deepest possible interpersonal relationships, they cannot accept the involuntary origins of homoerotic *interests* as a defense of voluntary homoerotic *behavior*. It would be logically possible to cede to Ulrichs and his intellectual heirs that homoeroticism occurs only because of involuntary reasons in development and yet still object to it on moral grounds. No one thinks genetic diseases and developmental disorders are worth protecting and celebrating merely because they are characteristic of and even predictable in individual or species development.[23]

There is no moral conclusion possible that the occurrence of a behavior or interest in nature is coextensive with its moral approbation, else there would be no independent means of discriminating between desirable and undesirable behaviors and interests. Sexual orientation science focused on the determinants of erotic interests cannot in principle and by itself establish the morality of homoeroticism. Neither can it describe the social accommodation that ought to obtain for people with homoerotic interests. Homoeroticism may be "in nature" for developmental reasons, but it remains a separate question whether and to what extent it is a morally valuable erotic form. Even if science were in possession of a full and complete account of why people have the erotic desires they have, still moral philosophy would be able to draw distinctions between valuable, less valuable, and condemnable forms of eroticism. The Catholic Church took full advantage of this conceptual space when it acknowledged that some aspects of sexual orientation appear to be involuntary but at the same time also declared that homosexuality is intrinsically disordered in a moral sense.[24]

In stressing the distinction between the developmental origins of erotic desires and their moral value, I should hasten to say that I do not find the objections to homoeroticism mentioned above convincing. It seems to me that homoerotic interests and behaviors as a matter of course ordinarily and fairly easily pass moral muster.[25] At the very least, there is no obvious reason why a defense of homoerotic behaviors should be held to higher standards than those governing heteroeroticism.[26] I agree with philosopher Alan H. Goldman that the same rules or precepts that inform our moral judgment in other domains of human life should also govern sex. Although I will not argue the point except in a very cursory way here, it seems to me that homoeroticism needs no special arguments applied to it that do not apply to heteroeroticism. To the extent that homoerotic interests are individually and mutually fulfilling and enlarge capacities for hope, happiness, and love, and do not involve social damages unparalleled in the pursuit of heteroeroticism, they meet a prima facie test of moral defensibility, and this would be true regardless of any specific biological or psychological mechanisms involved in their development. While I object, therefore, to any easy sliding between natural occurrence and moral approval in regard to homoeroticism, it seems to me that what moral justifications are needed by homoeroticism are both already available in abundance and credible in a philosophically rigorous way.

Before leaving the topic of natural development, I want to raise one issue that has currency in some explanations for the origins and worth of homoeroticism. Many gay people see their erotic nature as given by nature and offer as evidence their sense that they have never known a time without their homoerotic interests, that there was never a time when they were faced with anything like a choice about what kind of desires they would have. They feel that their homoerotic interests are coeval with their sexual awakening. Some say, further, that they always knew that they were somehow different from others as children, even before the awakening of their erotic interests properly speaking.[27] They therefore read biological sexual orientation research as confirming their view that sexual orientation is given biologically. It does not follow, however, simply because people have long memories of "being gay" that there are necessarily and only biological reasons for this state of affairs. Many learned human traits are so entrenched that they appear to be as fixed as traits of anatomy. For example, we hardly remember a time without language, and even less do we recall learning the basic sounds, grammatical structures, vocabulary, and cadences of our native languages. For all that, our abilities in speaking any given language are patently not biological in the sense that they are foreordained by genetic endowment or neuroanatomical structure, though these features will play a role in anyone's ultimate linguistic capacities. I continue to plead agnostic about the reasons people have the entrenched sexual orientations they have, but it is mistaken to conclude that long-standing traits are biologically dictated when in point of fact developmental history cannot but influence linguistics and erotics alike. The perception of a trait as "natural" in the sense of being continuously experienced does not indicate any exclusively biological causality of the trait.

Human Nature   Although the notions of nature discussed above are informative but ultimately silent about the normative worth and value of erotic matters, there *are* inherently normative conceptions of nature that do ground judgments about erotic interest. These conceptions of nature are metaphysical in kind and purport to identify goals inherent in the beings of the world, sometimes in the world itself and its history. The conceptions of humanity that underlie the ethical traditions of natural law, for example, describe the nature of human life not in terms of individual traits and interests but in terms of generalized goals said to pertain to human beings as such. These goals include, for example, maintaining bodily and mental integrity, discovery of the truth, the bearing and rearing of children, and participation in society. Natural law maintains that although these inclinations may be absent or distorted in specific persons they nevertheless typify in a metaphysically strong sense the kind of goals human beings have in virtue of the kind of beings they are. Religious beliefs may shape and inform views about the nature of human beings in these traditions, as they often do relative to views on the origins and destiny of human beings, but philosophical conceptions of human nature can in principle be constructed independent of any particular religious beliefs. In practice, however, religious beliefs are commonly alloyed with philosophical views about the nature of human beings, and they mutually inform one another.

In natural law traditions there has been considerable objection to homoeroticism on the grounds that its sexual acts are inherently sterile, that they distort the human inclination toward the begetting of children, and that they treat sexuality as an instrument of selfish pleasure unconnected to its potential for transcendent personal goals. It is also sometimes alleged that homoeroticism is a threat to the social underpinnings of human community. For all these reasons homoerotic behavior is to be discouraged, even if the emergence of homoerotic interests per se is beyond the reach of social correction. If one thought homoeroticism to be pathological, to say further, the restoration of heteroeroticism would be a morally desirable goal under natural law relative to the principle of maintaining bodily and psychic integrity. To be sure, that treatment should not itself involve unethical medical interventions that jeopardized psychic or bodily well-being. As many contemporary natural law theorists do not discuss homoeroticism in terms of pathology, I will myself forgo any discussion of pathology here and will treat homoeroticism only in relation to metaphysical claims about human nature.

One contemporary formulation of homoeroticism as contrary to human nature is that of philosopher John Finnis, who claims that homoeroticism is inherently incapable of achieving the sorts of moral goods available in genital intercourse between a married man and woman.[28] Among other things, Finnis objects to homoerotic sex because it is sterile, disposes its participants to an abdication of responsibility for the future of human kind, fails to actualize interpersonal devotion, is a selfish sexual pleasure, and dis-integrates personal reality. Although he argues that homoeroticism is bad in itself and its consequences, Finnis does accept the view that criminalization of truly private sexual acts between consenting adults is beyond the state's function. Yet he does say that the state has responsibilities to discourage the expression or manifestation of homoeroticism. Toward that end the state should not tolerate the marketing or advertising of homosexual services, the maintenance of places of resort for homosexual activity, the promotion of homosexual lifestyles by education and public media, same-sex marriages, or the adoption of children by gay parents. Society might also attach special penalties to homosexual prostitution not paralleled in heterosexual prostitution and recognize different ages of consent for same-sex and different-sex relations. These varied practices have as their common goal the suppression of the visibility of homoeroticism, thereby frustrating easy access to that allegedly immoral sexuality.

The success of this argument depends on two key propositions: (a) that the most morally fulfilling human sexuality is that of intercourse in marriage and (b) that the state has responsibilities to help promote a social environment conducive to virtue and to discourage morally bad conduct. The first proposition amounts to a metaphysical characterization of human genital sexuality. Finnis says, "Genital intercourse between two spouses enables them to actualize and experience (and in that sense express) their marriage itself, as a single reality with two blessings (children and mutual affection). Non-marital intercourse, especially but not only homosexuality, has no such point and therefore is unacceptable."[29] Finnis goes on to say homoeroticism falls short of those capacities insofar as it does not permit the actualizing and experience of self-giving of partners "in biological, affective and volitional union in mutual commitment, both open-ended and exclusive."[30]

The first thing to be noticed about this characterization is that it is offered independent of any causal analysis of erotic desires. The values and disvalues of homoeroticism are measured in metaphysical terms, i.e., in terms of their compatibility with the putative goals of marital sexuality per se, which are represented as the putative goals of human sexuality per se. There are no references to any scientific literature in Finnis's account, and there is nothing in this account that is logically dependent on homoeroticism having one cause or another: wherever it comes from, Finnis argues, it is bad sexuality. To be sure, against a metaphysical argument like the one here sexual orientation research is unlikely to have much impact because the primary sexual goods of human beings are defined independent of why anyone has the sexual interests he or she has. Yet empirical facts may be relevant in another way, as I will show after making a number of points about the adequacy of Finnis's characterization of moral human sexuality.

According to Finnis, the benefits of homoeroticism cannot approach heterosexual marital sexuality in the biological-personalizing effects of its sex acts: "For want of a *common good* that could be actualized and experienced *by and in this bodily union*, that conduct [homoeroticism] involves the partners in treating their bodies as instruments to be used in the service of their consciously experiencing selves; their choice to engage in such conduct thus dis-integrates each of them precisely as acting persons."[31] According to this view, homoeroticism is incapable of biological (i.e., reproductive) union and therefore incapable of the unifying effects of marital sex. The assertion of an intrinsic good, that of heterogenital sex acts in marriage, is always hard to evaluate, for intrinsic goods are by definition beyond assessment by the usual empirical means. One argumentative assessment that is in order is that this definition of human sexual achievement does not seem as radically distant from homoeroticism as Finnis suggests it is. He notes, for example, that some married couples will be sterile. This sterility is no objection to their sexual acts insofar as their behavior is suitable for generation, "so far as they can make of it." This qualification seems to open the door to gay sex if the licitness of the sex is conditioned not on the openness to fertility of the sexual act per se but only on the couples not willfully obstructing that openness to fertility.

It goes almost without saying that no intentional obstruction to reproductive capacity occurs in homoerotic sex. Like sterile couples, gay couples participate in sex that is open to reproduction "so far as they can make of it." Of course, Finnis might say that the sterility of homoeroticism is unlike the sterility of straight couples insofar as homoeroticism represents an *intentional* turning away from a moral good. Here the facts of sexual orientation research might prove him wrong. If it turns out that people have homoerotic interests for involuntary reasons, those interests would be blameless because beyond the domain of personal choice. Finnis might want to argue that acting on these interests does necessarily involve choice and therefore does permit judgments of moral blame insofar as that *behavior* is concerned. Nevertheless, it would still remain true that insofar as they willingly choose to act on their homoerotic interests gay people do not for that reason also intend their sexual acts to be sterile.

Finnis, moreover, quotes Plutarch to the effect that intercourse with a sterile spouse is a desirable mark of marital esteem and affection. To extend the issue to gay sex, it is unclear why a woman's continued desire to have sex with her beloved female partner would be no less a mark of that same kind of esteem and affection. Insofar as the instrumental goal of having children can *never* be achieved through having same-sex relations, same-sex partners can never be used as a selfish way to have children. In this regard it would seem that homoeroticism is morally free of one kind of human selfishness, one that is, moreover, possible *only* in heteroerotic sex. Given that gay sex is not in principle open to this kind of selfishness, and given that it is socially ostracized, is it not therefore all the more capable of being a vehicle of esteem and affection, all the more an invitation to personalizing union?

A third line of response to be made here is that surely not all heterogenital marital sex achieves the lofty goals Finnis sets out. Many of the objections Finnis attaches to homoeroticism are to be found in heterosexual relations, married and otherwise, both in kind and degree. To use one example to make both points: both gay and straight people are equally capable of using one's sexual partners as an instrument of selfish pleasures and gains. This observation about the failings of straight marital sex does not touch, of course, the ideal of marriage as Finnis has stated it, only the practice of marriage, but it does raise a question of civic consistency: if straight people have the political right to enter into marriages that do not embody high marital ideals, why should gay people not also have that same entitlement? Even if Finnis's definition of the nature of marital sexuality were true, it is unclear why a homoerotic falling off from this ideal is so immoral that it deserves the social burdens he would impose to discourage it when there is probably just as much falling off from this ideal in the totality of all straight marriages.

Finnis says that the state has a responsibility to promote virtue by minimizing the manifestation of homoeroticism, but this conclusion does not follow as neatly or broadly as he thinks. Properly speaking, Finnis's goal is or should be the maximization of good heterosexual marriages. In fact, it would seem more important that a state take steps to ensure marriages in which there can be the blessed biological commingling of souls he advocates rather than to prevent gay sex outright. It appears, then, that Finnis would have done better to raise obstacles to heterosexual marriages—making them harder to enter into—so that people entering into them would not use them as gay people allegedly use their relationships, as instruments of selfish pleasure no more or less morally distinguished than masturbation. Perhaps straight people should pass some kind of marriage test to show that they are likely to succeed in achieving the kinds of benefits Finnis thinks marriage holds out to them, benefits that are achievable only if marital sexuality is responsibly engaged. Or Finnis might try to identify those features, tractable to social intervention of one kind or another, that might improve the chances that people entering into marriage can achieve the values he thinks reside there. In the totality of things, the suppression of homoeroticism might not go very far in promoting the virtues of heterosexual marriage.

To extend this last point further, it does not follow necessarily that the suppression of the visibility of homoerotic sex will help achieve a more virtuous society. For example, suppose that the suppression of homoeroticism had the effect of channeling more and more gay people into marriage—because they had fewer and fewer social and sexual options available to them. To the extent that their erotic inclinations worked against the very goals of marriage, it cannot be in the interest of a virtuous society to foster the conditions under which people entered into sham marriages as adverse preferences, something they succumbed to as a matter of social pressure. In other words, the proposals that Finnis offers to discourage homoeroticism could also well cut against his marital ideals. There is some sense in thinking that reducing the public visibility of homoeroticism will lead to less gay sex, especially if gay people find it harder to locate one another. But it does not follow as a matter of course that this state of affairs would by itself necessarily help promote social virtue in its marital ideals. It remains to be shown whether Finnis's policy recommendations would work to enable more marriages to become better vehicles of the virtues he says reside there and in no other sexual-social relations.

Even if there were such an effect, it would not by itself be morally decisive unless weighed against the costs of Finnis's policy recommendations. Civic restriction of liberty interests can sometimes lead to greater social vice than accommodating an allegedly offensive practice. It seems to me that in their totality the burdens Finnis would impose on gay people would be so inimical to their well-being and so contrary to public interests in free speech and free association that any society governed by them is fundamentally compromised in its social responsibilities to protect the welfare of all its people. It is utterly astonishing that nowhere in this account does Finnis even attempt to measure the effect on gay people of the the restrictions he would impose on them. Surely the effects of restrictive policies on gay people are relevant to a consideration of the benefit those restrictions have to a society overall. It is utterly indefensible to assume that the impositions Finnis proposes are benign in regard to the human goods important to all people, gay people included. Here empirical research would be all to the point as it showed any and all harms that came to a people whose erotic interests are systematically suppressed as a matter of cultural policy. I do not assume, for example, that all the restrictions on the visibility and acceptability of openly gay people are less worse in their effects on gay people than the criminalization of consensual, private homoerotic relations, something Finnis says is beyond society's supervisory function. A society in which there are no social accommodations of any gay people is not ostensibly superior to one in which gay sexual relations are criminalized with the effect that some people are occasionally arrested and criminally punished. The moral interest gay people have in leading psychologically healthy lives should work against any universal suppression of the public visibility of gay sexuality. Finnis's argument is deeply flawed in this regard because it gratuitously assumes that the suppression of gay culture imposes no relevant moral harms.

Respect for disagreement in profoundly important matters such as sexuality also counts as a virtue that a society ought to promote and protect. This is not to say that the ideological camp opposed to homoeroticism cannot offer its educational suasions about the virtues of heterogenital marital sex, but it is to say that it is unclear why this position should dominate public policy to the extent Finnis envisions when an opposition party, with a sexual metaphysics of its own, has a competing political vision of human sexuality. At the very least, it does not follow automatically that of all the responsibilities a society might bear in regard to promoting virtue it should penalize homoeroticism when adults of goodwill and uncompromised intellect disagree about its value.

Finnis says his position is not a moral argument based on natural facts in the sense that it infers normative conclusions from natural-fact premises, and he is right about this because he does not argue from any facts of nature that heteroeroticism has the values it does or homoeroticism has the disvalues he says it does. He does not believe, that is, that we can read values off facts about physical objects or that natural objects have functions that determine what is good for their kind. On the other hand, he does say that his position is based on natural facts insofar as it applies "relevant practical reasons (especially that marriage and inner integrity are basic human goods) and moral principles (especially that one may never intend to destroy, damage, impede, or violate any basic human good, or prefer an illusory human good to a real instantiation of that or some other good) to facts about the human personal organism."[32] If there are facts here, they are not of the kind unearthed by scientific research. They are the putative facts of practical reasoning in the sense that such reasoning is thought to discover basic values. It is hard to see, however, that the "facts" at stake here are anything less than normative *ideals* raised not only to describe sexual relations but also to evaluate them. It is exactly the distance of these ideals from scientific facts that permits Finnis the opportunity to forgo paying attention to scientific research about the determinants of erotic interests or the effects of various social policies on gay people. Paying attention to the facts of homoeroticism would require empirical determinations of whether or not the proposals he makes would lead to a more virtuous society, whether most marriages reach the ideal he sets out for them, and whether some gay couples do not achieve more communion in their relationships than in those many, many empty marriages that Friedrich Nietzsche once called loneliness in pairs. Only social research could show what social practices in regard to gay people would actually bring about a more virtuous society as Finnis spells it out or whether his proposals would do gay people—and everyone else in that society—more harm than good. Finnis's proposals about what does and does not lead a society to virtue should be treated, then, as a set of hypotheses that may or may not bear up under empirical scrutiny. Even if Finnis's antigay policy recommendations were effective in some measure in promoting heterogenital marital sex, they seem ultimately less important than other social policies—and social virtues—that should prevail in their stead.

Pragmatic Effects   Some people do seem to be more favorably inclined toward homoeroticism if they believe it to be "biological," that is, if it seems to stand on its own as an inevitability of nature.[33] This effect may obtain for a number of reasons. Against the background of a century of psychological dispute about the origins of homoeroticism, biological accounts of homoeroticism seem attractive and compelling because they seem to bypass contested concepts and competing schools of psychology and seem therefore less prone to error, which is, of course, not true. In any case, the credibility of the biological sciences cannot by itself entirely account for the view that discovering, say, a genetic contribution to sexual orientation necessarily helps the cause of gay people, for there are many instances in which science is thought to confuse matters, as in matters of diet and health, for example, where contradictory and ever more complex studies offer no unitary message about the advantages and disadvantages of particular foods. In instances in which biogenetic explanations of sexual orientation are favored, then, there must be a supporting belief that there is something about these explanations that frees them from the limitations attributed to the workings of science elsewhere.

Part of this supporting belief may be found in the critical vacuum in which biological studies can appear. Because of the kind of findings it offers, biological studies may have no direct competing authority in politics or religion to offer contradictory judgments. That is, social opinion might hold that neither religion nor politics are in a position to offer credible competing hypotheses about the origins of sexual orientation. The acceptability of scientific explanations of homoeroticism may therefore chart the relative standing of science, religion, and politics as social authorities about a particular topic. This is all to say that the acceptance of biogenetic explanations of homoeroticism, then, may be rooted deeply in the methods by which a culture comes to believe what it believes.

At the present time it does seem that the public believes that genes are in an important way constitutive of an organism, of a person.[34] Implicit in the view that genes are constitutive of people is the assumption that genes are essential traits rather than sites of biological processes with variable outcomes, that they are activators rather than acted on, and that in some ways they are miniature people waiting to emerge in full somatic form and behavior. Genes are read as the molecular equivalent of manifest human traits—as little human beings pre-formed in the ribbons of DNA and merely awaiting fleshy instantiation in order to unfold according to a predetermined logic. In such a context biogenetic reports about sexual orientation may have a triggering effect and serve as a pre-text for asserting beliefs to which society is already predisposed. If, therefore, science is perceived as offering a genetic explanation of homoeroticism, that explanation may be taken to mean that a person is fundamentally and inalterably a lesbian or gay man by reason of genetic endowment. This view of genes as behaviors-waiting-to-happen is hardly true to the dynamics of gene activity, for it is a long explanatory way between the DNA sequences and the erotic behavior of mature human beings.[35] If, however, genes are treated as the biological equivalent of categories in nature, as elements of the language of nature itself, it will not be surprising that some people find the notion of a genetic basis for sexual orientation equivalent to a fixed decree that genes are sexual destiny.

For a combination of these reasons there may be a pragmatic benefit to gay people and their allies in advancing scientific accounts of erotic desire if it inclines people to see homoeroticism as merely another manifestation of the plurality and diversity in the great chain of being. To the extent to which this effect obtains, the biological study of homoeroticism could help rather than frustrate social and political accommodation of gay people. In a moral sense this political effect will always run afoul of the caution described above: that naturalistic explanations are not themselves moral explanations. From a moral point of view, too, this political effect might be superfluous insofar as advocacy of the morality of homoeroticism can go forward entirely independent of biological accounts of sexual orientation. Even if we knew nothing about biological determinants of sexual orientation, homoeroticism could still be defended by showing the compatibility of homoeroticism with happiness and well-being, by appealing to the rights of competent adults to make decisions about their sexual behavior, by invoking the moral limits to state oversight of behavior, and by showing the absence of objectionable consequences or at least objectionable consequences not different in kind or degree than are to be found elsewhere in the human sexual and social order. The best arguments in moral philosophy do not always translate into effective political strategies, however, and some gay advocacy is likely to find more practical benefit in appealing to biological aspects of homoeroticism than to the inadequacy of moral condemnations of homoeroticism, even if these appeals are grounded in strategies of social psychology rather than moral defenses properly speaking.

SEXUAL ORIENTATION RESEARCH AND THE LAW

Disagreeing with those who see the scientific study of homoeroticism as leading to improved social standing for gay people, Ruth Hubbard has observed that "grounding difference in biology does not stem bigotry" and offers left-handedness as an example.[36] Though left-handedness is ostensibly natural in the sense of being an event in nature and/or the consequence of biological development, it was nevertheless stigmatized, and decades of effort went into pedagogical efforts to "correct" this hand preference.[37] Hubbard is therefore skeptical that finding a biological basis for homoeroticism will necessarily improve its social standing. The underlying message of much of Hubbard's work is a caution against assigning too much power to biological inheritance: genetic explanations can be as confining as they are liberating, especially if they reflect or are used to reinforce objectionable social opinion and structures.[38]

While these cautions are well-placed in the sense that genetic explanations of behavior and traits have often been put to social purposes far beyond the powers of their data, some commentators have held that there is one legal way in which gay people might be served by a scientific demonstration that sexual orientation "is biological," and this involves the deference shown under the law to people in suspect classes. Because of constitutional guarantees of equal protection, courts take pains to ensure that socially marginalized groups receive heightened scrutiny in regard to their claims of injustice.[39] Toward this end the law can designate certain classifications of people as *suspect*, that declaration affording people in those classes the right to greater protection from state policies and law that may adversely affect them. Even though it is not the people in them but the classifications that are suspect, these matters are ordinarily referred to as matters of suspect class.

In order for courts to recognize a suspect class, the group in question must (a) have faced discrimination historically, (b) the discrimination must be intentional and irrational in the sense that it is unrelated to the ability of group members to participate meaningfully in social life, (c) members of the group must lack mechanisms of legislative redress, and (d) the group must be defined by some characteristic that is used as the rationale for ill or substandard treatment and that characteristic must be immutable. Because of the concern about ensuring equal protection in the face of systemic social adversity, laws that would abridge the rights of people in suspect classes must have a *compelling* state interest in order to pass constitutional muster. *Non-suspect* status applies to all persons outside suspect classes and courts must find only that the state has a *reasonable* interest to justify lack of equal opportunity (namely, differential treatment) of all persons (in, for example, denying driver's licenses to twelve-year-olds). By historical reason of their vulnerability and social marginalization, the law currently recognizes groups determined by race and national origin in the category of suspect classes because of the vulnerability and social marginalization that attach to those immutable characteristics.

Richard Green and Simon LeVay have argued that the extension of the category of suspect class to gay people would be a signal legal achievement.[40] In their view of things, status as a suspect class would position gay people to demand the highest level of scrutiny of laws that currently sustain the unequal treatment of gay people, including antisodomy laws, the exclusion of gay people from the military, and barriers to civil marriage. At present states can and do argue that they have a reasonable interest in maintaining these social practices—as necessary to the promotion, for example, of public morals—but it is unclear that these arguments would be equally convincing when assessed for burdens they differentially impose on gay people and no one else, when examined, that is, as matters of *compelling* state interest.

Are gay people candidates for the status of suspect class? As to the first requirement of that designation, there can be little disagreement that gay people have faced long-standing social discrimination both individually and as a group. Second, this discrimination has been intentional and not, for example, the accidental side effect of some other social policies, for prohibitions of antidiscrimination laws and, more recently, bars against same-sex marriage have been adopted expressly in regard to homoeroticism.[41] This ill-treatment is irrational, moreover, since homoeroticism is no barrier to the exercise of important human virtues and is compatible with both individual achievement and social contribution.[42] There is nothing about gay people that is so morally or otherwise bankrupt that society needs to be protected from, for example, their having private consensual sexual relations or applying as openly gay for employment. As to the question of ability to seek redress of ill treatment, Richard Green has pointed out that gay people remain vulnerable because their causes are politically unattractive to legislators.[43] Indeed, it is difficult to disagree that gay people have fewer options when it comes to legislative redress. It is the last point, however, the immutability of the trait by which a suspect class is defined, that has been the major topic at issue for sexual orientation research.

The relevance of immutability to social justice is based in the moral and legal belief that people should be held responsible for their actions and status only to the extent they have choice over them. As people hold no power over their race or national origin, society should not impose burdens attaching to those traits.[44] If homoeroticism were similarly immutable, then the state should—as a matter of ensuring equal protection to marginalized groups—strike down state-imposed or state-tolerated mechanisms of discrimination triggered by sexual orientation. I will not describe here the history of immutability as the concept has in fact been played out in court,[45] but I will consider what sexual orientation science has to offer by way of support for this view. Has or can sexual orientation science show that homoeroticism is an immutable trait?

The immutability of homoeroticism has always been a core question in sexual orientation research. Sexologists such as Richard von Krafft-Ebing, Sigmund Freud, and Havelock Ellis agreed that homosexuality could be either innate or acquired, with innate homosexuality being functionally inevitable and acquired homosexuality being avoidable or preventable in principle but occasioned by circumstances of chance and choice. In general, most therapists drawing a distinction between innate and acquired believed that innate homoeroticism was not tractable to modification but that acquired homoeroticism could be extinguished or modified.[46] These two senses of the immutability of homoeroticism, in its origin and in its susceptibility to therapy, have both proved considerations in the question of suspect class for gay people.

As to whether erotic orientations are immutable in their origins in the sense of being inevitable, the first thing to note is that the state of knowledge about the causal origins of erotic interests is far from complete, so that definitive judgments about the necessary and sufficient causes of erotic interests are at present impossible. Contemporary research has yet to reach a consensus on exactly how sexual interests are disposed by biological endowment, influenced by one's development, and controlled by choice. For example, William Byne and Bruce Parsons have described the determinants of sexual orientation as belonging to the interaction between biological and environmental and/or cultural processes.[47] Only a few years before John Money had said, "People become homosexual, bisexual, or heterosexual because of what happens to them partly in their prenatal history and partly in their postnatal history."[48] Even if researchers guardedly hold the belief that sexual orientation is genetically fated, they are nevertheless cautious in interpreting their data and describe their findings as *suggestive of* or *compatible with* a biological or genetic basis for sexual orientation. Richard Green, for example, says that biological research does not show that sexual orientation is genetically or hormonally determined; he concludes only that "the sexual science data, however, do point to some contribution from both these sources."[49]

Contemporary science seems to indicate that gay people may be probabilistically differentiated from straight people in regard to such traits as INAH3 size, patterns of sibling sexual orientation, fingerprint ridge density, or even birth order, but that same research does not indicate to what extent erotic interests are *necessarily* fated from particular biological events, psychological history, or genetic endowment, and no strict conclusions along these lines should be drawn from this research. It is unlikely in the extreme that the panoply of erotic interests of adult human beings are utterly immutable in the sense that they could not have emerged in their particulars other than they did. This is not to say that some people are not shifted toward one sexual orientation or another, but it is to say that a lot can happen to a human being between sexual conception and sexual interests.

Research about the origins of homoeroticism is not, moreover, uniform for men and women alike. Women have always been less studied than men in regard to their sexual orientation, and present research offers no major departure from that norm. There are fewer reports in the literature overall about the causality of sexual orientation in women. From this paucity of study very little can be concluded, but the possibilities are intriguing. In light of their investigations, for example, Dean Hamer and his colleagues have suggested that there may be different pathways to homoeroticism in women than in men.[50] It may be that homoeroticism in men and homoeroticism in women are two causally distinct phenomena. Moreover, some commentators have argued that homoerotic interests and identities in women are more fluid than they are in men, that homoerotic identities may ultimately be chosen for political reasons, though it is worth treating these claims skeptically in the sense that there may be some nonobvious disposition working to affect that kind of "choice."[51] If true, however, these voluntaristic accounts would work against any conclusion that sexual orientation is immutable in its origins. Faced with data different for men and women, courts might find themselves in a political predicament if they had to conclude that the scientific evidence suggested that men were gay for involuntary reasons but that lesbians are not entitled to heightened forms of judicial protection because there is less evidence that their erotic interests are involuntary.[52]

If present research is any indication, moreover, evidence regarding sexual orientation for both men and women alike will be probabilistic in nature.

Courts could then be faced with making decisions about the immutability of sexual orientation using data showing, to pick some numbers out of the air just for example, that 60 percent of gay men have an identified trait causally implicated in their erotic interests but that 37 percent do not, and 3 percent could not be assessed because of missing or ambiguous data. The data might also suggest entirely different numbers for the origins of sexual orientation in women, with the numbers perhaps going the other way: 37 percent of women show a causally implicated trait while 60 percent do not, and 3 percent of the subjects cannot be determined for one reason or another. It is also worth keeping in mind that even if the probabilities achieved in a particular study of sexual orientation science are impressive, the whole field will necessarily remain fallible. Certainly the historical record gives ample reason to be wary. Immured as we are in the present, convinced as we are of the progress of science, it is hard to avoid believing that contemporary science reports—like those of LeVay, Hamer, and Bailey—are the last word on the origins of erotic interests. One hundred years hence these studies may look as dated as the last century's accounts that attributed homoeroticism to, for example, degenerative effects of warm climates, neurological miswirings in the anus, or the overeducation of women.[53] In any case, from a judicial point of view, because scientific accounts are tentative and fallible, it may be hard if not impossible to know whether and when to accept scientific accounts as having confirmed that there is enough *fate* in sexual orientation to call it immutable in regard to its origins.

Some courts have wrangled with the questions of whether therapy can modify a homoerotic sexual orientation and whether that modification bears on the question of the immutability of sexual orientation. To get an answer to the first question, the courts have entertained dueling expert witnesses, witnesses who either defend or criticize the most prominent research about sexual orientation therapy.[54] As I have argued in chapter 3, even the most sympathetic reading of the scientific literature (as against religious testimonial literature on the same subject) reveals that only a handful of people were ever reported to have had their erotic orientation modified by therapy, and even then it is hard to know how exactly to credit these reports. This domain of study is characteristically impoverished with respect to standard control mechanisms and follow-up assessments.[55] So limited in value are these studies that Richard Green has characterized the data as showing overwhelming evidence *against* the possibility of sexual reorientation.[56] The vast majority of people find their sexual orientation entrenched and functionally immutable, whether those interests are gay or straight or in-between, and there is virtually no credible evidence that there exists an effective method of reorientation that works on randomly selected individuals, whether children or adults.

On the other hand, to say that there is no method of reorientation at present is not to say that one is inherently impossible. Sexual orientation science might well find a method of helping shift people from one sexual orientation to another, as I have said in chapter 3. Even if a treatment could shift people from one eroticism to another, however, it is unclear that that treatment should be seen as relevant in judgments about unlawful discrimination. That sexual orientation might be able to be altered through some form of therapeutic intervention does not mean, first of all, that that trait is voluntary in its origins. Immutability, moreover, need not mean permanence of a trait, as Richard Green has pointed out.[57] Even if a sexual orientation could be modified, it might nevertheless remain treated as socially immutable. Witness in this regard the social belief that men and women who undergo transgender therapy remain people of their sex at birth, that is, that transgendered people are gender imposters. Like race and sex, sexual orientation has a social permanence—an immutability—to it, all possible interventions and modifications of therapy notwithstanding.

The doctrine of suspect class is designed to protect people from unjust treatment attaching to a trait over which they have no control and consequently no way to escape the mistreatment, but even if people could slip in and out of sexual orientations without lingering social effects, no court should find that the existence of a therapy would be reason to conclude that an adequate mechanism existed for avoiding any and all social disvalues attaching to homoeroticism, that discriminatory laws in effect were ultimately benign. Passing as white or as male has afforded some people a mechanism of escaping social mistreatment, but these "opportunities" are not equally available to all and are merely escape hatches from social inequity, not remedies for social injustice. It would be wrong to conclude that the ability to change one's socially offensive trait renders society any less accountable for its objectionable opinion and treatment of those with that trait. At the very least, the existence of a therapy should not be taken to imply that discrimination on the basis of sexual orientation is legally insignificant because evadable. People should not have to seek recourse from social injustice through the transforming ministrations of their doctors and therapists.

Whether an argument that gay people represent a suspect class succeeds in court will depend on a number of factors, including the facts of the case at hand and the question of whether or not conduct is recognized as the basis of group membership. In making its judgments about whether or not Perry Watkins was entitled to continue serving in the military, one court panel reached divided conclusions about recognizing gay people as a suspect class. One judge held that gay people were a suspect class and that the military could not therefore justify its bar on gay service members. Another judge reached the conclusion that although he disagreed with the Bowers v. Hardwick decision, he was bound to recognize it as a precedent voiding a constitutional right to same-sex relations, with the effect that no group could be legally predicated on those nonconstitutionally protected sexual relations. A higher court did reinstate Watkins to the military, but it did so on the narrow grounds that the military had given Watkins sufficient reason to believe that his sexual orientation was not cause for discharge: to discharge him would be to subject him to double jeopardy.[58] That decision did not, then, depend on the broader question of whether and to what extent gay people constituted a meaningful group before the law and whether the classification of gay people as a general threat to the military should be treated as suspect.

Even if courts do recognize gay people as a suspect class, it goes almost without saying there is reason to believe that there will continue to be resistance to affording them equal status under the law. Victories for gay people often bring backlashes. For example, in direct response to the possibility that the state of Hawaii will permit gay marriages, a number of states have adopted legislation that would forbid same-sex marriages, and the U.S. federal government adopted a Defense of Marriage Act that forbids recognition of same-sex marriages in federal policies.[59] A similar sort of backlash could follow judicial recognition of gay people as a suspect class, with congresspeople on both side of the political aisle arguing that the presence of gay people in the military undermines unit cohesion even if sexual orientation is as involuntary as eye color. Recognizing gay people as entitled to heightened judicial scrutiny will not automatically end their woes before society and the law.

If I have spent time problematizing the benefits of suspect class for gay people, it is not because I think antisodomy laws or other laws that have discriminatory effects against gay people should remain standing. I think these discriminatory practices are objectionable for reasons independent of the criteria of suspect classifications above, though as I have tried to show, most of these criteria would seem to apply to gay people. In the end, I believe antisodomy laws and collateral discriminatory statutes should be struck down independent of whether or not gay people are entitled to the legal status of suspect class. When called upon to do so, courts should look to considerations of the Constitution that respect free speech, privacy, the right of assembly, the separation of church and state, which considerations in their totality go a great distance toward protecting the rights of gay people and do not depend on whether or not there is in the scientific literature a convincing report that sexual orientation cannot be changed or whether women and men are fated to homoerotic lives because of their genetic or neuroanatomical endowment. The utility of pursuing suspect classification for gay people may have come to an altogether abrupt end in 1996, because of the U.S. Supreme Court's decision in Romer v. Evans.[60]

In Romer v. Evans the court held that states may neither retroactively nor prospectively rule out antidiscrimination laws that protect people on the basis of sexual orientation. It rejected Amendment 2, as the amendment to the Colorado constitution at issue was universally known, because it "identifies persons by a single trait and denies them protection across the board. The resulting disqualification of a class of persons from the right to seek specific protections from the law is unprecedented in our jurisprudence." Because of Amendment 2, the court noted, "Homosexuals are forbidden the safeguards that others enjoy or may seek without constraint." The court went on to say that the amendment seemed to be motivated by animosity toward gay people because "in making a general announcement that gays and lesbians shall not have any particular protections from the law, [it] inflicts on them immediate, continuing, and real injuries that outrun and belie any legitimate justifications that may be claimed for it." Indeed, the court rejected the two main ways in which the state of Colorado defended the law: to protect the freedom of association and to conserve resources to fight other kinds of discrimination. The court sharply observed that "the breadth of the Amendment is so far removed from these particular justifications that we find it impossible to credit them."

In this landmark case the court held that the amendment did not embody a rational relationship to a legitimate governmental purpose. There are in the court's opinion no references to scientific research about the biology of sexual orientation, and there are no discussions of whether sexual orientation is immutable in regard to its origins or susceptibility to therapy. It is notable that, in its opinion, the court accepts without hesitation the notion that there is a class of gay people, and it uses exactly that language. This is striking because the court does not see before it people who can or not engage in homoerotic behavior as a matter of ultimate indifference to their identity, as indifferent as engaging in, say, croquet or reading. The court appears to accept that there is a class of people for whom an essential component of their identity or character consists in having—and by extension, acting on—homoerotic inclinations, regardless of the origin of those inclinations. Or, at the very least, the court implies that states may not refuse to deny that there is such a class.

As I have said, there are no references to scientific research in this opinion, and no legal finding depends on the origins of erotic interests, but it may be that the cumulative effect of sexual orientation research has influenced this court decision via the work it has done on public and judicial perception of gay people—by convincing the public that gay people are not victims of pathological disorders, that homoeroticism is an important component of individual identity, that there may be some biological contributions to the origins of erotic desire, and that homoerotic orientations are fairly common and compatible with important social station and contribution. This observation is speculative, of course, but it is hard to separate out this decision from an improved—but still tentative—understanding of the origins and effects of sexual orientation. It is hard to imagine this decision coming down in the way it did had there been no credible science investigating the nature and social effects of sexual orientation.

Three Supreme Court justices dissented from the majority opinion in Romer v. Evans, and one of the chief lines of argument in their dissent was that the opinion was at odds with the 1986 Bowers v. Hardwick decision. Bowers permits states to criminalize private consensual sex by same-sex adults. Why is it not also within a state's power, the dissent wonders, to discourage that very same sexuality by barring the extension of special rights to homosexuals? If the majority opinion passed over Bowers in silence, it is because the justices in the majority felt no obligation to its logic of using prevailing patterns of hostility to justify discrimination against gay people. Richard D. Mohr has rightly made the point that the logic of Romer v. Evans repudiates the logic by which Bowers v. Hardwick was upheld, namely, what he calls the bootstrapping of public policy off prejudice.[61] Depending on the cases that come before it and the judges sitting at the time, it might very well fall to the Court to confront the apparent contradiction between Romer v. Evans and Bowers v. Hardwick. A reconciliation is not necessarily in the immediate offing. Some states, after all, quite happily tolerate the dissonance of having both sodomy laws and antigay discrimination laws on the books at the same time.

In any case, it does not appear that the courts can offer broad protection to gay people only by finding that they possess an immutable characteristic that would invoke heightened judicial protection under the doctrine of suspect class. I think courts should continue to examine laws bearing on gay people primarily on the grounds of whether they have a rational relation to a legitimate government purpose. That kind of analysis should afford gay people the kinds of protections of equality and liberty they deserve, the immutability of their sexual orientation notwithstanding.

As Richard D. Mohr has wittily pointed out, if one means by nature the world with human beings in it, then homoeroticism is manifestly natural; if one means by nature the world without human beings in it, it is hard to know what creatures or processes should serve as exemplars for human morality.[62] It turns out in any case that one of the direct consequences of reading homoeroticism into nature is that it becomes thereby a legitimate topic of study in the life and social sciences. It is ironic that nineteenth-century efforts like those of Ulrichs to shield homoeroticism by locating it within the natural order have in the twentieth century opened it to worries that technological interventions could wipe it out. The value of reading homoeroticism into nature cannot therefore be assumed to have a uniform effect independent of culture. Perceptions of the value of sexual orientation research—like perceptions of sexual identities themselves—are subject to flux in their meaning for gay and straight people.

In illuminating the personal and social consequences of various erotic interests and identities, sexual orientation science can be eminently useful where it helps clear away false views that undergird wrongful heteronormative assumptions. Whether people hold antigay views because of empirically false information about gay people is, of course, a contentious question since dislike of gay people can drift along happily independent of facts. Heterosexism may be resistant to change and can assume new manifestations and rationales when confronted with data that confound central antigay beliefs. It is to be noted in virtually the same breath that science can also engender new errors about sexual orientation insofar as it is incomplete or distorted by the way in which it is received in public opinion. Nevertheless, to the extent sexual orientation science clarifies erroneous views about gay people it can, as I have already noted, help change prevailing social attitudes and thus work to enlarge the liberties and rights of gay people.

There may well be biodevelopmental features involved in shifting people toward the sexual orientations they have, though an exact accounting of the way in which those features work is far from complete, and this is not to say that erotic interests are only dependent on the workings of biology. The evidence is far more clear and convincing that entrenched adult homoeroticism is highly intractable to therapeutic modification. In the context of a history of discrimination and political powerlessness, findings that there are involuntary components to sexual orientation and that it is functionally immutable might convince some courts to conclude that laws prejudicially affecting gay people should be examined using the highest level of judicial scrutiny. It is not for me to say whether courts will in fact reach this conclusion. The fate of gay people as a suspect class will depend on the nature of cases that reach the courts and the logic of the judges hearing the cases. My own view is that the history of moral philosophy is redundant in credible defenses of homoeroticism and that most laws inimical to gay people should be struck down without recourse to the logic of suspect class, which is another way of saying that rights for gay people should not have to rely on stop-press science.

If one understands a liberal society as one that has a respect for the privacy of its citizens, that espouses neutrality in regard to conflicting visions of morality, and that tries to lift those social repressions unnecessary to the core functions of a society, it follows that a liberal state ought to respect the sexual privacy of its citizens regardless of gender, that it ordain no state sexual orientation by curtailing the liberty of gay people, and that it expect of and accord to gay people all duties and rights that belong to others. In such a state the findings of science in regard to the causality of sexual orientation science would by and large be moot.

That said, in the rough and tumble of real-world politics and court decisions it may be that as a political strategy a designation of suspect class would do more to advance the rights of gay people than having to enact antidiscrimination statutes brick by brick in every legislative jurisdiction. Yet the Romer v. Evans decision may have preempted the worth of invoking suspect class status for gay people because it struck down a highly prejudicial statute without first making any determination about the immutability of homoeroticism either in regard to its origins or its susceptibility to therapy. Henceforward, it is to be hoped, antigay laws will be assessed closely to determine whether they credibly assert a legitimate governmental goal. If there are pragmatic benefits of sexual orientation science in this process, they should be welcomed so long as generalizations about the facts of "nature" are not mistaken for principles of moral judgment. Respecting the difference between the data of science and moral principles will provide the critical space necessary for analysis and correction should it turn out that sexual orientation research is used in ways detrimental to gay people or should it turn out that scientific data is wrong in important ways.

7 |||||||||||||||||||||||||||||||||||||||||||||||||||||||||||||||||||||||||||||||

SCIENCE AND THE FUTURE

Suspicion of science and medicine is almost one of the foundational canons of gay culture, a suspicion born of the excesses of sexological science in the nineteenth century and revisited more recently in the real and perceived failures attributed to biomedicine in the AIDS epidemic.[1] Gay culture has often been predicated on mutually incriminating antagonisms with the institutions of medicine, law, government, and religion—even if individual gay people have found support from specific physicians, attorneys, legislators, and religious communities. There is continuing evidence of heterosexism in the health professions, and efforts at educational reform in those professions can hardly be described as robust.[2] The battle for equal protection under the law sees new skirmishes not only in the legacy of the Supreme Court Bowers v. Hardwick decision but also in the efforts of some jurisdictions to outlaw what they call special rights for homosexuals.[3] While members of a religion do not hold uniform views or behave uniformly, the most socially significant denominations in the United States and around the world continue to condemn homoeroticism as sinful and socially corrosive, this despite the presence of significant numbers of gay people in those denominations, not only in the rank and file laity but also in ecclesiastical office as well.

It will not be surprising therefore, in an age confident of its flourishing scientific abilities, that Richard Pillard, a psychiatrist working at a prominent urban university medical center, can still worry that because society does not treat homoeroticism like a neutral trait, as it does left-handedness, gay people may face extinction: "The price to pay for relaxing our guard is extermination."[4] Pillard's worry is worth taking seriously if only because it recurs among both advocates and detractors of gay people as they imagine the future of science. Will there be gay people in the future or will sexual orientation science abet the direct or indirect extinction of gay people, thereby fulfilling the most grim suspicions held by gay people in regard to biomedicine?

Suppose that adults could seek deliverance from their homoerotic desires by turning to therapy. Suppose too that parents could subject a fetus under suspicion of a homoerotic future to biomedical intervention or even abortion. Were these therapies and interventions safe, effective, and acceptable, would the number of gay people not fall? If so, would the diminished number of gay people count as a morally relevant constraint against the use of therapies and prenatal interventions or even against sexual orientation research whose goal was to produce them? Or would diminishing numbers of gay people be a morally indifferent matter, equivalent to the loss of social interest in a particular style of clothing or music, something to wax nostalgic about perhaps, but no loss or social deprivation so compelling as to forbid sexual orientation research or forbid people from taking advantage of therapies and prenatal interventions? And what would be the fate of the gay people who did endure? Would their decreasing numbers not open them to even greater social injustice?

These are all highly speculative questions, given that there now exist no therapies or prenatal interventions that offer the kind of control over sexual orientation imagined here. Some commentators have noted that it can be socially counterproductive to raise questions about practices that belong more to imagination than to clinical reality if these questions fill the public mind with illusory expectations. For my purposes it is enough to note that these *are* speculative questions—no one should mistake thought experiments for clinical or social reality—but also to observe that they remain instructive by reason of the issues they raise and the moral considerations they illuminate even if the therapies and interventions under discussion *never* emerge. Nonetheless, I hope that my consideration of these questions does not sap energy that ought to go toward protecting gay people from actual and present, not imaginary and future, discrimination. I do not consider the hypothetical discussions that follow the moral equivalent of attending to real social injustices.

That said, my own sense is that if therapies and interventions offering real or perceived control over sexual orientation were available some people would use these techniques with themselves and their progeny and the number of gay people would fall. It does not follow as a matter of moral logic that this outcome would necessarily worsen the fate of gay people, for people can be valued in kind even if they are few in number. Moral logic is not, however, the same as social and political process, and if there were fewer and fewer gay people all the time, durable historical antagonisms might swell up against a politically vulnerable because numerically small minority, especially if gay people were held responsible for grave social ills. These sorts of therapies and interventions would not, however, be the only determinants of the number of gay people in the future. Gay people might well respond to their diminished numbers by having more children and using prenatal interventions to ensure that their children were gay. This practice would certainly be anathema to people who oppose homoeroticism on moral or religious grounds, but if parents' rights to choose heteroeroticism for their children are to be respected, as I have argued in chapter 4, there is also a prima facie case for an equivalent right of parents to choose homoeroticism in their children were that option available.

In speculating about the future numbers of gay people, it is also important to pay attention to the social determinants of sexual interests and identities. One social historian has argued that socioeconomic trends are strongly implicated in the emergence of homoerotic interests, influencing as they do the erotic freedom that is available to people at any given time. Cultural attitudes toward sexuality will also play a contributing role in the emergence of erotic interests. John Money has speculated that cultural sexophobia actively contributes to the emergence of homoeroticism, quite contrary to its own goals. If this kind of analysis is accurate and current economic and sexual trends continue to prevail, there is likely to be more and not less homoerotic interest in the future.[5] If so, these trends will sustain a future in which there are gay people no matter how effective therapy and prenatal interventions prove.

In this chapter I will explore the context of the suspicion by gay people of science and try to think through the implications of sexual orientation science for the future. It turns out that the numbers of gay people in the future will not simply be a function of the state of science in identifying ways in which sexual orientation might be manipulated. Having looked at the meaning of sexual orientation science for individuals (who might be seeking therapy for themselves or interventions for their children), I will then consider the effects sexual orientation science might have on society as a whole. In all instances it is hard to imagine a future in which there would be no gay people. The decisive moral question in regard to the future of gay people turns, then, not on their numbers but on their treatment.

SUSPICION OF SEXUAL ORIENTATION RESEARCH REVISITED

One way to contextualize the suspicion of sexual orientation research is to consider whether there are at present any institutionalized mechanisms that promote the emergence, continued existence, and well-being of gay people. In fact, there is little familial, institutional, or social investment of any kind in the continued existence—let alone the generational emergence—of gay people. Prevailing social consensus about gay people goes entirely the other way. Literature professor Eve Kosofsky Sedgwick put the matter like this:

> The scope of institutions whose programmatic undertaking is to prevent the development of gay people is unimaginably large. There is no major institutionalized discourse that offers a firm resistance to that undertaking: in the United States, at any rate, most sites of the state, the military, education, law, penal institutions, the church, medicine, and mass culture enforce it all but unquestioningly, and with little hesitation at even the recourse to invasive violence.[6]

By way of caustic understatement she adds that "the number of persons or institutions by whom the existence of gay people is treated as a precious desideratum, a needed condition of life, is small."[7] Against a social background systemically imbued with hostility and indifference toward gay people and a society that imagines no place for gay people in its future, effective sexual orientation therapies and/or prenatal interventions provoke live worry about the ultimate fate of gay people.

Given a different social history, sexual orientation research need not have provoked the consternation it now does. Neither would its advocates and practitioners look to it for benefits they expect it to confer. Imagining that history could have taken different pathways is to open the door to speculation both profitable and unprofitable. At its best this kind of reflection does make it possible to imagine how homoeroticism could have been, for example, accommodated without hostility into culture, for which accommodation there are historical precedents, and to do so in order to have a criterion by which to evaluate the contemporary treatment of gay people. Had political, moral, and religious leaders taken a different view of things, homoeroticism could have avoided its cursed history, in much the same way genetics could have had a markedly different history had there been, for example, no Francis Galton or the widespread cultural expectations that genetic science could deliver social order and progress. It is at least *imaginable* that homoeroticism could have been incorporated into human culture without the moral sanctions and political and religious subjugation that have been its all-too-common fate. This is not to say that homoeroticism could have been accommodated culturally only in the sense of there being gay people in the sense we know them, but it is at least possible to imagine the last two millennia as having occurred without homoeroticism taking on socially durable meanings of immorality, sin, disorder, and criminality, however it came to be incorporated in social identities and roles. There seem to have been some clear historical moments in which social meanings of homoeroticism that did not involve condemnation were in fact explored, even if those social accommodations were ultimately rejected in the West.[8]

At its worst, speculation about matters contrary to fact can fuel escapist fantasies unrelated to actual world history, fantasies so remote that they encourage altogether dismissive and simplistic accounts of the past. It is not my intention to suggest other pathways history might have taken in fact so much as it is my goal to suggest the extent to which antigay prejudice is a social artifact. For purposes of this argument I assume that there is nothing developmentally necessary about antigay sentiments and beliefs as a condition of individual, social, or historical development. This assumption could prove unwarranted if it turned out that something about the psychology of human beings or the development of social institutions *required* heterosexism as a condition of psychic organization, development, and progress. In light of both individuals and cultures making their peace with homoeroticism, however, an assumption of inevitable psychological and cultural hostility toward homoeroticism seems altogether unwarranted. It does not follow, either, that if heterosexism were somehow necessary to human development in the past it would need to continue in the future.

What also remains in the realm of speculation is whether there can be a future other than one whose trajectory is continuous with the more or less calculated heteronormativity of the past. To be sure, one cannot assume that the future of gay people will be necessarily continuous with their achievements in staking out a place for themselves thus far. Nevertheless, neither can one assume that the future of gay people is foredoomed. Democratic societies, for example, do observe certain political safeguards that would work against the outright elimination of gay people, safeguards such as constitutional liberties including rights of association, speech, and reproductive privacy. Advocacy groups under democratic regimes can have, for example, a vital protective function for all beleaguered minorities, and privacy rights protect against a great many intrusions by the state. I do acknowledge that these are formal, procedural, and sometimes merely theoretical safeguards that are often frail and fallible in practice. In the United States, for example, there are reasons to be suspicious of the beneficence of a nation toward gay people when its highest court found a way to permit states to criminalize private sexual behavior between consenting adults of the same sex, when it sustains legal barriers to same-sex marriage, and when it tolerates the exclusion of gay people from military service. How far a step is it between these sorts of practices and efforts to reduce the numbers of gay people in the nation more systematically?

As I have tried to show in chapter 2, it does not seem wise to discuss sexual orientation research only as the project of a heterosexist science whose ultimate goal is the extinction of gay people. On the contrary, because inquiry into the nature and effects of sexual orientation has proven to falsify erroneous beliefs about the generalized psychological incapacity of gay people and because scientific study has proven to elicit some public support for gay men and lesbians, sexual orientation research must also be understood in its capacity for resisting rather than generating heterosexism and antigay prejudice. That sexual orientation research can have these kinds of beneficial results means, at the very least, that a blanket condemnation of such inquiry is unjustified. To make this observation is not, however, to address worries about the ill effects of sexual orientation research if it turns out that the number of gay people diminishes because of the therapies and interventions it makes possible. I now turn to consider exactly that issue.

HOW MANY GAY PEOPLE WILL THERE BE?

One of the central tasks of bioethics involves the anticipation and discussion of objectionable consequences of biomedical practices. This enterprise proceeds with the acknowledged risk of conjuring a parade of horribles to argue against a particular practice or policy.[9] It is easy to fall into a formulaic incantation of possible objectionable consequences when discussing new biomedical developments, especially those involving socially vulnerable minorities. Foreseeing the consequences of a practice or policy is important, of course, but many objectionable consequences may never come to pass or will fail to be as significant as originally estimated. Some imaginable ill effects can be offset by crafting social policies and statutes adequate to contain them. Acknowledging the limitations inherent in drawing conclusions about contemporary events by relying on expectations of the future, I want nevertheless to speculate about the fate of gay people in a hypothetical future in which sexual orientation science has produced an effective therapy for adults and prenatal intervention offering control over the sexual orientation of children. Will such developments really lead to the extinction of gay people or is this scenario an exaggeration of the likely future?

Sexual Orientation Therapy   If biomedicine were to discover a therapy for sexual orientation, offering control over the gender of one's erotic interests, there is no doubt that some health professionals would offer this treatment and that they would find willing clients. The stalwart 1978 Bell and Weinberg study shows that, depending on the race and gender of the respondents, between 29 and 38 percent of their homosexual subjects had considered "discontinuing homosexual activity."[10] Of those who had, between 40 and 75 percent made some conscious steps to do so, some making repeated attempts.[11] These attempts included withdrawing from gay sociosexual involvement, increasing heterosexual sociosexual involvement, stopping homosexual feelings, marriage, and seeking professional help.[12] Had there been a therapy available for gay sexual orientation during the time of the Bell and Weinberg study, it would have

been of interest to a subset of gay people wishing to discontinue their homosexual activity.

Is it reasonable to assume, then, that there would have been fewer gay people by the same percentages at which the Bell and Weinberg subjects made
attempts to give up homoeroticism? There is no simple answer to this question.
Most people in the group surveyed by Bell and Weinberg who wanted to give
up their homosexuality did *not* seek professional help, which means that they
relied on unproved folk methods alone. Among those men and women who *did*
consult professionals, less than 20 percent of them did so with the specific
intention of giving up their homosexuality.[13] It may be that most people did
not seek professional help for the same reasons that people attend to health
needs first through "self-care" and resort to professional assistance only when
genuinely unable to control suffering and disorders. Or there might be something about the economic and cultural stratification of the subjects that made
professional therapy impossible for monetary and cultural reasons. In any case,
having an interest in a therapy does not mean that one would have access to or
actually use that therapy.

The same limitations would apply if there were a therapy in the future that
could effectively modify sexual orientation. The use of any actual sexual orientation therapy will depend not only on whether people want it but also on
whether they can afford it. If unhappiness about having homoerotic interests
were either the cause or effect of some disorder, there would be a prima facie case
for health insurers to pay for it. As it is, with no major U.S. medical organizations
backing a pathological interpretation of homoeroticism per se, insurers might
leave it to the individual to pay for elective treatment since they have no obligation to provide every treatment that could contribute to a person's well-being.
Given the resistance of insurers to coverage for the costs of, for example, transgender treatment, I suspect that they would be equally disinclined to pay for
therapy for unwanted homoeroticism.[14] Some insurers might pay, though, if a
formal diagnosis of sexual orientation distress were involved, which diagnosis is
at present recognized by the A.P.A. At the very least, there would be a messy fight
about whether to pay for sexual orientation therapy generally, and it should not
be assumed that simply because there was a sexual orientation therapy that it
would be automatically accessible even to those with health care insurance.

If there were a direct parallel between having money and use of the therapy,
and this pattern prevailed for very long, there would eventually be, so it seems,
fewer gay people among wealthier groups, making homoeroticism disproportionately prevalent among the less well-to-do or those with the wrong kind of
insurance. But this outcome would ensue only if those with enough money to
afford the therapy were, as a class, generally disposed against homoeroticism.

This is an empirical matter, of course, but it may prove that wealthier people have fewer reservations about homoeroticism and would have fewer reasons to seek therapy, their ability to pay for it notwithstanding. After all, having significant amounts of money provides some degree of insulation against the social troubles visited on gay people, which is to say that the wealthy *already* have some insulation from the social problems that drive the search for sexual orientation therapy in the first place. One should not automatically assume, therefore, that the wealthy would be unremittingly eager to change their sexual orientation.

Another reason for being hesitant that the Bell and Weinberg figures (or other figures that might be more current) identify a meaningful percentage of people who would be interested in professional sexual orientation therapy goes in a different direction: those figures might underestimate an interest in therapy. Some would-be clients of sexual orientation therapy might simply be unaware that changing sexual orientation is the kind of thing they could pursue with therapists. Not knowing that therapists try to modify sexual orientation, some people might simply have failed to pursue that avenue of treatment. Some of the more scientifically sophisticated public might know that therapists do offer services of this kind but believe that such therapy is worthless because professionals lack hard evidence that it works. Only if there were clear evidence of an effective therapy would these hard-nosed clients seek it. Another limitation on the effectiveness of any therapy is that those who enter therapy do not always finish it, for all manner of reasons. For some, attempts at therapy will confirm them in their sexual orientation, with no small irony in that. The attractiveness of a therapy will also depend on its cost, its methods, and its outcome. If the therapy were, for example, extremely costly or involved surgery or offered only a 60 percent chance of success, its attractiveness would presumably diminish even among those most interested in it. Limitations of these sorts suggest that even among an adult population disenchanted by its sexual orientation therapy would be no universal panacea for both reasons of chance and choice.

Yet even a therapy of limited value would in all likelihood draw clients. There are ways in which the availability of a product creates its own market. If it became widely known that a certain class of health professionals could treat unwanted sexual orientation with some degree of success, that publicity could help shape a market. An effective marketing campaign and reasonable costs could put sexual orientation therapy within the sights of many people unhappy about their erotic interests. Most gay people, for example, experience a period of dissonance between the emergence and acceptance of their homoerotic interests. For people at that point sexual orientation therapy might appear as the path of deliverance, and a cagey marketing campaign could capitalize on that dissonance.

Though it is one of the most comprehensive empirical studies of homo-eroticism in history, the Bell and Weinberg report is, of course, dated by a quarter-century of social change and gay advocacy, and it is difficult to assess the significance of that report for the present. It would be a mistake to assume that its reported percentages of gay people attempting to give up their homoeroticism would be replicated today or in the future. For one thing, the world is in many ways more congenial to gay people, especially because they no longer grow up under the formal judgment of pathology and because there are social and political groups committed to protecting them from harmful treatment. Given that the largest majority of gay people in the Bell and Weinberg study reported little or no regret about their sexual orientation,[15] one would expect that general state of affairs to prevail in a world made incrementally safer for homoeroticism by the emergence of a gay culture complete with recreational, political, legal, educational, and religious components. This culture is bounded by clear limits in its ability to protect gay people from judgmental views, hostility, and inequality, but it affords men and women alike the opportunity to imagine their lives and futures in ways that do not require modification of their sexual orientation.

It would, of course, remain an empirical matter as to how many people in the future would experience regret about their sexual orientation, a regret so compelling that they would desire therapy. It would also be a separate empirical question whether people would actually pursue and receive sexual orientation therapy were it available: of a presumably shrinking number of gay people regretful of their sexual orientation, how many would have access to therapy and complete it successfully? In all likelihood the most that can be said is that the market for sexual orientation therapy for adults would be fluid, subject to contradictory movements diminishing the need for it, scientific developments perhaps improving prospects of success, and social developments widening knowledge about it.

It is far from clear in any case that the mere existence of such a therapy would decimate the ranks of gay people. Most self-identified gay people accept their sexual orientation and want *no* change, and, as treatment with adults is voluntary, it goes almost without saying that most gay people would not seek the therapy. It is therefore an indefensible overstatement to say that the development of an effective sexual orientation therapy could lead by itself to the extinction of gay people, for even if there were a completely effective therapy, it is by and large unwanted by most adult gay people and could not be imposed on them.

It is also unclear that gay advocacy would suffer irreparable damages if a sexual orientation therapy were to emerge. People who seek sexual orientation therapy are virtually never the same people who publicly commit their energy, lives, and money to improving the lot of gay people. If the ranks of gay people were thinned by people availing themselves of sexual orientation therapy, it is hardly likely that many activists would be lost. The people looking for therapy to escape homoeroticism are neither the front-line recruits nor the mandarins of gay advocacy. The fate of gay people in any society will depend, therefore, not on whether there exists a sexual orientation therapy but on gay people who shun therapy and who *are* willing to commit to social advocacy, however many of them there are.

Prenatal Interventions   Suppose researchers were to discover that a single gene strongly disposed an individual to adult homoeroticism. Suppose one could test for that gene prenatally and control it (i.e., suppress its effect entirely) by the administration of a single hormone injection in mothers at a particular point in pregnancy or by some treatment equivalently easy and cheap. How detrimental to the future of gay people would an intervention of this kind be? The answer to this question is to be found in the strength of parental desire to avoid having gay children and their access to these interventions. Predicting the significance of interventions like this is, as with forecasting the significance of therapy with adults, a complicated matter.

The Bell and Weinberg study shows that a certain percentage of self-identified lesbians and gay men would experience regret if their children were homosexual, not in the main because of something profoundly objectionable about homoeroticism but because of social intolerance.[16] Some gay and lesbian parents, perfectly content in their own sexual orientation, might therefore wish to spare their children homoerotic sexual identities not because they see anything wrong with that sexual orientation but because a heteroerotic sexual identity is less fearful given the workings of contemporary society. Some of them might therefore opt for the use of these interventions. Straight parents may be expected to have the same sorts of worries, only magnified, in confronting the possibility of gay children. It would be an empirical matter whether and to what extent gay and straight parents would avail themselves of an intervention that disposed against children being gay. Nevertheless, certain contours of such use may be roughly estimated.

As was the case with sexual orientation therapy, access to and success in the use of a prenatal intervention for sexual orientation would define the limitations of even an ideal method of sexual orientation control. For example, even though genetic tests exist for hundreds of conditions that may be diagnosed prenatally, many children are born each year with those genetic disorders because the mutations arise spontaneously in families without any history of the condition, because there are more genetic disorders than is reasonable to test for in the course of routine prenatal diagnosis, because many women do not have access to genetic prenatal diagnostics, and because there is a degree of error in conducting and analyzing tests. There is no reason to think that a gene for homo-eroticism would not prove as elusive as genes for cystic fibrosis or Down syndrome sometimes do. It should also be observed that the majority of children in the world are born without any sort of prenatal diagnostics or interventions of the kind imagined here. If there were a prenatal intervention available, its use would presumably follow current patterns of biomedical access. For the foreseeable future most children would continue to be born without any testing for sexual orientation. Availability and access of sexual orientation interventions would always be subject to constraints of class, economics, geography, and religious views about the acceptability of their use.

Contrary to the easy and cheap treatment suggested above, if the prenatal techniques involved in controlling the sexual orientation of a child were expensive, they would ordinarily be beyond the reach of low-income populations. If the techniques were sufficiently complex as to require being conducted in a major medical facility, people in outlying regions might find them beyond their geographic reach. Or if the techniques were dangerous, they might not be carried out in women with a history of spontaneous abortion or where they might somehow subject a pregnant woman to risk. It is important to keep in mind, too, that no procedure is without its errors of application. Even if control over sexual orientation were within the power of biomedicine, because of faulty technique there would still continue to be homosexual progeny.

One genetics counselor has pointed out that even if there were no barriers to the use of a prenatal diagnostic under the law, individual hospitals and clinics might well decline as a matter of institutional policy to make prenatal tests for sexual orientation available to parents, as some do now with respect to the disclosure of fetal sex. Some physicians have said they would refuse to offer a sexual orientation test whether or not the profession or medical institutions as a whole had a policy against using such a test.[17] Whether a manufacturer would be willing to produce and market sexual orientation tests would also affect the availability and use of a prenatal genetic marker for sexual orientation. Philip Reilly, a medical geneticist, has said of that kind of test,

> No company would touch it. They would perceive the market of potential users as, essentially, women who dislike homosexuality enough to consider terminating a pregnancy for that very reason—a very small market—and they could run the risk of being targeted by the gay community. Many of these companies are risk-aversive. It costs large amounts of money to develop these tests, and what would be the return on the investment?[18]

Absent a large and perhaps continually growing market for the product, some manufacturers might choose to develop products other than those that would bring gay activists marching in protest to their corporate headquarters.

I have presumed to this point in the discussion that a prenatal intervention for sexual orientation would be largely effective in its results. It may very well turn out that a genetic probe, for example, could *not* offer results with unequivocal certainty but could offer only probabilistic results. Parents might thus learn from their physician that there is a 40 percent chance that their female fetus is likely to be lesbian. Or they might learn that there is a 30 percent chance that their twin male fetuses are likely to be gay. Or there may be a 50 percent chance that one dizygotic twin will be gay, while the other twin faces only an 18 percent risk. One woman might find that her fetus stands a 72 percent chance of being gay, but she might also face an enormously difficult time in becoming pregnant again. In addition to uncertainties in the test, the effectiveness of a prenatal intervention might also be probabilistic in nature, complicating the matter even further. A woman knowing that her male fetus faces a 27 percent chance of being gay might learn that the proposed intervention—hormone therapy— offers her only 27 percent chance of altering that degree of risk. The complications of probabilistic assessment might well undercut, therefore, the desirability and use of prenatal tests and interventions for sexual orientation.

There would be no broad legal incentives to the use of sexual orientation tests either. At present, U.S. states do not—and probably could not—oblige health care practitioners to conduct prenatal genetic testing of any kind or compel women to submit to such tests. The United States has rejected unwanted testing on both moral and legal grounds. It is a guiding principle of medical ethics that competent people may decline unwanted testing and treatment, even lifesaving treatment. In the context of this tradition it is unclear that the state could—or should even aspire to—impose a mandatory sexual orientation test on all pregnant women. No guiding principle is without its exceptions, of course, and though some pregnant women have been ordered to undergo some forms of testing and treatment, these coerced interventions have largely been justified as protecting newborns from harm by reason of the woman's drug use. It is far from clear that letting a child be "born gay" is analogous to the damage a newborn faces as the result of a pregnant woman's use of alcohol or cocaine.[19] States may require that physicians *offer* certain tests and information to pregnant women, but offering is very different from requiring that the test be carried out independent of a woman's wishes.

It is also unclear that any general public health concern could justify imposing a sexual orientation test on pregnant women generally. Insofar as homoeroticism is not judged pathological, there is no disease to monitor and control. Moreover, gay people do not in the main regret their sexual orientation. This acceptance of sexual orientation seems to undermine any paternalistic viewpoint that would attempt a general "rescue" of people from homoeroticism and do so in the name of their own well-being. As AIDS is often raised in conjunc-tion with health and homoeroticism, I do acknowledge that gay men are over-represented among people with AIDS, but the greater susceptibility of gay men to AIDS would not count as a justification for a general screening for sexual ori-entation if that susceptibility is not a function of homoeroticism itself—which it surely is not. To try and prevent a communicable viral disease by attempting to reduce gay men as a class would be a highly idiosyncratic way of improving the public health. Consequently, there does not seem to be any compelling pub-lic health justification for imposing an involuntary sexual orientation test on pregnant women.

Legal worries on the part of health care practitioners would not either seem to be a significant force propelling widespread sexual orientation testing. There may be professional and legal incentives for health care practitioners to carry out some prenatal tests in order to protect against charges of professional wrongdoing, but these incentives are usually tied to the very specific familial or genetic circumstances of a particular patient and do not apply generally across the range of all possible prenatal tests. If a prenatal diagnostic test could predict sexual orientation but was not recommended by a particular physician, some parents of a gay child might pursue a wrongful birth suit, alleging that their physician failed to offer a test about future sexual orientation, a test they say would have permitted them to choose hormonal therapy or even abortion for a child with so objectionable a trait, objectionable to them and—they allege—to the child. Failure to offer or conduct prenatal tests is sometimes used as the basis for wrongful birth actions, yet U.S. courts have generally rejected these suits, and it is unclear how one might succeed in convincing a court that homo-erotic sexual orientation is an evil so grave that a child would have been better off having been aborted, especially when courts have already proved skeptical about these claims in regard to seriously debilitating diseases and disorders. It is therefore unlikely that an incentive for widespread prenatal testing is to be found in fear of wrongful birth suits.

Certainly an individual parent might successfully sue a physician for negli-gence in failing to conduct a sexual orientation test *properly* with the result that a parent ended up with a child of unwanted sexual orientation, if, for example, the physician botched the test and lost the window of opportunity for inter-vention in a child's sexual orientation. While this is a plausible outcome, it is difficult to see how courts could meaningfully estimate the damages of that "negligence" for purposes of compensation. A suit might have to wait till a child's adolescence in order to be sure that a homoerotic sexual orientation did in fact emerge, if courts wanted to know from children themselves whether their sexual orientation has proved an injury. Given the increasing ease with

which some adolescents declare themselves gay or lesbian, it is certainly imaginable that some teenagers would allege no injury, and thus the child on whose
behalf the suit has been filed might prove its undoing. On the other hand, the
courts might find damages of a psychological kind to the parents sufficient
grounds for awarding damages independent of the actual sexual orientation of
the child. Exact outcomes cannot be forecast here because of uncertainties
about the facts of suits that might be brought, the way in which they are argued,
and the logic that would prevail in the court's decisions.

There is, moreover, virtually nothing to be said in favor of an argument that
the state ought to impose a sexual orientation test on all pregnant women in
order to ensure straight children as a national policy goal. It is not obvious that
the state has a moral justification for enforcing an orthodoxy in sexual orientation any more than it does an orthodoxy in religion or the other domains in
which people differ. On the contrary, there may be important moral and political reasons for the state to protect diversity in sexual orientation. Foremost
among them is the basic intuition that one should resist unwarranted extensions of state influence in the domain of personal life, absent a compelling
rationale for doing so. Second, it can be argued that positive benefits follow
from diversity of sexual orientation in society. Richard Pillard put the matter
this way when he said that sexual orientation research will contribute to seeing
"that gay people will have a vital place in society; our orientation is in some
way favorably selected. Societies without gay people may not thrive as well as
those with gay people."[20] Whether gay people have been instrumental in the
survival of kinship groups is a matter related to the adequacy of sociobiological accounts of the origins of homoeroticism, some of which have been mentioned in chapter 3, and I will not revisit them here except to say that there
remains considerable work to be done before one accepts this view as well documented in an empirical sense.

Another sense in which it is better that there are gay people in a society does
not depend on arguments about the emergence and reproductive adaptation of
the species but on the moral qualities that typify a society and the moral life of
its members. I will stipulate here that a society is better off having gay people
insofar as that society seems better equipped to appreciate the moral importance of tolerance, sexual diversity, social diversity, and political restraint than
one without gay people.[21] My primary intuition that this view is correct rests on
the assumption that societies without gay people do not have the same opportunities for moral learning and growth as those in which there are gay people.
Whatever their instrumental value may be in the overall reproductive march of
the species, in a moral sense gay people are the occasion of lessons otherwise
unlearned. Differences in sexual orientation are thus as important as differences

in gender and race in learning what it is to be human and what duties a society has to its people. Diversity in sexual orientation is an occasion of lessons about the differences that occur in human beings, about the way in which societies have conscious and unconscious impulses toward conformity, and about the ways in which it is possible to achieve fulfillment in personal and social life. If this view is correct, there is a prima facie reason to have the state remove itself from trying to define a state sexual orientation or at least from trying to institute measures that would prevent the existence of gay people through some kind of universal testing and treatment policy.

There is a corollary to the discovery of a "gay gene," or whatever determinant might predispose people to being gay, that often remains underappreciated in discussions about the future of gay people. If the determinants of homoeroticism were to be discovered, they could just as easily be selected for as against. John Money put the matter rather extravagantly when he said society could use knowledge about the determinants of sexual orientation "to mass-produce homosexuality in a world not only overpopulated by breeding couples, but also in need of a new generation of creators of civilization like Leonardo and Michelangelo."[22] It is hard to imagine how society could be shifted from its current opinions about gay people and persuaded of the desirability of such a goal, but Money is in any case correct. Should social currents of opinion shift radically about the value of homoeroticism, the emergence of prenatal techniques offering control over sexual orientation would permit parents generally to select gay children. Given the choice, some parents might want to have a gay child for the same sorts of reasons that they want a mix of children in other ways, by sex, for example. Though it is uncertain with what frequency parents would make decisions in favor of gay children, it does not follow that prenatal interventions need always work to the detriment of gay people.[23]

It could be objected, of course, that while some parents might use prenatal techniques to select for gay children and while some adults might use therapies to enter into gay or lesbian sexual orientations, the prevailing use of these interventions will have the effect of diminishing—not increasing—the total number of gay people. As I have mentioned, however, the diminishment of a group is not prima facie evidence of unjust treatment. The diminishment of a group is unjust only if immoral practices are the root cause of the diminishment. I would be reluctant, therefore, to argue that people should be restricted in the use of prenatal diagnostics or therapies unless their use fundamentally damaged the interests of gay people in a way that only restrictions on these interventions could halt that damage. Before formulating policy decisions along these lines, it would be essential to determine whether gay people are damaged in that relevant way or whether their well-being might not be sustained in other ways. I want, therefore, to consider whether there are cultural forces that might help sustain the gay community despite the availability of prenatal interventions and therapies for sexual orientation.

Sociological Determinants   Historian John D'Emilio has argued that the most important factor in the social emergence of lesbians and gay men is not biology but economic sociology. By contrast to historical circumstances that confined erotic desire to gender roles compatible with patriarchal familial units, contemporary society is organized in such a way that economic and social independence permit both men and women to explore a wide variety of erotic interests and to embrace gay and lesbian identities.[24] If this argument is right, the economic trends of the nation—and the world at large for that matter so long as capitalistic values prevail—nourish increasing independence from a nuclear family grounded in patriarchal and heterosexist norms. These trends predict homoerotic interest and exploration in the future even if that interest is not always expressed in lesbian and gay identities as we now know them. Some support for such a view was found in one sex behavior study that determined people from large cities were more likely to be homosexual than people who were raised in suburbs, towns, or the countryside.[25] The researchers offer no causal account of this phenomenon, but one can reasonably speculate that urban life offers more economic, social, and therefore erotic freedom than is to be found in rural life. Because it is easier to be gay in these sorts of environments, these environments have more gay people in them.

Certainly the urbanization of social life has been essential for the emergence of gay identities in the contemporary sense. As historian George Chauncey has shown, the availability of affordable housing for single people was a key element in the emergence of gay communities in the sense we know them today.[26] In her history of lesbian life Lillian Faderman has shown how women in the last century sometimes adapted their homoerotic interests to the conventions of romantic friendship common to the day but that social changes, the effects of World War II most notably, brought about independent urban life that permitted the flourishing of lesbian lives properly speaking.[27] Historians Elizabeth Lapovsky Kennedy and Madeline D. Davis have likewise described how urbanization and the movement of women from the domestic sphere into the public realm also afforded women opportunities for the construction of lesbian identities and community.[28] For both men and women growing opportunities for leisure in commercial establishments such as bars and other public venues offered more opportunities for socializing in ways that affirmed notions of gay identity and community. There is more work to be done in investigating how particular social contexts influence social patterns of erotic interests and identities, but the point to be observed is that forms of social organization and economic independence play a hand in the emergence of gay people, which is to say in the way homoerotic interests are pursued and socially deployed. Whether patterns of increased social and economic independence could offset the effects of therapies and prenatal interventions designed to reduce homoeroticism is an empirical matter. There might very well be, though, counterweights in the trends of society that would increase the total number of people exploring homoerotic interests and assuming gay identities—or would at least keep the number of gay people from falling significantly even if sexual orientation therapies and prenatal interventions were used in some quarters.

D'Emilio has also observed that gay and lesbian advocacy groups have typically formed in response to particular social oppressions.[29] Widespread antigay uses of therapy and prenatal interventions—or the perception of their use as antigay—might similarly provoke the formation of advocacy groups that took as their task educating the public about factual errors in widely held views of homoeroticism and the heterosexist assumptions driving therapy and reproductive interventions. Advocacy groups could, for example, educate prospective parents that most gay people *do not* regret their sexual orientation and *would not want* a magic pill that would modify their sexual orientation to heterosexual. Such efforts might well reduce the number of parents using prenatal interventions, thereby stabilizing the total number of gay men and lesbians. These sorts of educational efforts would not, obviously, dissuade all parents from wanting and using prenatal interventions for sexual orientation. Nevertheless, gay advocacy groups would stand as one social barrier to a merely impulsive and unreflected use of prenatal sexual orientation interventions.

John Money contends that a culture that is generally fearful and repressive of sexuality is all the more so in regard to the sexual interests of children, with results exactly counterproductive to its intentions of discouraging homoeroticism. He suggests that harsh and repressive responses to sexuality, especially in childhood sexual exploration and play, may direct children away from heteroeroticism. Money believes that sexophobic cultures systematically deprive children of heteroerotic rehearsal play, that is, playful growth into heteroerotic interests. Not only that, but when sex play of children is discovered it is often "extravagantly punished and humiliated."[30] If heteroerotic interests are quashed, children will seek sexual exploration and gratification elsewhere in the less controllable—because less acknowledged—domain of homoeroticism. Same-sex play is often easier for children to achieve than different-sex play given that the same educational and social institutions that routinely segregate boys and girls to prevent sexual play simultaneously foster situations where homoerotic sex play may occur easily: shared sleeping facilities, shower rooms, field trips, camping, segregated youth groups, and so on. Thus, Money concludes, "Clandestinely and unspoken, one of the presuppositions of our society is that, before and apart from marriage, homosexual encounters are preferable to heterosexual, because they are sterile."[31] If male children are punished for sexual interest in females, for example, but are bedded down with their male friends and thrown in the shower with naked schoolmates, it will be little surprising if some of them begin to explore sexuality with their accessible friends and schoolmates rather than with the forbidden and less accessible females.

Money acknowledges the insufficiency of evidence to draw unequivocal conclusions about the relation between sexual orientation and cultural forces, but he does in general think that sexual science shows that the emergence of exclusive homoeroticism is an artifact of culture. He says that the "ethnographic evidence on record indicates that in societies where boy-girl sexual rehearsal play is not punished or prevented, adult homosexuality is absent or rare. Boy-boy or girl-girl sexual rehearsal play, where it is by custom not illicit, does not lead to homosexuality in adulthood, although it may lead to bisexual adaptability."[32] If a general thesis along these lines is true, to so assume for the sake of the argument, sexophobic attitudes and values might ironically contribute to the emergence of more lesbians and gay men even as they put the values of heteroeroticism on constant parade.[33] Again, this particular thesis deserves study and assessment as to what role the quashing of childhood sexual interest plays in the emergence of nonheteroerotic interests, but whatever the particulars of this kind of study, it is important to bear in mind that it cannot be biology *simpliciter* that decides the erotic interests of any given individual or population. Consequently, the number of people with homoerotic interests will not be entirely amenable to prenatal manipulations, and the very heterosexism that drives interest in prenatal interventions might also undercut their value by contributing to the emergence of gay people elsewhere.

That heterosexist practices may contribute to the continued existence of gay people has also been observed by Dean Hamer, who has pointed out that if homoerotic sexual orientation is governed by genetic factors a society that restricts gay identities may force people into straight relationships by default, thereby *increasing* the number of children born to gay people, assuming those people bear more children than they would have had they entered exclusively gay relationships. If that happened, the prevalence of genes for gay interests in a population would remain stable over time rather than decrease. Societies that forbid and discourage gay relations could, ironically, be contributing to the perpetuation of any genes that underlie homoeroticism.[34] If this contention is correct, a society that permitted, even fostered, same-sex relationships might reduce the total number of gay people in the future, assuming that gay couples have fewer biologically related children of their own than do male-and-female couples. Thus should the truly antigay take up common cause with advocates of gay marriage! In any case, the point to be observed here is that there may be social influences on the emergence of homoeroticism that prenatal interventions could not by themselves entirely thwart.

As I have been arguing all along, there is no reason to think that the pathway to erotic interests is the same for all people or that there is a single factor that will prove decisive. Because the incidence and prevalence of sexual orientations will be tied to a number of biological and social factors acting in tandem, it is unlikely that one kind of obstacle, prenatal or otherwise, would prevent the emergence of gay people when there are countervailing sociological forces encouraging people to explore and commit to homoerotic identities. It does not follow, therefore, that the mere existence of therapies and prenatal interventions for sexual orientation will wipe out gay people on the planet. By the same token, though, the prospect of diminishing numbers of gay people is alarum enough to examine the importance of gay people to society and to debate what, if any, social obligations there are to protect gay people in numbers sufficient to make community possible in meaningful ways and to sustain the benefit of gay people to society at large. In the next section I therefore consider what obligations society has to protect gay people from falling numbers and whether those obligations would justify interventions of some kind to counteract any diminishments brought about by the use of techniques for the control of sexual orientation.

SOCIAL OBLIGATIONS TO GAY PEOPLE

The case for free use of sexual orientation therapies and prenatal interventions rests primarily on respect for individual autonomy, an autonomy respected at the core of Western moral philosophy and law. While respect for autonomy goes a long way in ethics, and in protecting the interests of gay people in particular, it is by no means the only consideration relevant to an assessment of the ethics of sexual orientation therapy and interventions. The question must also be asked whether the emergence of sexual orientation therapies and prenatal interventions would create indirect social harms that would justify limiting the availability of sexual orientation controls or, perhaps, even restricting sexual orientation research. My view is that sexual orientation interventions do not appear to be in a position to produce objectionable social harms so grave as to justify their restriction. This is not to say that these interventions would leave gay people untouched in number or that social hostility toward gay people will dissipate as mechanisms of erotic development are elucidated. It is to say that sexual orientation interventions do not of themselves imply necessary social harm that could only be avoided by forbidding those interventions or the science behind them.

To make this case I will assume for the sake of the argument that the total number of gay people *will* fall as the result of uses of sexual orientation interventions including therapy and prenatal diagnostics. There is no compelling reason to choose one figure over another, but in order to countenance a serious challenge to gay people I will assume that the total number of gay people will fall by approximately one-third within one generation after the development of effective therapies and prenatal interventions. A precipitous drop of this kind would be a damaging blow to any minority. Would this turn of events, though, constitute a moral harm the magnitude of which leaves only the option of shutting down sexual orientation research or forbidding sexual orientation tests, therapies, and prenatal interventions? The answer depends on what the loss of approximately a third the current number of gay people would mean for society.

For people with views inimical to homoeroticism, it almost goes without saying, this sort of decline would not only be no loss, it would be interpreted as an important moral gain for society, albeit one achieved through medicine rather than moral reformation, and there are serious questions to be asked about the legitimacy of trying to achieve moral reform via biomedical engineering. Nevertheless, were there a loss of gay people in numbers this large there would be a strong political opinion that no social damage had occurred, making the imposition of any legal restrictions on sexual orientation interventions a politically daunting prospect. I want to argue the point further, though, from a moral point of view.

Apart from the contentious if politically potent belief that a society is better off the fewer gay people it has, do gay people confer on society some benefit that would be lost as their numbers diminished?[35] I have already argued above that there is a valuable moral benefit that gay people confer on the society in which they live. Even so, it is hard to know exactly how to identify and quantify the social benefits contributed by gay people qua gay people, because the social contributions gay people make are diverse given the breadth of a population that numbers in the millions and that includes all ages, genders, races, ethnicities, and social strata. For all that variability, it is a widely held view that gay men as a class possess superior artistic and creative capacities, just as attributions of superior physical skills are made to lesbians as a class. Attributions of this sort are difficult to assess. Are gay men really more creative than straight men or do social roles permit gay men to pursue creative activities in ways not available to straight people?[36] Or is it that gay men are visible to the public largely through the creative arts (as against corporate responsibilities or educational roles) and therefore stereotyped as artistic? Are lesbians really more adept at the sorts of jobs ordinarily held by men or are they simply more visible to the public that way? If the attribution of creativity is in some way correct, and the total number of gay men fell by one third, society could as a matter of course expect to suffer diminishment in its total creative and artistic powers. If the attribution of lesbians' capacities in doing "men's work" is correct, and the total number of lesbians fell by one third, society could expect to find fewer women to fill jobs favored by lesbians.

While these losses might be felt sharply by individual artistic and work communities, it is unclear that these losses would justify abrogating the rights of adults to make decisions about conducting sexual orientation research or using sexual orientation therapies and prenatal interventions. In the first instance it should be noted that these losses might be offset by social adaptation. The vacuum of opportunity created by the diminution of one group's disproportionate presence in the creative arts might well lure others into the fold, i.e., into a vacuum of opportunity. Perhaps the loss of lesbian employees could be accommodated simply by restructuring jobs in ways that made them more accessible to people, straight women and men alike, who would not have otherwise pursued them. Society can absorb an almost infinite variety in the people it folds into its communities and shared goals, if only it wants to, and it is unclear that any particular minority is necessary for its continued survival and/or flourishing. It is unclear that there is any social institution so fragile that it could not survive the loss of even a third of its gay citizens, as the AIDS epidemic has made poignantly clear with the wide swath it has cut through the aspects of society supported and sustained by gay people. This remark should not be construed at all to mean that AIDS has not been socially damaging, for it clearly has been devastating. By making this observation I mean to note merely that society is polymorphously diverse, and it adjusts all the time to changing demographics. It is therefore hard to make the case that society, in losing a third of its gay men and lesbians and their direct social contributions as gay people, would face a loss so socially catastrophic that restricting the autonomous pursuit of sexual orientation science or sexual orientation interventions would be justified.

I have said above that coming to grips with diversity in sexual orientation can help in the appreciation of tolerance and social diversity, all of which functions as a spur to moral growth. Diversity in sexual orientation goes right to the heart of important questions about the relationship between erotic interests, sexual identity, gender identity, and social identity. It appears to me that the existence of gay people does offer a unique and unparalleled opportunity for moral growth that would not be easily replicated by reference to some other social or sexual minority. By the same token, it is unclear exactly how many gay people are necessary in order to frame these questions so that they can prove the important occasions of learning that they are. Certainly, more gay people would be better than fewer, but, again, the question to be asked is whether the loss of a certain percentage of gay people would be sufficient reason to constrain the choices of adults in regard to the science they would pursue or the therapies they used. This seems a hard argument to make, especially when some gay people will continue to exist no matter the existence of therapies and prenatal interventions.

It almost goes without saying that diminished numbers would in fact pose great challenges for gay people themselves, especially those related to the prospects for community and political advocacy. Diminished numbers overall could lead to unhappier lives since, as a vanishing minority, gay men and lesbians might be even less capable of defending themselves against violence and discrimination, as individuals and as communities. For all the good work of present lesbian and gay advocacy groups, discrimination and suspicion of gay people continues unchallenged in many quarters. Those advocacy groups, moreover, often depend on but a tiny fraction of the total number of gay people in order to do their work. The relevant moral question is whether an increasingly difficulty advocacy on behalf of gay people constitutes a sufficient reason to bar sexual orientation research and therapies or prenatal interventions. I think it does not so long as the mechanisms of democratic society remain available to gay people and so long as educational efforts remain possible to urge people not to use sexual orientation interventions. If adults do not want homoerotic interests, and parents do not want gay children, it is hard to see why the political needs of gay people in the future should override these fundamental and autonomous interests even if their use slows—but does not make impossible—political progress for gay people.

In the main we are not obliged to deliver a specific kind of future to generations that follow; we do not seem, by extension, obliged to guarantee certain patterns of sexual orientation in future generations. It is certainly wise to prepare a future free of toxic environments and the threat of nuclear war, and I want to make perfectly clear that I think a world liberated from heterosexism very much belongs to the vision of what a better world looks like. It nevertheless does not follow that men and women who do not yet exist have the right to impose on people who *do* exist the duty to prepare exactly that future. It may be wise and generous to prepare a particular kind of world for future generations, just as it is important to reverence certain aspects of past generations, but it seems impossible to owe anything to people who do not and may never exist. Neither is it owed to people who no longer exist the duty of continuing forever the social forms they set in place. Insofar as future generations have little authority in regard to the kind of world they receive, about the kinds of people they will be, restrictions on the use of sexual orientation controls will not be justified by an argument that the people of the future have a right to expect the same distribution of sexual orientations that exists now, to the same number of gay and straight people.

Worries about widespread use of sexual orientation controls may be ampli-fied by the apparent lack of any social requirement of social justice to ensure that there be any lesbians or gay men at all, in the present or the future. It is indeed unclear that justice requires that there be a specific number of gay men, lesbians, or even any total amount of homoeroticism in a particular society. To the extent that sexual orientations are distributed more or less randomly across a population, it does not seem that anyone could identify a quota of the popu-lation that ought to be lesbian or gay as a matter of social moral duty. To use philosopher John Rawls's methodology, it is hard to imagine that in the formu-lation of the ethical principles that should govern an ideal society people would unanimously consent to establishing quotas according to sexual orientation.[37] This is not to say that questions of justice cannot be raised with respect to the distribution of social duties and benefits according to sexual orientation within a particular society,[38] but it is to say that it is unclear how moral philosophy might define and defend standards governing the overall incidence and preva-lence of sexual orientations within a particular population or society. Because moral philosophy is unable to offer a convincing account of why a particular percentage of the population ought to be gay or lesbian, it does not seem that any social injustice is necessarily committed by diminishing (or increasing) the numbers of gay men and lesbians, if that diminishment occurs through prac-tices that are morally defensible as matters of autonomous choice and so long as those practices do not impinge on the rights of gay people who do now exist.

Let me extend this argument through the use of a comparison. Members of a religious faith might find it discouraging to behold a future in which there would be fewer and fewer believers all the time, perhaps even beholding the extinction of the faith and its attendant culture altogether, but that loss—com-ing as it does through the exercise of choice—would not by itself create a duty on the part of society to maintain a thriving community in that faith. If people give up a faith by moving to other religious views, society loses any benefits that faith may have conferred in terms of altruism or social stability. It is unclear, however, that these losses constitute a reason why society has an *obligation* to prevent the loss of those religious communities by imposing obstacles to, for example, learning about alternative religious beliefs by adults or by requiring that parents raise children in certain religious beliefs alone. If the diminishment of a particular faith were due to objectionable social practices, such as system-atic suppression of the faith, a moral injunction should be raised against those acts of suppression, but the issue at stake here is not the total number of people in the faith properly speaking but wrongful social acts. The same issues are involved in regard to considerations of sexual orientation. If people walk away from a social orientation for reasons of their own and not for reasons of wrongful interference by society, there is no inherent injustice in the diminution of that sexual orientation, or at least none that requires the imposition of barriers to the ways in which people might control their own erotic interests and those of their children.

A society may act, of course, to salvage any particular group or endangered species it wishes to maintain, from crustaceans to avians to cetacean mammals.[39] If, for supererogatory reasons, a society wished to sustain gay people against diminished numbers, it might well try to do so, so long as its efforts were not incompatible with its other duties and obligations. If society found, for example, that important values in tolerance and appreciation of diversity were being undercut by falling numbers of gay people, it might take some measures to shore up those numbers. Unless one takes a strictly libertarian view that the state should not concern itself with the kinds of children being born, there is nothing objectionable about the state offering inducements favorable to gay people. One might even argue, too, that insofar as the heterosexism of its own past helped create the diminishment of gay people, society owes a positive obligation now to sustain gay communities. For example, the state might offer tuition waivers or high tax deductions for gay children. Employers might offer incentives to gay people who come out at work. Affirmative action programs might make it attractive to affirm gay identities. It would be an empirical matter whether or not these sorts of inducements had the effect of sustaining a desired number of gay people, but society could do any and all of these things to make it easier for people to choose to forgo the use of sexual orientation therapy for themselves and sexual orientation interventions with their children. It *could* do these things to foster the emergence of more gay people, but it is hard to see that it *must* do so as a matter of moral duty unless the continued existence of gay people in their present numbers were vital to some essential social goal that could not be otherwise achieved.

I should immediately add that political reaction to the pro-gay proposals I have just described here would likely be as swift as it would be fatal. If simple antidiscriminatory measures designed to protect gay people from capricious treatment in employment and housing are rhetorically characterized by their opponents as creating "special rights," one could imagine how poorly state-sponsored efforts to *increase* the number of gay people would fare. If homo-erotic art sponsored by the National Endowment for the Arts has no political constituency to save it from legislative wrath, it is hard to imagine that a broad political constituency would coalesce behind the state-sponsorship of gay people themselves. I raise this point not because I mistake the politically possible as an argument against the morally desirable but merely to suggest that state-sponsored efforts to protect gay people from vanishing might prove counterproductive, as opposed to educational efforts that help people understand that gay and lesbian lives can be full and rewarding in their own right. Educational efforts that diminished the number of people seeking sexual orientation therapy and control over the sexual orientation of their children, it seems to me, are much more favorable in the long run to the interests of gay people than would be any state policies that foment resentment and hostility toward gay people by closing down avenues of scientific research, closing off rights of access to sexual orientation controls, or even trying to increase the number of gay people by artificially created inducements.

This entire discussion of sexual orientation interventions has thus far presupposed their investigation and use in a vigorously democratic society. Perhaps the question of the moral legitimacy of sexual orientation controls would find a different reception in societies under dictatorships or other authoritarian forms of rule. One might question the wisdom of sexual orientation research in a society governed by a dictator or military cabal hostile as a matter of principle to gay people. This question is hardly as pressing as it might appear. As it is, powerful dictatorships make tests and treatments for homoeroticism relatively redundant, at least on any grand scale: these authoritarian regimes can simply forbid the public expression of offensive views and behaviors. Were they sufficiently powerful at forbidding public expression of homoerotic interests, these governments would pretty much already have what they wanted: no publicly visible homoeroticism. They would by extension have little need to subject all pregnant women to diagnostic tests and prenatal interventions in order to eliminate public expressions of gay culture. Finely reticulated networks of informants also endanger private homoerotic behaviors even if they cannot extinguish homoeroticism altogether. A suppressed gay culture fosters the atmosphere of fear, secrecy, and blackmail on which authoritarian rule thrives. In authoritarian states de facto and de jure barriers to "offensive" sexual acts, public associations, and free speech would provide such a state with all the barriers to public manifestations of homoeroticism it would usually need. Such a state might nevertheless wish to ensure the heteroeroticism of all its citizens through some widespread testing program, but it is hard to see what would be gained by such an expensive operation if in fact no public accommodation tolerated any open expression of homoeroticism. The testing program would be wastefully redundant.

A very wealthy and very paranoid authoritarian state might wish, despite what I have just said, to use prenatal diagnostics on all pregnant women, but unless it also has a mechanism for compulsory treatment and/or abortion of fetuses under the suspicion of homoeroticism, it will continue to have gay people. It is easy to imagine that a state might want to test certain public officials to be sure they are free from the offending trait of homoeroticism, but the state might find itself mightily embarrassed if the ruling family or key military and government officials were found to be gay by such an examination. A dictatorship might also find itself embarrassed if much larger percentages of its people had homoerotic traits than anticipated, thus causing—to their way of thinking—a national scandal. Unless the authoritarian state is prepared to submit to scandal and has some means of dealing with the people and offspring it decides are gay, it is unclear that it has a strong interest in widespread testing.

Authoritarian states could always use sexual orientation tests and treatments not en masse but in selective instances, subjecting those identified as gay to highly prejudicial treatment. It might subject, for example, those convicted of sexual crimes to involuntary sexual orientation therapy. Would such uses of a sexual orientation test in politically repressive societies justify a moratorium on sexual orientation research?[40] Accepting the rationale that the moral acceptability of biogenetic research into sexual orientation depends on its effect on citizens in repressive societies leads one into quandaries of moral consistency. The question "What does scientific investigation augur for oppressed (and possibly further oppressible) members of dictatorial societies and other authoritarian regimes?" is one that can be put to all research, not just sexual orientation research. In order to be consistent one would have to subject all developments in engineering, communication, and computational science to an assessment of whether and how they might be used in authoritarian societies, for there is nothing consequentially dangerous in sexual orientation science that might not also emerge from advances in other research domains. For example, research in phototechnology and electronic eavesdropping might even be more important as instruments of statist dominion of gay people than a sexual orientation marker, because of the opportunities they open for spying on citizens. The development of sophisticated computer systems and weapons are even more obvious examples of research that might serve oppressive regimes by affording more control over citizens and destabilizing entire geographical regions of the world.

The United States and other nations do observe bans on the export of certain technologies to various nations around the globe, and they should continue to do so, but these bans do not forbid research in any particular domain at home. If autocratic governments use sexual orientation research and its resultant technologies in order to discriminate against lesbians and gay men, those kinds of prejudicial uses ought to be condemned and resisted on ethical grounds as violations of human rights rather than seeing them as necessary extensions of research itself. Objections to the wrongful treatment of citizens should be met with the sorts of economic sanctions that this nation routinely imposes on countries around the world. This model of distinguishing between research and its dissemination could be deployed in regard to sexual orientation science if it proved that authoritarian and heterosexist regimes were interested in, for example, some ill-advised plan to screen all their citizens for a gay gene and use test results to implement grossly inhumane policies against gay people. The real question to be settled before one could make the determination that sexual orientation technology should not be exported is not simply its imaginable uses but a realistic assessment of whether it poses the same kind or degree of evil that justifies bans on exports of weapons and computational technology. This is to say that the solution to the problems of gay people under an authoritarian regime is far more complex than could be remedied by simply halting sexual orientation research.

In making all the arguments in this section, I do not want to appear insensitive to the fate of gay people in the present or the future. In fact, I do think it is important that there be gay people now and in the future and that gay people exist in numbers sufficient to produce communities capable of self-protection, advocacy, and cultural development. As I do not know, however, what number of gay people must exist for these conditions to be met, I would not want to restrict adults' rights to use therapies and interventions for sexual orientation. Neither does it seem to me that the social obligations society has to gay people can be met by imposing a moratorium on sexual orientation research. In regard to measuring the morally relevant consequences of diminishing numbers of gay people, I think the default should be set this way: unless there are demonstrated harms to gay people of a magnitude that impinge on meaningful prospects for self-protection, advocacy, and community, adults should be free to use therapies and prenatal interventions to select against unwanted erotic interests in themselves and their children and to research matters of sexual orientation. Those who would wish to restrict the use of therapies and prenatal interventions bear, it seems to me, the burden of proving that gay people are protectable only through limitations on sexual orientation research and interventions as against what I consider the front line of defense: full civic and legal equality for gay people.

Despite acknowledging the suspicions gay people have of contemporary society and offering a threshold for justifying limitations on the use of sexual orientation therapies and technologies, it may yet seem extraordinarily naive and optimistic of me to say that the future of gay people need not be abject simply because there are fewer gay people. Does it not just seem plain that it would be bad all around if there were fewer gay people? For all the ease with which images of a deplorable future may be conjured, I believe it is the social and legal climate of the future that will be decisive in regard to the fate of gay people, not their total numbers. Having large numbers of gay people does not guarantee that an effective political base will necessarily emerge. Most gay people in the United States—the country that is the largest exporter of gay culture around the globe—do not join or support political action groups financially let alone support them with their direct involvement in demonstrations, lobbying, volunteer work, and so on. The efficacy of political action does not depend, therefore, on the absolute number of gay people that are in a society. Neither do gay advocates have to be gay. Some of the greatest advocates of gay people have been straight judges ruling in cases that have broad social significance. The U.S. Supreme Court judges who ruled in 1996 against Colorado's statutory ban on antidiscrimination laws did far more for the social future of gay people than the average patron of the average gay bar. It is also to be remembered that some of the most liberal laws in regard to gay people occur in countries where the total number of gay people is Lilliputian by comparison to the absolute number of gay people in the United States. The social accommodation of gay people in, for example, the Netherlands and Denmark has occurred all out of proportion to the number of gay advocates available to press the cause forward in those nations. As is sometimes the case in moral development, it is not masses of people that are necessary to change a political landscape so much as ideas acting quietly but as inevitably as leaven. For this reason the fate of gay people cannot be predicted by merely forecasting a census of their numbers.

It is a commonplace that culture attributes to science far-reaching powers of transformation, witnessed by our ever increasing dependence on mechanical, communication, engineering, biomedical, and computational technology. The expectation that science cannot but transform society carries over to the expectation that science will extend its dominion over people in ways hardly yet imaginable. Contemplating the future of genetics, theologian Paul Ramsey worried more than a technologically remote quarter of a century ago that there would "come a time when there will be none like us to come after us."[41] He was concerned about the future of the human species as we know it, but the refrain also bespeaks the fears of gay people as they contemplate a biomedical science abundantly more powerful than that imagined even by Ramsey. Simultaneous with growing powers of science, there is a moral consensus emerging that people should be respected in their autonomous choices about the use of those powers, including having the political right to choose the traits of their children, to the extent this choice is possible and so long as there are no manifest harms from doing so.[42] Does the confluence of these social and moral trends foredoom gay people? For the reasons I have urged above, it need not.

What is most important to the future of gay people is that social policy recognizes them as the civic equals of all others both in regard to their rights and duties,[43] at a minimum ensuring that gay people do not suffer from wrongful discrimination in the law, politics, education, medicine, and even religion. The future of gay people depends less on biomedical science than on whether the state has mechanisms for protecting them from ill-founded discrimination and whether society values gay people in its day-to-day practices, whether society wants to have gay people in its future. It would be dismal to see people flocking to therapists to rid themselves of homoerotic desires or to see parents using prenatal diagnostics and possibly abortion to select against gay children. These trends would be dismal because most of the reasons for making these choices are morally unfounded even if they should be respected as a matter of political right. The future of gay people depends not only on theoretical civic equality but on adults choosing to live as gay and on parents accepting the notion that a gay child is very much a "perfect" child. The future of gay people depends, that is, on people making choices that are not informed by false, prejudicial, and invidious conclusions about the value of homoeroticism and lesbian and gay lives.

Some progress toward that goal can be achieved simply by the presence of gay people in the research community.[44] Had the authors of the reports on the INAH3, the Xq28 chromosomal region, and dermatoglyphic studies been named Bieber, Socarides, or Nicolosi, there would be reason to worry about the motives driving their labors. For this reason it is significant that many of the researchers of sexual orientation science are themselves gay people who do not see their findings as undermining the value of a gay sexual orientation. Simply, though, because some of the most prominent sexual orientation researchers identify themselves as gay does not mean that *their* views of the meaning of homoeroticism or the value they attribute to their research will prevail as that research is disseminated to every reach of society having an interest in sexual orientation. Whoever elucidates the developmental mechanisms of sexual orientation, therefore, the social question will remain the same: whether the science will be used to the ill or gain of gay people.

It is exactly because of the ways in which causal accounts of sexuality can be misused that the case for the social equality of gay people is made all the more urgent, for if under the systems of law, medicine, and education there were no stratification of worth by sexual orientation, then the effects of a sexual orientation science brought to completion would be moot, the question of invidious effects dissolved outright. We do not need to wait for sexual orientation science to complete its tasks before confronting heterosexist inequalities of the present. The legal and social protection of gay men and lesbians in the present will offer more protection in the future than any attempts in the present to curtail biogenetic study of sexual orientation or attempts to impose restrictive bans on sexual orientation therapy, prenatal diagnostics, and prenatal interventions.

At the very least, the future of gay people will depend on the rights of adults to protect themselves from unwanted diagnostic tests and treatments, protection from prejudicial uses of biomedical tests, and the freedom to seek judicial and political remedy from social injustice. So long as these liberties prevail, there will continue to be people with homoerotic interests whether they are open about them or not. Whether gay people survive and flourish openly will depend on whether there are individuals willing to work against the heteronormative grain of history and culture and on whether there are social institutions whose dedicated purpose is the well-being of gay people. Political advocacy groups will be the mainstay of such institutions, but the emergence of gay families will be equally important, not because gay parents will recruit their children into homoeroticism but because gay families are one way to dissipate heterosexism across generations, to prepare a future more accommodating to gay people, whether the children in these families are gay or straight. Thus do political and legal efforts to secure equal rights for gay people assume an importance as questions of social justice not only in a time in which we are largely ignorant of the causal determinants of sexual orientation but also for the time in which we might be able to identify and manipulate some of those determinants. Granted the same social liberties accorded everyone else and having a place under the umbrella of social institutions interested in their survival and well-being, there will always be gay people no matter how far scientific explanation and control eventually reach.

||||||||||||||||||||||||||||||||||||||||||||||||||||||||||||||||||||||||||||||||

EPILOGUE

Barring almost unimaginable shifts in religion, politics, and science, people will continue to be interested in the determinants of homoeroticism, if not sexual orientation more generally. The nature and origins of erotic desire will remain of interest to moralists and theologians wondering about the relation between biological explanations, moral accountability, and the standing of gay people in society. Researchers looking at a general theory of human development will have an abiding interest in sexual orientation research, as they try to account for the broad array of human erotic interests. Those who think there is something psychologically wrong with homoeroticism will look to its causes in order to fix it. The market for sexual orientation research is bullish.

There are many ways in which sexual orientation research can go wrong, but there is nothing inherently unscientific in asking how people come to have the entrenched patterns of erotic interest they have. Sexual orientation science has ranged before it a host of legitimate questions. What determinants—accidents of circumstance and conscious choice among them—produce the habituated erotic interests that a person has at any given time? How do these take shape developmentally in any given culture? How do prevailing gender roles inform individual psychosexual development? How do erotic interests come to be distributed as they are across a given population? Why does homoeroticism predominate in some people but appear only transiently in others, while being altogether absent in others yet? How do children survive environments hostile to homoeroticism with same-sex interests fully intact? How and to what extent are social prohibitions against homoeroticism implicated in producing the very behavior they ostensibly proscribe? How amenable to change are habituated erotic interests? Can they be modified through a pioneering sense of erotic adventure or only through psychological or biomedical treatment? Or are adult erotic interests so deeply habituated that they are beyond substantive modification? All these questions can be formulated in ways that can be tested, even if difficultly so, and even if the course of investigation produces as many failures as advances.

These kinds of questions mark out a domain of research that is not inherently ideological or reductionist, research that is not necessarily captive to morally tendentious judgments about homoeroticism. Well-posed questions can pay due attention to the influences of culture and family on psychosexual development while also attending to the role of accident and choice. Far from being a narrow line of inquiry, sexual orientation science has before it a robust agenda. On an agenda that is not narrowly and tendentiously focused homoeroticism will be but one component of the study of human erotic interests and their interplay with moral theory, social institutions, and the political order. Homoeroticism will be, to be sure, an important item for investigation, if only because it has prominence in the sexual sky, but in the totality of questions that one may ask about human sexual life it is not a privileged question and should not be treated as such.

To make this foregoing point more clearly, let me note that other psychobehavioral traits may be studied by asking similar questions. There is nothing inherently unscientific, for example, in asking why some people have profound antipathies toward erotic interests different from their own. Why is it that some people can easily welcome the existence of people with homoerotic interests while others deploy hostility toward any suggestion of homoeroticism in others or themselves? Do antigay feelings emerge from fear of one's latent homoerotic interests, as some have suggested, or from some other aspect of psychological and moral development?[1] In an age of advanced psychosexual science, people worried about their antigay feelings might seek treatment, just as treatment is sought for any number of unwanted somatic traits. Sexual orientation research would rightly encompass this kind of project as well.

We are creatures easily fascinated by what is novel, odd, and unusual. Whether homoeroticism is novel, odd, or unusual in the species or not, it is certainly that in a cultural sense, so much so that it will continue to be questioned in regard to its determinants. A research agenda focussed on the determinants of homoeroticism will remain troubling because of many features of contemporary culture, features that are inimical to gay people and even to those people with transient and merely exploratory homoerotic interests and behaviors. Although, in industrialized democracies, certain social adversities against gay people are less pronounced than they might have been even one or two generations ago, antigay discrimination, intolerance, hostility, and indifference are nevertheless prevalent at all social strata and are important reminders about the lack of value accorded to homoeroticism in its own right and to gay people as a social class. In the greatest part of the world still today, discrimination against people because they are gay is perfectly legal and socially acceptable. Not only that, but social institutions routinely presuppose that people are straight and that there will be gay people only sometimes, accidentally, and in ways that require no modification of underlying social assumptions. Thus do legal and medical institutions, for example, routinely fail to provide mechanisms for the accommodation of gay relationships—treating gay people as fundamentally incidental and well outside the realm of cognizable professional and social obligation. Not only do existing social institutions routinely disregard homo-erotic interest and identities, there is hardly a social institution that prepares the way for gay people, that values them in all the ways straight people are valued. It is exactly this daunting array of antigay forces that spurs worry about sexual orientation research. This worry says as much about *current* failures in the social treatment of gay people as about expectations of the future. If there were no hostility toward homoeroticism at the present time, it is hard to think why people would imagine the future more hostile toward gay people simply because sexual orientation research got closer and closer to the determinants of erotic interests. Until proven otherwise, sexual orientation research seems therefore under the suspicion that its purposes are not substantively different from those of a prevailing order that has not found an equitable place for gay people in its midst.

A more subtle worry is that discrimination, intolerance, hostility, and indifference toward gay people may be disappearing from overt policies and public discourse only to reemerge functionally intact in private decisions and discourse protected from public scrutiny and criticism. Though greatly tamed in U.S. public policies and rhetoric, a great deal of racism, for example, has not so much vanished as gone underground and taken less obvious forms in decisions about where to live, where to send one's children to school, with whom to socialize, what kinds of jobs to pursue, and so on. These decisions often preserve deep veins of racism. For all the public successes of gay advocacy, it may be that like racism before it antigay sentiment will continue to exerts its influence even where it is apparently absent. Will sexual orientation science extend possibilities of invisible and uncontrollable heterosexism by abetting, for example, decisions about the employment of gay people or controlling the erotic interests of children? Will it permit socially invisible patterns of heteronormativity to prevail in place of the overt policies that are increasingly hard to defend? Even a vigorous pro-gay public policy could not protect against

226

antigay sentiments and heterosexism diffused beyond its reach in the domain of the private.

Certainly there are many reasons to ask whether sexual orientation research will serve as the bridge between an antigay past and the future. In the past a sexual orientation science brought to completion on the scale imagined by contemporary researchers would have proved a boon to those interested in the eradication of "homosexuals." Nazi S.S. Reichsfuhrer Heinrich Himmler, for example, believed with a passion that "the homosexuals must be entirely eliminated."[2] Given the genocidal campaigns of the Nazis, any biological techniques available for the identification and prevention of gay people might have been attractive to them, if sufficient resources were worth deploying in that regard over and above the power the Nazi state already had over gay people. We need not, though, imagine a Nazi revisitation to appreciate how biological markers and theories of psychosexual development might work against the interests of gay people. Visions of a world in which there will be no gay people may be found in virtually every developed country, in every decade, and in every social quarter. To choose just one example from U.S. history, psychiatrist Karl Menninger took the opportunity in a 1963 preface to an American edition of the *Wolfenden Report* to undercut the value of that British proposal to liberalize the criminal treatment of homosexuality. For the record, Menninger repeated ritual statements of homosexual abnormality, saying it ranks high in the kingdom of evils, ruins the lives of millions, and breaks the hearts of millions more. In the face of psychiatry's inability to cure this affliction, he muses rhetorically how the world might benefit if only science assumed its full responsibilities for the tragedy of homosexuality and produced the necessary treatment.[3] In so saying, one of the most preeminent psychiatrists of his time envisaged a world and future altogether devoid of gay people if only biomedicine rose to the challenge. This blithe and easy vision of a future rid of gay people has echoes enough in the rhetoric used by prominent religious and political groups today, even if these groups no longer always use the language of pathology to animate that vision.

Barring almost unimaginable shifts in human psychology, sexual science, and society, there is no reason to believe that there will cease to be men and women with homoerotic interests. There will continue to be, that is, some analogue of gay identity in the future, regardless of whether that identity is socially closeted in nature, fully incorporated into society at every level, or something else. Even the most aggressive "search and destroy" program using prenatal diagnostics and interventions would reach only a portion of the world's population and would not obstruct all the mechanisms by which people come to have homoerotic interests and behaviors. Sexual orientation therapies would remain unwanted by the vast majority of gay and lesbian adults. Questions of the just social treatment of gay people must remain, therefore, very much on the moral agenda. We are long since past the time in which medical professionals or moralists can reflexively invoke the vision of a future with no gay people in it.

Nevertheless, the rhetoric of contemporary science invokes the image of unlimited control over the most elemental units of biological causality, a rhetoric that raises questions about manipulation and control of a vast range of human traits. Biologist and codiscoverer of the structure of DNA James D. Watson characterized the ambitions of the Human Genome Project this way: "A more important set of instruction books will never be found by human beings. When finally interpreted, the genetic messages encoded within our DNA molecules will provide the ultimate answers to the chemical underpinnings of human existence."[4] Despite the fact that the majesty and benefits of the Human Genome Project are typically couched in the language of improved health and freedom from disease, which seems all to the good, it was inevitable that the project would raise questions about eugenic purposes and applications, about implications for privacy, social control, and biological manipulation.[5] If society as a whole rightly has abiding worries about the impact of the Human Genome Project, minorities such as gay people will be especially worried by efforts to uncover genetic determinants of human traits. The rhetoric of science is pungently ripe when it comes to auguring the future powers that will be handed to ordinary citizens.

It is to be noted that some of the most atrocious applications of sexual orientation science took place not in global backwaters but in the world's most advanced cultures, advanced not only in science and the arts but also—according to their own lights and rhetoric—in morality as well. The mistreatment of gay people deserves lengthy chapters in British, German, and United States history, cultures that loom large in any history of human accomplishment. Is it fair to expect that the same Constitution that held sway in the United States during periods of the involuntary treatment of gay people to "cure" their homoeroticism will in the future protect gay people from the harms that might ensue an ever more powerful sexual science? This is a difficult question to answer, but there are several reasons to be somewhat optimistic that society will not fall victim to antigay atavism. First of all, there now exist gay advocacy groups that, although limited in political clout, are nevertheless instruments of social correction. Because of the evolution of culture in general and of gay culture in particular, gay people are also now less willing to be complicit in their own mistreatment. Second, a burgeoning historical appreciation of the mistreatment of entire classes of persons offers cautionary tales for our own times, even if it is sometimes difficult to recognize oppression in and of the present. To be sure, a heightened appreciation of sufferings in the past may not translate easily into an appreciation of suffering in the present, especially when one's status may be threatened by any shift in the social order of things, but attention to the mis-treatment of women, Jews, and even gay people can be an educational vehicle by which to sensitize the present to its own ills. Thus armed with moral tales, the world can try to choose less oppressive social policies.

I fully acknowledge that there are reasons to be cautious about the social standing of gay people in the future. To put it another way, I believe there is need for vigilance about the uses of sexual orientation science. The burden of this vigilance will most likely fall to gay people and their allies. In most instances the prime movers for the protection of gay people have been gay people themselves. Historically speaking, gay rights has not been the kind of cause that has ener-gized politicians, social reformers, medical practitioners, or the judiciary—sometimes not even the most radically revisionist among them. One of the few major efforts to protect gay people that went forward in the United States with-out significant lobbying by or input from gay people involved the Model Penal Code recommendations that were drawn up by the American Law Institute. These recommendations were predicated on the decriminalization of most con-sensual sexual acts between adults and therefore made no mention of sodomy.[6] When Illinois became the first state to adopt these recommendations in 1960, it did so despite the fact that there were no gay political rights organizations in existence in the state at the time, and the 1969 New York Stonewall riots that are frequently taken as the starting date of the contemporary gay rights movement were still almost a decade away.[7] Most other policy shifts favorable to gay peo-ple, though, have required considerable lobbying efforts by gay people, and pro-tection from any malicious uses of sexual orientation science will require dili-gence from that quarter again. The 1996 Supreme Court decision in Romer v. Evans hardly seems conceivable without thirty years of public gay advocacy behind it. Failing the emergence of a utopian state, gay people and all people subject to sexual orientation science can and ought to seek the protection of informed consent policies and adequate privacy and confidentiality standards. In this sense the courts and everyone with an interest in protecting people from undue social intrusion, ill-treatment, and prejudicial classification can be an ally of gay people.

I believe that researchers who conduct research with implications for the the-ory of sexual orientation have a duty to attend to the use of their science. At the very least, this duty takes the form of ensuring that their reports are as accurate and "hard" as possible. Unfortunately, publication of one's research in a scientific journal does not ensure that the best data have been selected, that the best repre-sentation of data has been made, that the best research questions have been asked. As I have said earlier in this book, we are probably better off at this stage of his-tory without yet another tentative, ill-supported, potentially false report about the determinants of sexual orientation. For this reason researchers should be more ambitious in the quality of their science even as they are more modest in interpreting what that science means for the standing of gay people in society. Interpreting biological data as evidence of the "naturalness" of homoeroticism, for example, only confuses the issue and the public as well. In the long run ensuring a bigger subject population will probably be more useful to sexual orientation research than a researcher appearing on a television talk show to "spin" the social meaning of his or her data. That said, researchers should be mindful of the context in which their research will be received. They should ask themselves, for example, who will benefit from their research and whether—if people stand to be harmed—their research is important enough to move forward given any oppression it could invigorate.

Even though I think that visions of genocidal campaigns against gay people are far-fetched, I do continue to worry that sexual orientation science will be ill used in specific instances. There are enough historical precedents to know that we should be suspicious of attempts to formulate scientific explanations of why one group differs from another, especially when those attempts are imbued with moral judgments about the comparative worth of those groups. For example, it is reasonable to believe that the attempt to differentiate between homosexual and heterosexual grew in the conceptual ground of trying to differentiate male and female, an enterprise that was itself used in defense of the social standing of men and women. Anne Fausto-Sterling has rightly argued that the presumptive "biological" differences between male and female are often artifacts of the projection of value-laden social expectations onto biological reality.[8] This same kind of projection has too often been the rule in documenting alleged differences between gay and straight people. The search for biological differences has therefore often amounted, both in regard to gender and sexual orientation, to an investigation of social stereotypes, which is to mistake social appearance for biological or psychological reality.

Yet for all its susceptibility to error, science need not be an instrument of oppression if it differentiates empirical fact from cultural fantasy. Science can debunk false claims about sexual orientation even if it is science that offers these false claims in the first place. This process of conjecture and refutation can go forward even if science does not ultimately achieve a veridically true characterization of the world. Moral philosophy is the most developed and sophisticated method for the clarification and assessment in matters of value. As sexual science moves forward, it is the task of science to be its own most demanding critic, just as it is the task of moral philosophy to examine the values connected with science and its social uses even if it does not either achieve a veridical window on moral truth. Both science and moral philosophy should proceed with the highest order of intellectual diligence in order to stave off any prejudicial use of research.

Some commentary on sexual orientation research makes it appear that ethics must control what is otherwise a scientific effort running amok. That science and ethics come into conflict—or appear to be in conflict—about matters of sexual orientation is worrisome because both science and ethics have a common ancestry and common interests as guides to rational action; they have their roots in capacities all human beings share.[9] The question now before us is whether science and ethics can be brought together in a way that emphasizes the commonality of their origins rather than their differences. Can science and ethics work in shared awareness of their mutual concerns and thereby achieve consensus about the purpose and uses of sexual orientation research? When Friedrich Nietzsche chose *Gay Science* as the title of his reflections on culture and morality, he did so in order to contrast a spirit of robust and adventurous inquiry to the oppressive and limiting conventions he found prevalent in science and scholarly inquiry of the day.[10] The entrenched contemporary use of the word *gay* to describe various homoerotic identities and political causes is founded on a remarkably similar self-conscious opposition to oppressive conventions and values, in this case, those conventions and values that hold homoeroticism to be pathological, criminal, and sinful.[11] Gay ethics has built on a rejection of heteronormative values and gone on to criticize formalistic, rigid, and inhumane social principles. It may be that science and ethics can join forces in their opposition to unfounded beliefs whether those beliefs occur in regard to the origins of erotic interests or the value of gay people to society. If so, this conjunction would go a long way toward showing that the study of erotic desire can be not only a human activity but a profoundly humane activity as well.

||||||||||||||||||||||||||||||||||||||||||||||||||||||||||||||||||||||||||||||||||||||||||||||||||

NOTES

INTRODUCTION

1. In that account three primordial sexes, each with two conjoined human bodies, were halved by an angry Zeus when they tried to scale the heavens. Desolate, lonesome "males" sought out their separated male halves, halved "females" sought one another, and, following the split of "hermaphrodites," male halves sought reunion with their separated female halves. Making erotic orientation a heritable feature of human nature, this mythical account explains erotic couplings as the search for a lost half: "When we are longing for and following after that primeval wholeness, we say we are in love." Plato, *Symposium*, 189c–193d, in Edith Hamilton and Huntington Cairns, eds., *The Collected Dialogues of Plato* (Princeton: Princeton University Press, 1961), pp. 526–574, 542–545. Certain commentators read the creation of Adam and Eve in a similar way. See Marie Delcourt, *Hermaphrodite: Myths and Rites of the Bisexual Figure in Classical Antiquity* (London: Studio, 1961), p. 74. David M. Halperin has objected to an interpretation of the *Symposium* as involving "homosexuality," asserting that the concept of homosexuality should not be applied before the era in which it emerged. This point may be granted, though the account is nevertheless and in any interpretation an account of homoeroticism. See *One Hundred Years of Homosexuality and Other Essays on Greek Love* (New York: Routledge, 1990).

2. For one account of such differences, see Aaron J. Rosanoff, "Human Sexuality, Normal and Abnormal, from a Psychiatric Standpoint," *Urologic and Cutaneous Review* 1929(33):523–530.

3. William H. Masters and Virginia E. Johnson say that in twenty years in their sex clinic they saw only two men who sought conversion to homoeroticism and that the motive had to do with impotence in opposite-sex relations. Masters and Johnson, *Homosexuality in Perspective* (Boston: Little, Brown, 1979), p. 408. Frederick Suppe has described one young man who felt trapped in his heterosexuality and who wanted to "become a homosexual" because he thought it would offer more opportunities for sex. See "The Diagnostic and Statistical Manual of the American Psychiatric Association:

Classifying Sexual Disorder," in Earl E. Shelp, ed., *Sexuality and Medicine* (Dordrecht: D. Reidel, 1987), 2:133n7.

4. William A. Henry III, "Born Gay?" *Time*, July 26, 1993, pp. 36–39.

5. Henry, "Born Gay?"

6. It would remain, of course, a separate question on this account whether that blamelessness would also extend to homoerotic *behavior*, since moral analysis rightly distinguishes between involuntary inclination and willful behavior. See discussions by Michael Ruse, *Homosexuality: A Philosophical Inquiry*, pp. 176–202 (Oxford: Basil Blackwell, 1988).

7. Simon LeVay, *Queer Science: The Use and Abuse of Research Into Homosexuality* (Cambridge: MIT Press, 1996).

8. Dorothy Nelkin and Laurence Tancredi, *Dangerous Diagnostics: The Social Power of Biological Information* (New York: Basic, 1988), p. ix.

9. This statement was made by Dean Hamer, as quoted in Chris Bull, "Drawing the Line," *Advocate*, April 5, 1994, pp. 27–28. Whether it will be possible to control genetic information in this way is far from clear at this point. The question of patentability of genetic profiles will depend on a number of technical questions, including the novelty of the technique in question and the utility of the product. It may be that the techniques used to identify gene sequences may not meet these tests or that same information may be obtainable using other techniques. For a discussion of gene patenting, see Timothy F. Murphy, "Ethical Aspects of the Human Genome Project," in Peter Singer and Helga Kuhse, eds., *A Companion to Bioethics* (Oxford: Basil Blackwell, in press).

1. SCIENTIFIC ACCOUNTS OF SEXUAL ORIENTATION

1. Many bisexual people identify themselves according to their erotic interests at a given moment: as gay or straight. Sometimes men who have sex with men and women who have sex with men nevertheless describe themselves as straight or lesbian respectively. Without wishing to dispute the political legitimacy of identifications like these, I mean the term *bisexual* to describe people who exhibit at any point across a lifetime erotic interest in male *and* females, however these people describe themselves at a given moment.

2. As to the cross-cultural occurrence of homoeroticism, see Clellan S. Ford and Frank A. Beach, *Patterns of Sexual Behavior* (New York: Harper and Row, 1951); and Frederick L. Whitam and Robin M. Mathy, *Male Homosexuality in Four Societies: Brazil, Guatemala, the Philippines, and the United States* (New York: Praeger, 1986).

3. The Kinsey report advised that "it would encourage clearer thinking on these matters if persons were not characterized as heterosexual or homosexual, but as individuals who have had certain amounts of heterosexual experience and certain amounts of homosexual experience. Instead of using these terms as substantives they may better be used to describe the nature of the overt sexual relations, or of the stimuli to which an individually erotically responds." Alfred C. Kinsey, Wardell B. Pomeroy, Clyde E. Martin, *Sexual Behavior in the Human Male* (Philadelphia: Saunders, 1948), p. 671. See also Gilbert Herdt, *Third Sex, Third Gender* (New York: Zone, 1994), p. 2.

4. See the discussions in, for example, LeVay, *Queer Science*, pp. 41–55; and Chandler Burr, *A Separate Creation: The Search for the Biological Origins of Sexual Orientation* (New York: Hyperion, 1996), pp. 163–181.

5. In fact, serious sex research does not try to count "homosexuals" or "heterosexuals" as if those were mutually exclusive categories. Most serious research studies sexual practices and perhaps self-applied labels and, in light of that data, usually offers some assessments about how people divide functionally into gay, straight, and bisexual groups. These categories have permeable boundaries. See, for example, Edward O. Laumann, John H. Gagnon, Robert T. Michael, and Stuart Michaels, *The Social Organization of Sexuality: Sexual Practices in the United States* (Chicago: University of Chicago Press, 1994).

6. This is, I take it, the position of David M. Halperin. See *One Hundred Years of Homosexuality*, especially pp. 27–29, 41–53.

7. Someone looking to review the breadth of research from the 1950s onward, would do well to begin with D. Michael Quinn's long listing of titles in *Same-Sex Dynamics Among Nineteenth-Century Americans: A Mormon Example* (Urbana: University of Illinois Press, 1996), pp. 18–22n8.

8. Richard C. Pillard and J. Michael Bailey, "A Biological Perspective on Sexual Orientation," *Psychiatric Clinics of North America* (1995), 18:71–84.

9. For further discussion on the implications of sexual orientation for psychological and behavioral study, see John P. DeCecco, "Definition and Meaning of Sexual Orientation," in Noretta Koertge, ed., *Philosophy and Homosexuality* (New York: Harrington Park, 1985), pp. 51–67.

10. Frederick Suppe, "What Causes Homosexuality? And Who Cares Anyhow?" in Timothy F. Murphy, ed., *Gay Ethics: Controversies in Outing, Civil Rights, and Sexual Science* (New York: Haworth, 1994), pp. 223–268.

11. Some researchers think that erotic interests do divide neatly into sex-specific types. See for example, the discussions offered by Burr, *A Separate Creation*, p. 243–247.

12. Claudia Card, *Lesbian Choices* (New York: Columbia University Press, 1994), pp. 47–57.

13. Edward Stein, "Introduction," in Edward Stein, ed., *Forms of Desire: Sexual Orientation and the Social Constructionist Controversy* (New York: Routledge, 1992), p. 4n5.

14. I do grant that there may be a political utility in deploying one term rather than another. Some political causes may succeed more readily if they advance under the banner of *sexual preference* (which language vitiates the connections of homoeroticism and pathology) or under the banner of sexual orientation (which language reads erotic interests into the protections afforded involuntary traits).

15. Sigmund Freud, *Three Essays on the Theory of Sexuality*, in James Strachey, ed., *The Standard Edition of the Complete Psychological Works of Sigmund Freud* (London: Hogarth, 1953), 7:138. Though he made the particular remark here almost as a digression to a discussion about the origins of homoeroticism, Freud's theoretical account of psychosexual development would require an account of how *any* person moved from a functionally bisexual libidinal capacity to his or her specific sexual orientation.

16. Adrienne Rich, "Compulsory Heterosexuality and Lesbian Existence," *Signs* (1980), 5:631–660. See also the discussion by Quinn, *Same-Sex Dynamics Among Nineteenth-Century Americans*, pp. 16–18n17.

17. John Money, *Gay, Straight, and In-Between: The Sexology of Erotic Orientation* (New York: Oxford, 1988), pp. 4–5.

18. For a useful discussion of social constructionism, see Stein, *Forms of Desire*, especially Edward Stein, "Conclusion: The Essentials of Constructionism and the Construction of Essentialism," pp. 325–353.

19. Consider the case of the Sambia, described by Gilbert Herdt in *Guardians of the Flutes: Idioms of Masculinity* (Chicago: University of Chicago Press, 1994). It appears that because of Christian and other Western influences, homoerotic *practices* are disappearing among the Sambia. It would be interesting to know to what extent homoerotic *interest* is also disappearing among the Sambia.

20. Richard D. Mohr, *Gay Ideas: Outing and Other Controversies* (Boston: Beacon, 1992), pp. 221 ff.

21. Halperin, *One Hundred Years of Homosexuality*, p. 28n.

22. Mohr, *Gay Ideas*, p. 235. Mohr also says rightly that "claims that same-sex relations are embedded in varying forms of social life cut not a whit against the realist" (p. 235).

23. Some social constructionists do deny the existence of sexual orientations as natural kinds, while others do not. The best discussion of these matters is to be found in Stein, "Conclusion," pp. 325–353.

24. Halperin, *One Hundred Years of Homosexuality*, p. 49.

25. Such are the questions asked by sociobiology. While sociobiological accounts have been criticized, and fairly so, those criticisms do not seem to me to raise insurmountable obstacles as to why questions of this kind could not be formulated and adequately answered if evidence were available to do so. Whether that evidence exists at present is extremely doubtful. See Ruse, *Homosexuality*, pp. 130–149.

26. One line of research, for example, that I do not take up in detail here concerns birth order and the number of male siblings in a family. It has been suggested that late birth order increases the likelihood of a homoerotic sexual orientation in males. See for example, Ray Blanchard and Kenneth J. Zucker, "Reanalysis of Bell, Weinberg, and Hammersmith's Data on Birth Order, Sibling Sex Ratio, and Parental Age in Homosexual Men," *American Journal of Psychiatry* (1994), 151:1375–1376, and Ray Blanchard and Anthony Bogaert, "Homosexuality in Men and Number of Older Brothers," *American Journal of Psychiatry* (1996), 153:27–31. The results in these studies are probabilistic and no specific causal mechanism is offered to account for sexual orientation differences according to paternal age, birth order, or number of previously born male siblings, though several conjectures are raised.

27. Simon LeVay, "A Difference in Hypothalamic Structure Between Heterosexual and Homosexual Men," *Science* (1991), 253:1034–1037.

28. Simon LeVay, *The Sexual Brain* (Cambridge: MIT Press, 1993); LeVay, *Queer Science*. Some of the questions that were raised in media reports about his original research findings are the questions that will be taken up in the following chapters: is sexual orientation research inimical to gay people or will it somehow advance the cause of gay rights? LeVay casts his lot with the latter interpretation. See also David Nimmons, "Sex and the Brain," *Discover*, March 1994, pp. 64–71.

29. Interview with Diane Sawyer, *Prime Time*, ABC, December 1991. See also LeVay, *The Sexual Brain*, pp. xiii–xiv.

30. See LeVay, *Queer Science*, pp. 83–95.

31. LeVay does not say in his article how he determined the sexual orientation of his subjects. My guess is that in at least some instances he determined sexual orientation from medical records on the basis of whether or not homosexuality was indicated as a risk factor for HIV infection. As lesbianism is not identified as a risk factor for any cause of death in medical records, it would be understandable why he claims that no identifiable lesbians were available for the study.

32. LeVay has nevertheless not categorically ruled out the possibility that there could be some AIDS-related effect on INAH sizes. See LeVay, *The Sexual Brain*, pp. 120–123.

33. LeVay acknowledges that the study may be limited to the extent that it deals only with postmortem tissue. See LeVay, *The Sexual Brain*, p. 44, 122.

34. Ibid., p. 122.

35. Ibid.

36. For example, because of the way in which some men are at pains to conceal their homoerotic interests and behaviors, they might well extend their efforts to their medical records. If so, some of the heterosexual men in the sample might well have had homoerotic lives, the information in their medical records notwithstanding.

37. Nimmons, "Sex and the Brain." See also LeVay, *Queer Science*, pp. 129–147.

38. Nimmons, "Sex and the Brain."

39. I should note that in his *Queer Science* LeVay seems more attentive to the issue of defining eroticism by categories or continuum. See pp. 42–52.

40. Burr, *A Separate Creation*, pp. 43–44.

41. Ibid., pp. 69; 37–41. LeVay says Byne now accepts the existence of INAH. See *Queer Science*, pp. 146, 321*n*47.

42. Ruth Hubbard and Elijah Wald, *Exploding the Gene Myth* (Boston: Beacon, 1993) p. 95.

43. Ibid., pp. 93 ff.

44. Ibid., p. 104.

45. See J. Michael Bailey and Richard C. Pillard, "A Genetic Study of Male Sexual Orientation," *Archives of General Psychiatry* (1991), 48:1089–96; and J. Michael Bailey, Michael C. Neale, and Yvonne Agyei, "Heritable Factors Influence Sexual Orientation in Women," *Archives of General Psychiatry* (1993), 50:217–223.

46. Twins have always held fascination for sexual orientation researchers. For discussions about the meaning of twins for theories of genetic involvement in sexual orientation see Pillard and Bailey, "A Biological Perspective on Sexual Orientation," and J. D. Haynes, "A Critique of the Possibility of Genetic Inheritance of Homosexual Orientation," *Journal of Homosexuality* (1995), 28:91–113.

47. Dean H. Hamer, Stella Hu, Victoria Magnuson, Nan Hu, Angela M. L. Pattatucci, "A Linkage Between DNA Markers on the X Chromosome and Male Sexual Orientation," *Science* (1993), 261:321–327. See also Robert Pool, "Evidence for Homosexuality Gene," *Science* (1993), 261:291–292. For media accounts of this study see Natalie Angier, "Report Suggests Homosexuality Is Linked to Genes," *New York Times*, July 16, 1993, pp. A1, C18; and Jerry E. Bishop, "Research Points Toward a 'Gay' Gene," *Wall Street Journal*, July 16, 1993, pp. B1, B4.

48. But see Angela M. L. Pattatucci and Dean H. Hamer, "Development and Familiality of Sexual Orientation in Females," *Behavioral Genetics* (1995), 25:407–420. This study of 358 women (heterosexual, homosexual, and bisexual) did not yield adequate data to distinguish clear genetic or environmental patterns in the distribution of female sexual orientation.

49. Dean Hamer and Peter Copeland, *The Science of Desire: The Search for the Gay Gene and the Biology of Behavior* (New York: Simon and Schuster, 1994).

50. Small sample size remains a problem with a number of studies of sexual orientation. See John Gallagher, "Getting Small," *Advocate*, December 27, 1994, pp. 26–27.

51. Ruth Hubbard, "The Search for Sexual Identity: False Genetic Markers," *New York Times,* August 2, 1993, p. A11. A similar point was made by Anne Fausto-Sterling and Evan Balaban in a letter to *Science.* See "Genetics and Male Sexual Orientation," *Science* (1993), 261(5126):1259. Fausto-Sterling and Balaban note that some of the linkage analysis data in the study was estimated rather than measured directly, and they also point out that changing assumptions about the baseline rate of the occurrence of male homoeroticism would undercut the significance of some of the findings.

52. As of this writing, Hamer is under investigation by the National Institutes of Health Office of Research Integrity on matters having to do with data selection and subject recruitment. See Eliot Marshall, "NIH's 'Gay Gene' Study Questioned," *Science* (1995), 268:1841.

53. Stella Hu, Angela M.L. Pattatucci, Chavis Patterson, Lin Li, David W. Faulkner, Stacey S. Cherny, Leonid Kruglyak, Dean H. Hamer, "Linkage Between Sexual Orientation and Chromosomal Xq28 in Males But Not in Females," *Nature Genetics* (1995), 11:248–256.

54. One study did show, however, that homosexual women were more likely than heterosexual women to have homosexual sisters, which result the researchers took to suggest a cofamilality to sexual orientation. See J. M. Bailey and D. S. Benishay, "Familial Aggregation of Female Sexual Orientation," *American Journal of Psychiatry* (1995), 150:272–277.

55. David L. Wheeler, "Study Suggests X Chromosome Is Linked to Homosexuality," *Chronicle of Higher Education,* July 21, 1993, pp. A6-A7. For further analysis see William P. Byne, "The Biological Evidence Challenged, *Scientific American,* May 1994, pp. 50–55.

56. For continuing discussion of the scientific credibility Hamer's work, see "More on Genes and Homosexuality," *Science* (1995), 268:1571; and Marshall, "NIH's 'Gay Gene' Study Questioned."

57. J. A. Y. Hall and D. Kimura, "Dermatoglyphic Asymmetry and Sexual Orientation in Men," *Behavioral Neuroscience* (1994), 108:1203–1206.

58. In another study Hall and Kimura also report that gay men with a leftward asymmetry were more likely than straight men to be adextral, meaning that they less consistently favored a single hand for single-handed tasks. J. A. Y. Hall and Doreen Kimura, "Sexual Orientation and Performance on Sexually Dimorphic Motor Tasks," *Archives of Sexual Behavior* (1995), 24:395–407. Of this study the authors say it "adds evidence that sexual orientation and motor/cognitive predispositions have early biological contributions."

59. Joseph Nicolosi, *The Reparative Therapy of Male Homosexuality: A New Clinical Approach* (Northvale, N.J.: Jason Aronson, 1991).

60. Ibid., p. 132.

61. Ibid., p. 149.

62. Ibid., p. xviii. In his view not only are there inherent deficits in homoerotic desire itself, but Nicolosi sees nothing but insuperable obstacles to gay relations because these are inherently volatile, unstable, and promiscuous—which traits Nicolosi sees as the consequence of the antisocial and narcissistic character of homoerotic sexual interactions.

63. Ibid., p. 13.

64. Of men who want to be free of their homoerotic interests, Nicolosi says that psychology "chooses to devalue their struggles and to counsel them instead for what it invariably interprets to be self-hatred due to internalized homophobia." Ibid., p. xvi.

65. Nicolosi's characterization of homoeroticism is reminiscent of the litany of woes attributed to it by such therapists as Edmund Bergler and Irving Bieber and Charles Socarides before him, with a dose of David Reuben thrown in for good measure. Ostensibly interested in clinical matters, Nicolosi fails to offer any sort of empirical account of the accuracy of his views. Second, it is unclear why Nicolosi thinks the psychological professions have failed his clients when, for example, the American Psychiatric Association retains a diagnostic category that would apply to the very men whom he wants to treat: those persons suffering from an unwanted sexual orientation could properly be diagnosed with "sexual orientation distress." Given Nicolosi's characterization of homoeroticism as a whole, it cannot but follow that he wants to return to a classification of all adult male homoeroticism as disordered in a pathological sense. I assume he would make the same case in regard to female homoeroticism.

66. Ibid., p. 25–35.

67. Ibid.,, p. 34.

68. Ibid., p. 42.

69. Ibid., p. xvi.

70. See also Joseph Nicolosi, *Healing Homosexuality: Case Stories of Reparative Therapy* (Northvale, N.J.: Jason Aronson, 1993).

71. D. Michael Quinn has offered a substantial review of the issues at stake on this particular point, namely, the failure to control the studies for psychic injury of a male child at the hands of his father. See *Same-Sex Dynamics Among Nineteenth-Century Americans*, pp. 4–6, 22–23n12.

72. Irving Bieber, Harvey J. Dain, Paul R. Dince, Marvin G. Drellich, Henry G. Grand, Ralph H. Gundlach, Malvina W. Kremer, Alfred H. Rifkin, Cornelia B. Wilbur, and Tony B. Bieber, *Homosexuality: A Psychoanalytic Study* (Northvale, N.J.: Jason Aronson, 1988).

73. Nicolosi, *Reparative Therapy*, p. xvi.

74. This would certainly be a question worth asking, however, since a transcultural finding of eroticism being linked to comparative INAH3 size would offer considerable evidence that that neuron group was implicated in the development of erotic interests.

75. Freud, *Three Essays on the Theory of Sexuality*, p. 148.

76. Ibid., pp. 140–141.

77. Suppe, "What Causes Homosexuality?"

78. Richard Green, *The "Sissy Boy Syndrome" and the Development of Homosexuality* (New Haven: Yale University Press, 1987).

79. Daryl J. Bem, "Exotic Becomes Erotic: A Developmental Theory of Sexual Orientation," *Psychological Review* (1996), 103:320–335.

80. Karl Popper, *Conjectures and Refutations: The Growth of Scientific Knowledge* (New York: Harper and Row, 1968).

81. See Clarence P. Oberndorf, "Diverse Forms of Homosexuality," *Urologic and Cutaneous Review* (1929), 33:518–523.

82. In their 1993 *Science* letter (see note 51 above), Anne Fausto-Sterling and Evan Balaban have said of Dean Hamer's 1993 report that "the scientific debate about the origins of homosexuality is taking place in the midst of a highly political one about the place of gay men and lesbians in our social fabric. Given the increased frequency of hate crimes directed against homosexuals, it is fair and literal to say that lives are at stake. We applaud, therefore, the expression of concern by Hamer and colleagues for the potential use of their data in the social arena; but we believe that the responsibility of scientists to

guard against the misuse of their results goes farther than words: it ultimately must rest in decisions about how and when to publicize preliminary data of the sort produced by these linkage studies. We wonder whether it might not have been more prudent for the authors and the editors of *Science* to have waited until more of the holes in the study had been plugged (or not, as the future will tell)." If the work specified here by Fausto-Sterling and Balaban had been done by Hamer and colleagues before publication, it would have in fact produced a stronger original research report. Would it have delayed or better countered possible prejudicial uses that could follow publication of this kind of research? It is unclear just exactly what social ill effects would have been avoided had *Science* not published this admittedly preliminary and incomplete report. Certainly, no lives seem to have been lost or prejudicial policies instituted, contrary to the implications of the rhetoric employed here. Better science will not by itself stave off prejudicial uses, but better science will be of more use than incomplete science in resisting those who would use it in prejudicial ways.

83. I borrow these possibilities from Marx Wartofsky, *Conceptual Foundations of Scientific Thought: An Introduction to the Philosophy of Science* (New York: Macmillan, 1968), pp. 293 ff.

84. Money, *Gay, Straight, and In-Between*, p. 122.

85. Ibid., p. 228.

2. THE VALUE OF SEXUAL ORIENTATION RESEARCH

1. Richard von Krafft-Ebing, *Psychopathia Sexualis, with Especial Reference to the Antipathic Sexual Instinct: A Medico-Forensic Study* (New York: Stein and Day, 1965).

2. On the shift in the United States from seeing homosexuality as a moral matter to a medical matter, see George Chauncey, *Gay New York: Gender, Urban Culture, and the Making of the Gay Male World, 1890–1940* (New York: Random House, 1994), pp. 123, 231.

3. Chandler Burr has said that in the past five years researchers in three biological disciplines—neuroanatomy, endocrinology, and genetics—"have created an entirely new field of scientific inquiry." See "The Destiny of You," *Advocate*, December 26, 1995, p. 37. This claim is simply wrong, as is the claim he makes that Simon LeVay's 1991 neuroanatomical report was the first major biological investigation of sexual orientation. See Burr, *A Separate Creation*, p. 3. The lineage of inquiry into the determinants of sexual orientation is as scientifically old as the nineteenth century and as mythologically old as the dialogues of Plato. It is true that techniques never before available have now been applied to sexual orientation, but this has historically been the prevailing trend: scientific techniques have been applied to matters of sexual orientation as they have emerged. There were many "biological" investigations of sexual orientation prior to the work of LeVay.

4. American Psychiatric Association, *Diagnostic and Statistical Manual: Mental Disorders* (Washington: American Psychiatric Association, 1952).

5. American Psychiatric Association, *Diagnostic and Statistical Manual: Mental Disorders*, 2d ed. (Washington: American Psychiatric Association, 1968).

6. American Psychiatric Association, *Diagnostic and Statistical Manual: Mental Disorders*, 3d ed. [*DSM-III*] (Washington: American Psychiatric Association, 1980). The American Psychological Association followed their psychiatrist colleagues' lead when they depathologized homosexuality in 1975. See Douglas C. Haldeman, "Sexual Orientation Conversion Therapy for Gay Men and Lesbians: A Scientific Examination," in John C.

Gonsiorek and James D. Weinrich, eds., *Homosexuality: Research Implications for Public Policy* (Newbury Park, Cal.: Sage, 1991), pp. 149–160.

7. American Psychiatric Association, *Diagnostic and Statistical Manual of Mental Disorders*, 4th ed. [*DSM-IV*] (Washington, D.C.: American Psychiatric Association, 1994), p. 538.

8. Aras van Hertum, "Many Psychiatrists Still See Homosexuality as an Illness," *Washington Blade* (1994), 24(40):31.

9. See, for example, Ellie T. Sturgis and Henry E. Adams, "The Right to Treatment: Issues in the Treatment of Homosexuality," *Journal of Consulting and Clinical Psychology* (1978), 46:165–169.

10. Burr, "The Destiny of You," p. 38.

11. Bert Hansen, "American Physicians' Earliest Writings About Homosexuals, 1880–1900," *Milbank Quarterly* (1989), supplement 1, 67:92–108.

12. See the account by Evelyn Hooker in Eric Marcus, ed., *Making History: The Struggle for Gay and Lesbian Equal Rights, 1945–1990* (New York: HarperCollins, 1992), pp. 16–25.

13. George Rousseau, "Queering the Pitch: American Psychiatry and the History of Homosexuality," paper presented at the 1993 Triennial Meeting of the European Association for the History of Psychiatry, London.

14. Richard Green, *Sexual Science and the Law* (Cambridge: Harvard University Press, 1992), pp. 87–98.

15. Lynda I. A. Birke has said of biomedical researchers committed to a view of homosexuality as medically disordered that "they maintain a popular set of assumptions about gender and sexuality and thereby serve to perpetuate the view that homosexuality is sick. In this sense, they serve a specifically ideological role." See Birke, "Is Homosexuality Hormonally Determined?" in Koertge, *Philosophy and Homosexuality*, p. 47.

16. Daniel J. Kevles, *In the Name of Eugenics: Genetics and the Uses of Human Heredity* (Berkeley: University of California Press, 1985), p. 3.

17. See Bieber et al., *Homosexuality*, and Charles Socarides, *Homosexuality* (New York: Jason Aronson, 1978).

18. Quoted in Edward Stein, "The Relevance of Scientific Research About Sexual Orientation to Lesbian and Gay Rights," in Murphy, *Gay Ethics*, p. 295.

19. Jeffrey Williams, "Sedgwick Unplugged," *Minnesota Review* (1993), 40:52–64. In the course of her conversation with Williams, Eve Kosofsky Sedgwick rightly rejects the notion that homophobic and queer-eradicating forces are collapsible into the essentialist-constructionist debate. To her mind, the appropriate question to ask about homoeroticism is not about its origins but about how it is valued.

20. Leo Bersani, *Homos* (Cambridge: Harvard University Press, 1995), p. 11.

21. Michel Foucault, *History of Sexuality* (New York: Vintage, 1990), 1:98.

22. Quoted in Stein, "The Relevance of Scientific Research," p. 295.

23. Bersani, *Homos*, pp. 2–3.

24. Udo Schüklenk, "Is Research Into the Cause(s) of Homosexuality Bad for Gay People?" *Christopher Street* (1993), no. 208, pp. 13–15. This piece also appeared as "Editorial," *Bioethics News* (1993), 12:1–5.

25. Evelyn Hooker, "The Adjustment of the Male Overt Homosexual" (1957), 21:18–31; Evelyn Hooker, "Male Homosexuality in the Rorschach," (1958), 22:33–54; Evelyn Hooker, "What Is a Criterion?" (1959), 23:278–281, all in *Journal of Projective Techniques*.

26. David W. Dunlap, "Homosexual Parents Raising Children: Support for Pro and Con," *New York Times*, January 7, 1996, p. A:13.

27. For a discussion of the way in which courts sometimes set aside the clear evidence that gay parents do not jeopardize their children, see Green, *Sexual Science and the Law*, pp. 18–49. Green points out that one question at issue in such cases is poorly studied: whether and to what extent children of lesbian and gay parents suffer because of taunting peers.

28. The U.S. military itself has, from time to time, conducted examinations of the nature and degree of disruption of homosexuals in its ranks only to conclude that no systemic problems can be identified. See, for example, discussion of the Crittenden Report and the so-called PERSEREC report in Randy Shilts, *Conduct Unbecoming: Lesbians and Gays in the U.S. Military, Vietnam to the Persian Gulf* (New York: St. Martin's, 1993), pp. 281–283 and 647 ff.

29. F. D. Jones and R. J. Koshes, "Homosexuality and the Military," *American Journal of Psychiatry* (1995), 152:16–21.

30. This observation is quoted in Burr, "The Destiny of You."

31. Masters and Johnson, *Homosexuality in Perspective*.

32. Kinsey et al., *Sexual Behavior in the Human Male*, and Alfred C. Kinsey, Wardell B. Pomeroy, Clyde E. Martin, Paul H. Gebhard, *Sexual Behavior in the Human Female* (Philadelphia: Saunders, 1953), p. 475.

33. Alan P. Bell and Martin S. Weinberg, *Homosexualities: A Study of Diversity Among Men and Women* (New York: Simon and Schuster, 1978); Alan P. Bell, Martin S. Weinberg, and Sue Kiefer Hammersmith, *Sexual Preference: Its Development in Men and Women* (Bloomington: Indiana University Press, 1981).

34. Money, *Gay, Straight, and In-Between*, p. 153. See also Ruse, *Homosexuality*, pp. 19–20.

35. Green, *The "Sissy Boy" Syndrome*.

36. Frederick Suppe, "Explaining Homosexuality: Philosophical Issues and Who Cares Anyhow?" in Murphy, *Gay Ethics*, p. 261.

37. Quoted in Burr, *A Separate Creation*, p. 273.

38. To make this point is to say nothing, however, about the relative merit of such inquiry compared to other inquiry competing for both researcher interest and financial sponsorship, a point I consider more fully below.

39. See Michael Ruse, *Is Science Sexist: And Other Problems in the Biomedical Sciences* (Dordrecht: Reidel, 1981), pp. 240, 264–268.

40. Schüklenk, "Is Research Into the Cause(s) of Homosexuality Bad for Gay People?"

41. See, for example, Gerald C. Davison, "Homosexuality: The Ethical Challenge," *Journal of Consulting and Clinical Psychiatry* (1976), 44:686–696.

42. Frederick Suppe, "Curing Homosexuality," in Robert Baker and Frederick Elliston, eds., *Philosophy and Sex*, 2d ed. (Buffalo: Prometheus, 1984), pp. 391–417.

43. Robert M. Cook-Deegan, *The Gene Wars* (New York: Simon and Schuster, 1993).

44. See LeVay, *Queer Science*, pp. 195–209.

45. Arthur L. Caplan, "Handle with Care: Race, Class, and Genetics," in Timothy F. Murphy and Marc A. Lappé, eds., *Justice and the Human Genome Project* (Berkeley: University of California Press, 1994), pp. 30–45.

46. See Timothy F. Murphy, "Is AIDS a Just Punishment?" *Journal of Medical Ethics* (1988), 14:154–160. See also "Graham Sorry He Said AIDS is God's Curse," *Washington Blade*, October 22, 1993, p. 19.

47. Bowers v. Hardwick, 478 U.S. 186 (1986).

3. THE PRACTICE OF SEXUAL ORIENTATION THERAPY

1. Edward Stein and Richard Pillard, "Evidence for Queer Genes: An Interview with Richard Pillard," *GLQ* (1993), 1:98.

2. Van Hertum, "Many Psychiatrists Still See Homosexuality As an Illness." Those countries included Brazil, China, India, Egypt, Korea, and Saudi Arabia.

3. Charles Socarides, *A Freedom Too Far* (Phoenix: Adam Margrave, 1994).

4. Cal Thomas, "Do Homosexuals Have a Choice?" *Champaign-Urbana News-Gazette*, October 4, 1992, B2.

5. Hamer et al., "A Linkage Between DNA Markers on the X Chromosome and Male Sexual Orientation."

6. See Paul R. Billings, Mel A. Kohn, Margaret de Cuevas, Jonathan Beckwith, Joseph S. Alper, and Marvin R. Natowicz, "Discrimination as a Consequence of Genetic Testing," *American Journal of Human Genetics* (1992), 50:476–482.

7. See Sturgis and Adams, "The Right to Treatment: Issues in the Treatment of Homosexuality."

8. In chapter 7 I do consider questions whether the consequences of sexual orientation therapy would be relevant in making moral judgments about its use. Here I want to restrict the analysis to the nonconsequential issues implicit in an analysis focused on autonomy.

9. For a survey of techniques used to try and change sexual orientation, see Timothy F. Murphy, "Redirecting Sexual Orientation: Techniques and Justifications," *Journal of Sex Research* (1992), 29:501–523.

10. Frank Z. Warren and Walter I. Fischman, *Sexual Acupuncture* (New York: Dutton, 1978).

11. Mark F. Schwartz and William H. Masters, "The Masters and Johnson Treatment Program for Dissatisfied Homosexual Men," *American Journal of Psychiatry* (1984), 141:173–181.

12. See Frederick Suppe, "The Diagnostic and Statistical Manual of the American Psychiatry Association: Classifying Sexual Disorders," in Earl E. Shelp, ed., *Sexuality and Medicine* (Dordrecht: Reidel, 1987), 2:133n7.

13. Stephen Sansweet, *The Punishment Cure* (New York: Mason/Charter, 1975), pp. 63–81. See also Sylvère Lotringer, *Overexposed: Treating Sexual Perversion in America* (New York: Pantheon, 1988).

14. I. Oswald, "Induction of Illusory and Hallucinatory Voices with Consideration of Behaviour Therapy," *Journal of Mental Science* (1962), 108:196–212.

15. Sansweet, *The Punishment Cure*, pp. 63–80.

16. See Murphy, "Redirecting Sexual Orientation," and LeVay, *Queer Science*, pp. 67–107.

17. Graeme M. Hammond, "The Bicycle Treatment in the Treatment of Nervous Diseases," *Journal of Nervous and Mental Disease* ([1892, vol. 17] 1968), 19:36–46. Unnamed medications were also administered as part of this bicycle therapy.

18. Sansweet, *The Punishment Cure*, p. 67. See also Johan Bremer, *Asexualization: A Follow-Up Study of 244 Cases* (New York: Macmillan, 1959), p. 308. Certain deaths in the Nazi camps should also be attributed to attempts to "cure" homosexuality, though given the brutal conditions of those camps it is often hard to tell what is objectionable experimentation, what is malignant neglect, and what is murderous intent. See Richard Plant, *The Pink Triangle: The Nazi War Against Homosexuals* (New York: Holt, 1986).

19. Martin Duberman has offered a first-person account of his own experiences in therapy of this kind in *Cures: A Gay Man's Odyssey* (New York: Dutton, 1991). Some of the potential side effects have been described by A. Damien Martin, "The Emperor's New Clothes: Modern Attempts to Change Sexual Orientation," in Emery S. Hetrick and Terry S. Stein, eds., *Innovations in Psychotherapy with Homosexuals* (Washington, D.C.: American Psychiatric Press, 1984), pp. 23–57. See also C. A. Tripp, *The Homosexual Matrix* (New York: McGraw-Hill, 1975), p. 246.

20. See in this regard Newdigate M. Owensby, "Homosexuality and Lesbianism Treated with Metrazol," *Journal of Nervous and Mental Disorders* (1940), 92:65–66.

21. Joseph Cautela and Albert J. Kearney, *The Covert Conditioning Handbook* (New York: Springer, 1986).

22. J. N. Marquis, "Orgasmic Reconditioning: Changing Sexual Object Choice Through Controlling Masturbation Fantasies," *Journal of Behavior Therapy and Experimental Psychiatry* (1970), 1:263–271.

23. Schwartz and Masters, "The Masters and Johnson Treatment Program."

24. Neither should one assume that a genetic trait can only be modified by genetic therapy: some genetic traits or dispositions are amenable to dietary, behavioral, endocrinological, and other kinds of treatment.

25. Edmund Bergler, *Counterfeit-Sex: Homosexuality, Impotence, and Frigidity*, 2d ed. (New York: Grune and Stratton, 1958), p. 186.

26. Havelock Ellis and John Addington Symonds, *Sexual Inversion* (New York: Arno, 1975 [1879]).

27. British Medical Association Council, *Homosexuality and Prostitution* (London: British Medical Association, 1955), p. 43.

28. R. E. Hemphill, A. Leitch, J. R. Stuart, "A Factual Study of Male Homosexuality," *British Medical Journal* (1958), 1:1317–1322.

29. C. A. Tripp, *The Homosexual Matrix* (New York: McGraw-Hill, 1975).

30. Timothy F. Murphy, "The Ethics of Sexual Conversion Therapy," *Bioethics* (1991), 5:123–138.

31. Henry Abelove, "Freud, Male Homosexuality, and the Americans," *Dissent* (1986), 33:56–69. See also Herb Spiers and Michael Lynch, "The Gay Rights Freud," *Body Politic*, May 1977, pp. 8–10, 25.

32. Timothy F. Murphy, "Freud and Sexual Reorientation Therapy," *Journal of Homosexuality* (1992), 23:21–38. Joseph Wortis describes conversations in which Freud characterized homosexuality as pathological and as arrested development, comparing it to failure to achieve an ideal height, and discussed instances in which homoerotic fixations might be undone. See *Fragments of an Analysis with Freud* (New York: Jason Aronson, 1984), pp. 38, 53, 55–56, 93.

33. Murphy, "The Ethics of Sexual Conversion Therapy."

34. Ronald Bayer, *Homosexuality and American Psychiatry* (Princeton: Princeton University Press, 1987).

35. Ibid., p. 103. See also LeVay, *Queer Science*, pp. 92–93, 211–230.

36. For a case report of aggressively imaginative therapy, see Basil James, "A Case of Homosexuality Treated by Aversion Therapy," *British Medical Journal* (1962), 1:768–770. A forty-year-old man submitted to isolation, deprivation of food and drink, emetics, recorded sounds of vomiting, and testosterone injections. According to James, he managed not only to survive but became "in all respects a sexually normal person," and, as a surprising side effect, wrote several short stories and a full-length novel!

37. James D. Steakley has pointed out that the Nazi response to homosexuality was primarily one of prevention and extermination: *The Homosexual Emancipation Movement in Germany* (New York: Arno, 1975). This mindset did not obstruct, however, efforts at "cure." See Plant, *The Pink Triangle*; Heinz Heger, *The Men with the Pink Triangle* (Boston: Alyson, 1980); Walter Poller, *Medical Block, Buchenwald* (Secaucus, N.J.: Stuart, 1960); and George L. Mosse, *Nationalism and Sexuality: Respectability and Abnormal Sexuality in Modern Europe* (New York: Howard Fertig, 1985).

38. National Institute of Mental Health Task Force on Homosexuality, *Final Report and Background Papers* (Washington, D.C.: Department of Health, Education, and Welfare, 1972). This report did not rule out the legitimacy of sexual orientation therapy on either moral or psychological grounds.

39. See Frederick Suppe, "The Diagnostic and Statistical Manual," 2:111–135; 112–120.

40. Council on Scientific Affairs, American Medical Association, "Health Care Needs of Gay Men and Lesbians in the United States," *Journal of the American Medical Association* (1996), 275(17):1354–1359.

41. Members of one such group were profiled in Laura Blumenfeld, "On the Straight and Narrow Path," *Washington Post*, May 6, 1991, pp. C1, C12–13. There are numerous religious books to be found on the topic. See, for example, John W. Drakeford, *A Christian View of Homosexuality* (Nashville, Tenn.: Broadman, 1977).

42. Sylvia Pennington, *Ex-Gays? There Are None* (Hawthorne, Cal.: Lambda Christian Fellowship, 1989).

43. E. Mansell Pattison and Myrna L. Pattison, " 'Ex-Gays': Religiously Mediated Change in Homosexuals," *American Journal of Psychiatry* (1980), 137:1553–1562.

44. Green, *The "Sissy Boy Syndrome,"* p. x. As Schwartz and Masters note, the term *failure* is relative in meaning since some of the men who entered the program looking for conversion to heteroeroticism left the therapy confirmed in the value of their homoerotic interests. Schwartz and Masters, "The Masters and Johnson Treatment Program."

45. LeVay, *Queer Science*, pp. 260–261.

46. LeVay, "A Difference in Hypothalamic Structure Between Heterosexual and Homosexual Men."

47. LeVay, *The Sexual Brain*, p. 122.

48. Edward O. Wilson, *On Human Nature* (Cambridge: Harvard University Press, 1978), pp. 142–147. For a critical overview of sociobiological accounts, see Michael Ruse, "Are There Gay Genes? Sociobiology and Homosexuality," in Koertge, *Philosophy and Homosexuality*, pp. 5–34.

49. One of the first apparent successes occurred only in 1995. See Gina Kolata, "Scientists Claim Gene Therapy's First Success," *New York Times*, October 20, 1995, p. A13. See also Jeffrey M. Leiden, "Gene Therapy: Promise, Pitfalls, and Prognosis," *New England Journal of Medicine* (1995), 333:871–873.

50. Nicolosi, *The Reparative Therapy of Male Homosexuality*, p. xviii.

51. See Kevles, *In the Name of Eugenics*, and Sheila Faith Weiss, "The Race Hygiene Movement in Germany, 1904–1945," in Mark B. Adams, ed., *The Wellborn Science: Eugenics in Germany, France, Brazil, and Russia* (New York: Oxford University Press, 1990), pp. 8–68.

52. See, for example, Eric S. Lander and Nicolas J. Schork, "Genetic Dissection of Complex Traits," *Science* (1994), 265(5158):2037–2048.

53. See Bremer, *Asexualization*, and M. J. McCullough and M. P. Feldman, "Aversion Therapy in Management of 43 Homosexuals," *British Medical Journal* (1976), 2:594–597.

54. In his "The Psychogenesis of a Case of Homosexuality in a Woman" Freud never considers the ethics of treating a woman at her parents' request and contrary to her own judgments. Fortunately, this young woman had sufficient sangfroid to resist Freud's attempts to treat her; he subsequently dismissed her from his care. *Standard Edition*, 18:147–172.

55. Andrew Hodges, *Alan Turing: The Enigma* (New York: Simon and Schuster, 1983).

56. Tripp, *The Homosexual Matrix*.

57. See Timothy F. Murphy, "Homosex/Ethics," in Murphy, *Gay Ethics*, pp. 9–25. My argument is that most purposes of homosex are functionally equivalent to heterosex and that heterosex relationships can be just as dependent on similarity as homosex seems to be. The alleged narcissism of homosex is just as pervasive in heterosex relations, even if it is less obvious.

58. I am not saying here that no public money should ever be expended along these lines, only that other lines of research may more often than not prove more important.

59. Joseph Sartorelli, "Gay Rights and Affirmative Action," in Murphy, *Gay Ethics*, pp. 191–196.

60. Twenty-three percent of 334 WHM (white homosexual males), 23 percent of 56 BHM (black homosexual males), 18 percent of 156 WHF (white homosexual females), and 11 percent of 37 BHF (black homosexual females) said that they had consulted a professional in order to try and give up their homosexuality. Bell and Weinberg, *Homosexualities*, table 12, p. 338, and table 21.22, p. 461.

61. I assume here, of course, that the experimental treatment is safe. If undue risks or fraud attached to the therapy, the state and professions would have a compelling interest to regulate and perhaps even forbid the treatment.

62. Historian Bert Hansen describes the emergence of sexual orientation therapy in the United States as co-constructed by physicians who offered and people who sought treatment. He is surely right that a mere decree of homosexuality as pathological did not produce the effect of people seeking treatment. On the other hand, Hansen does not consider the asymmetry of power between gay people and straight people. The pursuit of therapy probably should be considered as an artifact of systemic social deprivations attaching to homoeroticism. Even if the pathological label did not by itself produce supplicants at physicians' offices, the people showing up there looking for help could still be considered coerced, making the process ultimately involuntary. See "American Physicians' Earliest Writings About Homosexuals, 1880–1900," *Milbank Quarterly* (1989), supplement 1, 67:92–108.

4. CONTROLLING THE SEXUAL ORIENTATION OF CHILDREN

1. Sigmund Freud, *Three Essays on the Theory of Sexuality*, in *Standard Edition*, 3:229–230.

2. Gunter Dörner, *Hormones and Brain Differentiation* (Amsterdam: Elsevier, 1976), p. 138.

3. LeVay, *Queer Science*, pp. 266–267.

4. Joe Dolce, "And How Big Is Yours?" *Advocate*, June 1, 1993, pp. 38–44; 40.

5. Money, *Gay, Straight, and In-Between*, pp. 9–50.

6. Bayer, *Homosexuality and American Psychiatry*.

7. Frank X. Acosta, "Etiology and Treatment of Homosexuality: A Review," *Archives of Sexual Behavior* (1975), 4:9–29.

8. Edward Stein, "Evidence for Queer Genes," pp. 104–105.

9. For example, the American Academy of Pediatrics has declared that "therapy directed specifically at changing sexual orientation is contraindicated, since it can provoke guilt and anxiety while having little or no potential for achieving changes in orientation." American Academy of Pediatrics, Committee on Adolescence, "Homosexuality and Adolescence," *Pediatrics* (1993), 92:631–634.

10. In talking about treatment and/or therapy, I do not presume that homoeroticism is pathological or that any condition need be pathological in order to be the object of biomedical research or interventions. Lacking words for interventions for traits that are nonpathological and that do not carry connotations of pathology, I use the terms *treatment* and *therapy* with the above proviso.

11. Alexander C. Rosen, George A. Rekers, Peter M. Bentler, "Ethical Issues in the Treatment of Children," *Journal of Social Issues* (1978), 34:122–136. Stephen F. Morin and Stephen J. Schultz, "The Gay Movement and the Rights of Children," *Journal of Social Issues* (1978), 34:137–148.

12. Some people who underwent therapy as adolescents have as adults started organizing resistance to this sort of therapy. See Carole Rafferty, "Homosexuality or 'Disorder'?" *Chicago Tribune*, August 1, 1995, sec. 5, pp. 1, 2.

13. This is not to say, of course, that they have no choice about the expression of those dispositions. A deterministic account of erotic interests does not by itself determine the morality of actions carried out consonant with these interests. There could well be duties in regard to the expression of one's erotic dispositions that conflict with the nature of one's erotic interests.

14. See Wilson, *On Human Nature*, pp. 142–147.

15. These factors I borrow from Helen Singer Kaplan, *The Evaluation of Sexual Disorders* (New York: Brunner/Mazel, 1983), p. 253. Other factors identified as predictors of success in sexual orientation therapy may not be in place in very young children, e.g., some evidence of heteroerotic desire and behavior and a high motivation for change.

16. I do not assume that these reports show that homoerotic interests are ever fully extinguished. The nature of these successes is often unclear. Success may have occurred for a number of reasons unrelated to the therapeutic intervention itself: the workings of the placebo effect, misidentification of original sexual orientation, psychosexual development that was occurring for reasons unrelated to therapy, the unfolding of a latent bisexuality, or the addition of new sexual skills rather than the dismantling of existing ones.

17. In the past some researchers saw the treatment of gender atypical behavior as necessary to avoid homoeroticism in adult life. See, for example, G. A. Rekers, P. M. Bentler, A. C. Rosen, O. I. Lovaas, "Child Gender Disturbances: A Clinical Rationale for Intervention," *Psychotherapy: Theory, Research, and Practice* (1977), 14:2–11.

18. Green, *The "Sissy Boy Syndrome,"* pp. 263, 292 ff., especially 295–296.

19. I say this because homoeroticism involves no inherent incapacity for relationships or happiness or achievement. I take Frederick Suppe's "Curing Homosexuality" to be convincing on these points.

20. For accounts of the ways in which society does not value the lives of gay men and lesbians—and the damaging effects of that disparity for gay people, see Joseph Sartorelli, "Gay Rights and Liberalism," paper presented at the American Philosophical Association meeting in San Francisco, April 1995; and Joseph Sartorelli, "Gay Rights and Affirmative Action," in Murphy, *Gay Ethics*, pp. 185–196.

21. Schwartz and Masters, "The Masters and Johnson Treatment Program for Dissatisfied Homosexual Men."

22. This is the method proposed by Cautela and Kearney, *The Covert Conditioning Handbook.*

23. Lawrence Crocker, "Meddling with the Sexual Orientation of Children," in Onora O'Neill, ed., *Having Children: Philosophical and Legal Reflections on Parenthood* (New York: Oxford University Press, 1979), p. 145.

24. Some parents might be exempted from this duty if the pill were beyond their economic means to provide or if they had some principled moral and/or religious reasons for refusing to us it. Otherwise, Crocker's governing assumptions seem to warrant the use of the pill he describes.

25. Crocker, "Meddling," p. 146.

26. Crocker, "Meddling," p. 149.

27. Bell and Weinberg, *Homosexualities*, pp. 124, 339.

28. Responding in the affirmative to the question "Want a Magic HT [Heterosexual] Pill Today?" were 28 percent of 569 WHM, 23 percent of 109 BHM, 16 percent of 228 WHF, and 11 percent of 89 BHF. Bell and Weinberg, *Homosexualities*, table 12, p. 339.

29. Those who said they would be somewhat or much upset if their child became homosexual were 25 percent of 570 WHM, 26 percent of 111 BHM, 33 percent of 226 WHF, and 27 percent of 64 BHF. Bell and Weinberg, *Homosexualities*, table 12, p. 339. The subjects were not asked specifically why they would feel this way.

30. Rafferty, "Homosexuality or 'Disorder'?"

31. American Psychiatric Association, *Diagnostic and Statistical Manual of Mental Disorders*, 4th ed., p. 538.

32. In fact, even before gay and lesbian efforts at parenting began in earnest to help both men and women have children through adoption, artificial insemination, and even the more elaborate mechanisms of in vitro fertilization and embryo transfer, Bell and Weinberg reported that many self-identified gay men and lesbians had children, especially if they had at one point married. See Bell and Weinberg, *Homosexualities*, pp. 164–165, 391.

33. I have elsewhere developed this point with reference to prenatal interventions governing sexual orientation. See Timothy F. Murphy, "Prenatal Interventions and Sexual Destiny," *Bioethics* (1990), 4:121–142.

34. In this category were 76 percent of 570 WHM, 73 percent of 111 BHM, 69 percent of 226 WHF, and 77 percent of 64 BHF. Bell and Weinberg, *Homosexualities*, table 12, p. 339.

35. Parthenogenesis could only produce females since males could not be produced from gametes containing only an X or Y chromosome.

36. Dolce, "And How Big Is Yours?" p. 40.

37. Nimmons, "Sex and the Brain," p. 66.

38. Measuring the INAH3 of an adult at twenty-five years of age would, of course, require permission of that adult and not merely that of his parents.

39. Congregation for the Doctrine of the Faith, *Letter to the Bishops of the Catholic Church on the Pastoral Care of Homosexual Persons* (Washington: United States Catholic Conference, 1986).

40. M. J. Buckley, *Morality and the Homosexual* (Westminster, Md.: New Press, c. 1959), p. 184.

41. The text of the Congregation for the Doctrine of the Faith, *Instruction on Respect for Human Life in Its Origin and on the Dignity of Procreation: Replies to Certain Questions of the Day*, was reprinted in the *New York Times*, March 11, 1987, pp. A14–A17.

42. Charles Larère, "Passage of the Angel Through Sodom," in P. Flood, ed., *New Problems in Medical Ethics* (Cork: Mercier, 1953), pp. 108–123.

43. See Murphy, "Reproductive Controls and Sexual Destiny," pp. 134–135.

44. Congregation for the Doctrine of the Faith, *Letter to the Bishops of the Catholic Church*, p. 9.

45. The case, Planned Parenthood v. Casey, was reported in Linda Greenhouse, "High Court, 5–4, Affirms Right But Allows Most of Pennsylvania's Limits," *New York Times*, June 30, 1992, pp. A1, A7.

46. Such is also apparently the view of clinical geneticist Philip Reilly. See Burr, *A Separate Creation*, p. 278.

47. This point has been made in regard to gender selection by Betty B. Hoskins and Helen B. Holmes, "Technology and Prenatal Femicide," in Rita Arditti, Renate Duelli Klein, and Shelley Minden, eds., *Test-Tube Women* (London: Pandora, 1984), pp. 237–255.

48. See President's Commission for the Study of Ethical Problems in Medicine and Biomedical and Behavioral Research, *Screening and Counseling for Genetic Conditions* (Washington: Government Printing Office, 1983).

49. Martin P. Golding, "Ethical Issues in Biological Engineering," in Ronald Munson, ed., *Intervention and Reflection*, 2d ed. (Belmont, Cal.: Wadsworth, 1983), pp. 402–414.

50. Jeffrey R. Botkin, "Fetal Privacy and Confidentiality," *Hastings Center Report* (1995), 25:32–39.

51. Botkin does seem to believe that the potential personhood of embryos and fetuses is sufficient to require a prima facie respect toward them in health care relationships.

52. It is unclear to me that prenatal diagnostic information should be modeled this way rather than, for example, as a matter of parental beneficence.

53. Botkin, "Fetal Privacy and Confidentiality," pp. 37–38.

54. This is not to say that the costs could be extraordinary relative to a particular family's finances. Long-term psychobehavioral treatment might well be beyond the means of many families. In making this observation, however, I do not wish to imply that I think there is any such treatment that parents should routinely be sending their children to receive. I am merely treating the question as one of finances, its psychological and moral merit bracketed for that purpose.

55. Doe v. Bolton, 410 U.S. 1973.

56. For example, the American Medical Association has adopted a number of opinions that do not prevail as matters of policy at the present time. See Council on Ethical and Judicial Affairs, American Medical Association, *Code of Medical Ethics* (Chicago: American Medical Association, 1996).

57. Botkin, "Fetal Privacy and Confidentiality," p. 35.

58. Ibid., p. 35.

59. See on this same point, LeVay, *Queer Science*, pp. 264–265.

60. Botkin, "Fetal Privacy and Confidentiality," p. 39.

61. It would make an interesting analysis to consider the morality of a "magic pill" that could ensure that a child had Catholic or Jewish beliefs. On the presumption that religious views are meaningful insofar as they are purposefully and consciously chosen, it is unclear that a magic pill for religious belief would be theologically desirable. On my analysis here, looking at the matter in terms of parental interest in moral/religious development, there would be no impediment to its use so long as a child had no interest that was compromised by being magically disposed toward one religion over all others.

62. Mary Warnock, *The Uses of Philosophy* (Oxford: Basil Blackwell, 1992), p. 82.

5. THE USE OF SEXUAL ORIENTATION TESTS

1. Allan Bérubé, *Coming Out Under Fire: The History of Gay Men and Women in World War Two* (New York: Plume, 1991).

2. Ibid., pp. 16–17.

3. This attempt at differentiation was described by William C. Menninger, who himself believed the efforts at reclaiming those who engaged in homosexuality for reasons allegedly accidental or due to some lapse of judgment largely failed. *Psychiatry in a Troubled World* (New York: Macmillan, 1948), pp. 222–231.

4. Bérubé, *Coming Out Under Fire*, pp. 153–158.

5. Lillian Faderman, *Twilight Girls and Twilight Lovers: A History of Lesbian Life in Twentieth-Century America* (New York: Penguin, 1992), p. 188.

6. Bérubé, *Coming Out Under Fire*, pp. 28 ff. See Shilts, *Conduct Unbecoming*, pp. 490 ff.

7. Bérubé, *Coming Out Under Fire*, p. 33. It is hard to see that a cost-benefit analysis could show this practice to have been economically worthwhile unless the costs of having gay people in the military were extraordinarily high. To this day it is unclear that the expenditures required to discharge gay service personnel confer a benefit equal in value to their cost. It might be less expensive and confer a benefit of equal value to the military if inappropriate sexual acts were individually disciplined rather than to have an entire class of people universally subject to surveillance and exclusion.

8. By calling the results of the surveillance negligible, I do not mean to minimize the very real and damaging consequences of those who are discharged for erotic interests allegedly incompatible with military service. The results are negligible only in the sense that the surveillance of gay people fails to deliver what is expected of it. Dana M. Britton and Christine L. Williams cite a General Accounting Office report to the effect that between 1980 and 1990 an annual average of fifteen hundred service members were discharged for homosexuality but observe that "despite this high discharge rate, these numbers are far below those that should obtain if *all* men and women who 'engage in, desire to engage in, or intend to engage in homosexual acts' were separated from the military." See " 'Don't Ask, Don't Tell, Don't Pursue': Military Policy and the Construction of Heterosexual Masculinity," *Journal of Homosexuality* (1995), 30:1–22.

9. If a service member denies homosexuality, then the military will make efforts to falsify that claim and to substantiate their own claim to the contrary. By contrast and in contradiction of the methods of truth finding, if the service member asserts his or her

homosexuality, the claim is taken at face value, and the military need not offer corroborating evidence.

10. Steffan v. Perry, 41 F. 3d 677, 689–690

11. Robert Nugent, "Homosexuality and Seminary Candidates," in Jeannine Gramick, ed., *Homosexuality in the Priesthood and the Religious Life* (New York: Crossroad, 1989), pp. 200–218.

12. Bérubé, *Coming Out Under Fire*, p. 14.

13. Havelock Ellis, *Sexual Inversion*, in *Studies in the Psychology of Sex* (New York: Random House), 1:299, part 4. Green "is very rarely the favorite color of adults of the Anglo-Saxon race, though some inquirers have found it to be more commonly a preferred color among children, especially girls, and it is more often preferred by women than by men" (p. 299). See also pp. 289–299.

14. Ibid., pp. 290–291.

15. Ibid., p. 292.

16. Brian Gladue, Richard Green, Ronald E. Hellman, "Neuroendocrine Response to Estrogen and Sexual Orientation," *Science* (1984), 225:1496–1499.

17. See Suppe, "Explaining Homosexuality," Murphy, *Gay Ethics*, pp. 229–230.

18. I make this latter point because there is only one bisexual man identified in LeVay's study. There is, therefore, no basis for characterizing the size of the INAH3 in bisexual men relative to its size in gay men or straight men.

19. Sometimes this defense goes so far as to invoke the notion of "homosexual panic," namely the condition in which some individuals are so psychologically fragile in regard to their sexual identities that their volatile response to unwanted sexual advances is the consequence of diminished capacity. Diminished culpability is the legal objective of such a defense. Courts have not generally accepted this diminished mental status argument. See Green, *Sexual Science and the Law*, pp. 246–251.

20. American Medical Association, *Code of Medical Ethics*, p. 76.

21. Some of these considerations are raised in David J. Mayo and Martin Gunderson's "Privacy and the Ethics of Outing," in Murphy, *Gay Ethics*, pp. 47–65. But see Richard D. Mohr, *Gay Ideas: Outing and Other Controversies* (Boston: Beacon, 1992), pp. 11–48.

22. This is the gloss Richard D. Mohr puts on the outing of Gerry Studds, a U.S. congressman from Massachusetts who had a sexual relation with a male congressional page. There is an asymmetry in Mohr's analysis of outing. If favorable results that follow being outed can be used as evidence to support outing, as the analysis of Studds suggests, it is unclear why evidence of prejudicial effects of outing (such as being harmed in relationships, jobs, social standing, etc.) cannot count as evidence against outing. Beneficial results of outing should not count *for* outing if detrimental results cannot count *against* it. See Mohr, *Gay Ideas*, pp. 41–43.

23. Such indeed was the proposal made in Patricia Illingworth, *AIDS and the Good Society* (London: Routledge, 1990).

24. See Joseph Sartorelli, "Gay People and Affirmative Action," in Murphy, *Gay Ethics*.

25. Male-to-female transsexuals are sometimes viewed as extending the dominion of male influence over women's lives and identities. See Janice C. Raymond, *The Transsexual Empire: The Making of the She-Male*, 2d ed. (New York: Teachers College Press, 1994).

26. Loretta M. Kopelman, "Informed Consent and Anonymous Tissue Samples: The Case of HIV Seroprevalence Studies," *Journal of Medicine and Philosophy* (1994), 19:525–552.

27. For a case along these lines see Robert L. Spitzer, Miriam Gibbon, Andrew E. Skodol, Janet B.W. Williams, Michael B. First, *DSM-III-R Casebook* (Washington, D.C.: American Psychiatric Press, 1989), pp. 349–351.

28. "Gay military personnel are among the graduates of Annapolis, West Point, and the Air Force Academy in Colorado Springs. At least one gay man has served in the astronaut program. Recent gay general-staff officers have included one Army four-star general, renowned in military circles, who served as head of one of the most crucial military missions of the 1980s. In the past decade, gay people have served as generals in every branch of the armed forces. The Marine Corps has also had at least one gay person at four-star rank since 1981, and at least one gay man has served on the Joint Chiefs of Staff in that time." Shilts, *Conduct Unbecoming*, p. 3.

29. Ibid., pp. 726–734.

30. For a discussion of the need for and general rules governing gene banking, see George Annas, "Rules for Gene Banks: Protecting Privacy in the Genetics Age," in Murphy and Lappé, *Justice and the Human Genome Project*, pp. 75–90.

31. Richard D. Mohr, "The Case Against Clinton," *Windy City Times*, November 16, 1995, p. 12.

32. Philip Shenon, "Armed Forces Still Question Homosexuals," *New York Times*, February 27, 1996, p. A1.

33. U.S. Congress, House of Representatives, Sixteenth Report by the Committee on Government Operations, *Designing Genetic Information Policy: The Need for an Independent Policy Review of the Ethical, Legal, and Social Implications of the Human Genome Project* (Washington: U.S. Government Printing Office, 1992), p. 24.

34. I am not saying that people should feel this way, only that some might. The same caution applies to the speculations that follow.

6. SEXUAL ORIENTATION RESEARCH, NATURE, AND THE LAW

1. Interview with Diane Sawyer, *Prime Time*, ABC Television, December 1991. For other examples of those who think that biological study of sexual orientation bodes ill for improving the social standing of gay people, see those cited by Aaron S. Greenberg and J. Michael Bailey, "Do Biological Explanations of Homosexuality Have Moral, Legal, or Policy Implications?" *Journal of Sex Research* (1993), 30:245–251.

2. Nimmons, "Sex and the Brain," p. 68.

3. Faderman, *Odd Girls and Twilight Lovers*, pp. 57–61.

4. See Marcus, *Making History*, p. 18.

5. Green, *Sexual Science and the Law*.

6. This is not to say that all people have the same rights in this domains. A person's rights to procreation or even to adopt children, for example, may be conditioned on marital status or sexual orientation. The rights of married couples are more constitutionally secure than those of others. See John A. Robertson, "Surrogate Mothers: Not So Novel After All," in Kenneth D. Alpern, ed., *The Ethics of Reproductive Technology* (New York: Oxford University Press, 1992), pp. 45–56.

7. Green, *Sexual Science and the Law*, pp. 50–61.

8. Bowers v. Hardwick, 478 U.S. 186 (1986).

9. For a discussion of Plato's views that homosexuality did not occur in animals, see Ruse, *Homosexuality*, pp. 178–181, 188–192.

10. LeVay, *Queer Science*, pp. 206–207.

11. Because of the cognitive component of human erotic desire in human beings, there is legitimate concern about whether and to what extent the homoeroticism of human beings is a conceptual and behavioral analogue of erotic practices of other animals, but an appreciation of differences between species should not overshadow an appreciation of commonalities either. See discussions of these matters in Kinsey et al., *Sexual Behavior in the Human Male*, pp. 612–615, and Burr, *A Separate Creation*, pp. 29–35.

12. LeVay, *Queer Science*, p. 209; Hamer and Copeland, *The Science of Desire*, pp. 14–15.

13. Greenberg and Bailey have rightly argued that there is a sense in which homoeroticism—indeed all eroticism—is biological. Unless one is prepared to defend the view that there are uncaused behaviors, biology must of necessity play a role in all behavior. Unless sexual orientation research uncovers the kind of causal mechanisms that are relevant to moral determinations of responsibility and policy, biological studies of sexual orientation are themselves morally inert. See "Do Biological Explanations of Homosexuality Have Moral, Legal, or Policy Implications?"

14. Quinn, *Same-Sex Dynamics Among Nineteenth-Century Americans*, p. 4 (references omitted).

15. Karl Heinrich Ulrichs, *The Riddle of "Manly Love,"* trans. Michael A. Lombardi-Nash (Buffalo: Prometheus, 1994), 2:603.

16. Ibid., 2:553 ff.

17. Ibid., 2:621.

18. Ibid., 2:362 ff.

19. Ibid., 2:614. Arguing in a different way, Simon LeVay has observed that the rejection of homoerotic behavior seems to be altogether absent in nonhuman species, and he therefore concludes, like Ulrichs before him, that it is homophobia rather than homoeroticism that is, if anything is, contrary to nature. Levay, *Queer Science*, p. 209.

20. Ulrichs, *The Riddle of "Manly Love,"* 2:611.

21. Ibid., 2:611.

22. This view is popular in ecclesiastical quarters and in the opinions of political candidates. Patrick J. Buchanan espoused exactly this distinction during his 1996 run for the U.S. presidency. *Meet the Press*, ABC, Feb. 11, 1996.

23. Michael Levin more or less accepts that there is a strong biological basis for homoerotic orientation, but he does not rush therefore to embrace civil rights for gay people. Far from it. He points out that even genetic traits can be objectionable if they are not adaptive in an evolutionary sense. Moreover, some discrimination against genetically based traits will still be defensible if there are good independent reasons for sustaining it. He believes a biologically based dislike of homosexuality would be exactly one such reason for sustaining antigay discrimination, as would be discrimination that used sexual orientation as a proxy marker for objectionable traits associated with gay people. See Michael Levin, "Homosexuality, Abnormality, and Civil Rights," *Public Affairs Quarterly* (1996), 10:31–48.

24. Congregation for the Doctrine of the Faith, *Letter to the Bishops of the Catholic Church*.

25. Murphy, "Homosex/Ethics," in Murphy, *Gay Ethics*, pp. 9–25.

26. Alan H. Goldman, "Plain Sex," *Philosophy and Public Affairs* (1976/77), 9:267–287.

27. For a biographical report on this felt difference, see Andrew Sullivan, *Virtually Normal: An Argument About Homosexuality* (New York: Knopf, 1995).

28. John M. Finnis, "Law, Morality, and 'Sexual Orientation,'" *Notre Dame Journal of Law, Ethics, and Public Policy* (1995), 9:11–39.

29. Ibid., p. 26.

30. Ibid., p. 30.

31. Ibid., p. 29.

32. Ibid., p. 31.

33. Nimmons, "Sex and the Brain," pp. 64–71. See also LeVay, *Queer Science*, pp. 3–4.

34. In *The DNA Mystique: The Gene as Cultural Icon* (New York: Freeman, 1995), Dorothy Nelkin and M. Susan Lindee have documented both the temptation and cultural prevalence of "genetic" explanations, especially in regard to the traits of people.

35. For a journalistic account of how genes, insofar as they function to produce proteins, might be involved in the determination of sexual orientation, see Burr, *A Separate Creation*, pp. 238–269.

36. Ruth Hubbard, "The Search for Sexual Identity: False Genetic Markers," *New York Times*, August 2, 1993, p. A11.

37. Ruth Hubbard and Elijah Wald, *Exploding the Gene Myth: How Genetic Information Is Produced and Manipulated by Scientists, Physicians, Employers, Insurance Companies, Educators, and Law Enforcers* (Boston: Beacon, 1993), p. 94.

38. Biologist Anne Fausto-Sterling has offered an analysis of gender in exactly this regard, arguing that the search for biological differentiation between men and women has reflected and reinforced prevailing—but erroneous—notions of what roles women ought to play in society. Fausto-Sterling, *Myths of Gender*.

39. As grounded in the fifth and fourteenth amendments. See William E. Nelson, *The Fourteenth Amendment: From Political Principle to Judicial Doctrine* (Cambridge: Harvard University Press, 1988).

40. Green, *Sexual Science and the Law*, pp. 62–87; LeVay, *Queer Science*, pp. 239–254, especially pp. 251–254.

41. On states that have passed laws forbidding the recognition of gay marriages, see David W. Dunlap, "Foes of Gay Marriage Foiled in California Senate," *New York Times*, September 4, 1996, p. A12. On federal action on the same issue, see Eric Schmitt, "Senate Delays Vote on Same-Sex Marriage Measure," *New York Times*, September 6, 1996, p. A12.

42. In describing discharge after discharge, Randy Shilts's *Conduct Unbecoming* documents the way in which it is in fact merely hypothetical disruption that serves as the basis for the exclusion of gay military personnel.

43. Green, *Sexual Science and the Law*, p. 63. It should be noted, though, that the lack of access to mechanisms of redress may not be as stringent as it once was, as Simon LeVay points out (see *Queer Science*, pp. 237–238). Though not in great numbers, openly gay people have been elected to federal, state, and local political office. Despite waxing and waning in membership and financial clout, gay advocacy organizations are also a political force and mechanism of social reform. While gay people did suffer the 1986 setback of the U.S. Supreme Court decision, Bowers v. Hardwick, a number of sodomy laws have been repealed in states around the country both by legislative and judicial action. There has also been some political support for a federal nondiscrimination bill, the Employment Non-Discrimination Act, that would outlaw most discrimination on the basis of sexual orientation. It may be that these sorts of considerations diminish the claim to systematic lack of access to political redress, as was the case with, for example, women and black people denied the right to vote.

44. For similar reasons, the U.S. federal government has also decided that people should not be ordinarily barred from employment by reason of their disabilities. See *Americans with Disabilities Act (ADA): Basic Facts about the Law* (Washington, D.C.: Department of Justice, Civil Rights Division, 1993).

45. See LeVay, *Queer Science*, pp. 238–239; and Hamer and Copeland, *Science of Desire*, p. 211 ff.

46. I read Sigmund Freud's account of "The Psychogenesis of a Case of Homosexuality in a Woman" as evidence he held, in at least some instances, that the primary reasons for the emergence of homoeroticism were congenital rather than psychodevelopmental. *Standard Edition*, 18:147–172.

47. William Byne and Bruce Parsons, "Human Sexual Orientation: The Biologic Theories Reappraised," *Archives of General Psychiatry* (1993), 50:228–239.

48. Money, *Gay, Straight, and In-Between*, pp. 4–5.

49. Green, *Sexual Science and the Law*, p. 85. He has said further that homosexual orientation is immutable in the sense that it "is not consciously chosen but, rather, that sexual and affectional feelings are a basic part of an individual's psyche and are established by early childhood." Quoted in LeVay, *Queer Science*, p. 287.

50. Hamer et al., "A Linkage Between DNA Markers"; Hu et al., "Linkage Between Sexual Orientation and Chromosomal Xq28 in Males But Not in Females"; Pattatucci and Hamer, "Development and Familiality of Sexual Orientation in Females."

51. See Card, *Lesbian Choices*, pp. 47–57. See also Vera Whisman, *Queer by Choice: Lesbians, Gay Men, and the Politics of Identity* (New York: Routledge, 1996), p. 6.

52. In court testimony the psychologist Judd Marmor was pressed to make exactly this distinction between the involuntary nature of male homoeroticism and the elective nature of female homoeroticism. See LeVay, *Queer Science*, p. 245.

53. Many of these theories have been surveyed in the introduction to Bieber et al., *Homosexuality*.

54. For an account of these witnesses competing with one another, see LeVay, *Queer Science*, pp. 231–232, 234, 241–246; and Mark Wolinsky and Kenneth Sherrill, eds., *Joseph Steffan Versus the United States* (Princeton: Princeton University Press, 1993).

55. Among the most repeatedly cited studies having to do with sexual orientation therapy are Bieber et al., *Homosexuality*; Masters and Johnson, *Homosexuality in Perspective*; Pattison and Pattison, " 'Ex-Gays': Religiously Mediated Change in Homosexuals"; and Schwartz and Masters, "The Masters and Johnson Treatment Program for Dissatisfied Homosexual Men." While the Bieber account is profoundly compromised in its research methodology, the Masters and Johnson efforts are also limited in their own way and therefore suspect as an indication of what men wanting change in the nature of their erotic lives might reasonably expect from clinical practitioners. For a discussion of some of the limitations of these studies, see Murphy, "The Ethics of Conversion Therapy."

56. Green, *Sexual Science and the Law*, pp. 77–84. For a similar view, see William Byne, quoted in Burr, *A Separate Creation*, p. 81.

57. Green, *Sexual Science and the Law*, p. 85.

58. Arthur S. Leonard, *Sexuality and the Law: An Encyclopedia of Major Legal Cases* (New York: Garland, 1993), pp. 507–519. See also Green, *Sexual Science and the Law*, p. 85; and LeVay, *Queer Science*, pp. 239–240.

59. See Eric Schmitt, "Senators Reject Gay Marriage Bill and Job-Bias Ban," *New York Times*, September 11, 1996, p. A1.

60. Romer v. Evans, 116 S. Ct. 1620 (1996).

61. Richard D. Mohr, "Romer v. Evans: A Blow for Justice," *Harvard Gay and Lesbian Review* (1996), 3:6.

62. Richard D. Mohr, "Homosexuality," *Encyclopedia of Ethics* (New York: Garland, 1992), 1:552–554.

7. SCIENCE AND THE FUTURE

1. See Randy Shilts, *And the Band Played On: AIDS, Politics, and People* (New York: St. Martin's, 1987); and Charles Perrow and Mauro F. Guillén, *The AIDS Disaster: The Failure of Organizations in New York and the Nation* (New Haven: Yale University Press, 1990). The most extreme claims allege that the epidemic was fostered directly by the government for the express purposes of eliminating undesirable people. See Alan Cantwell, *AIDS and the Doctors of Death* (Los Angeles: Aries Rising, 1988).

2. See Vern L. Bullough, "Homosexuality in Health Professions Education," unpublished ms.

3. The logic of Romer v. Evans bodes favorably for gay people on other fronts where they face discrimination because the Court held that the widespread prevalence of a view of a certain class of people does not by itself justify a rational governmental interest in sustaining that view. One commentator has gone so far as to say that the logic of this decision could be the basis for overturning Bowers v. Hardwick. See Richard D. Mohr, "Homosexuality: Legal Issues," unpublished ms. Whether it has that effect will remain to be seen. After all, it did appear that the logic of privacy that sustained many of the Court's decisions in regard to reproductive liberty (cases bearing on contraception and abortion specifically) would extend to sexual liberty, but that logic did not prevail in Bowers v. Hardwick, which argued against sodomy apart from issues of privacy.

4. Quoted in Stein, "Evidence for Queer Genes," p. 97. See also Henry, "Born Gay?" and Jerry Bishop, "Research Points Toward a 'Gay' Gene," *Wall Street Journal*, July 16, 1993, p. B1.

5. I should say that I do not take this to be a settled question. For a discussion of the need for evidence for such a claim, see Ruse, "Are There Gay Genes? Sociobiology and Homosexuality," p. 28.

6. Eve Kosofsky Sedgwick, "How to Bring Your Kids Up Gay," in Michael Warner, ed., *Fear of a Queer Planet: Queer Politics and Social Theory* (Minneapolis: University of Minnesota Press, 1993), pp. 69–81, especially p. 76.

7. Ibid.

8. I understand John Boswell to read the history of Christianity this way. See John Boswell, *Homosexuality, Christianity, and Social Tolerance* (Chicago: University of Chicago Press, 1980).

9. See James Rachels, "When Philosophers Shoot from the Hip," *Bioethics* (1991), 5:67–71.

10. Responding in the affirmative were 29 percent of 575 WHM, 25 percent of 111 BHM, 38 percent of 229 WHF, and 30 percent of 64 BHF. Bell and Weinberg, *Homosexualities*, table 12, p. 337.

11. Responding in the affirmative to the question "If considered giving up homosexuality, ever attempted?" were 63 percent of 166 WHM, 39 percent of 26 BHM, 75 percent of 84 WHF, and 58 percent of 19 BHF. Bell and Weinberg, *Homosexualities*, table 12, p. 337. In

response to the question "If attempted to give up homosexuality, number of attempts?" the answers were as follows. One attempt: 53 percent of 105 WHM, 30 percent of 10 BHM, 70 percent of 63 WHF, and 73 percent of 11 BHF. Two attempts: 23 percent of 105 WHM, 40 percent of 10 BHM, 16 percent of 63 WHF, and 9 percent of 11 BHF. Three or more attempts: 24 percent of 105 WHM, 40 percent of 10 BHM, 14 percent of 63 WHF, and 18 percent of 11 BHF. Bell and Weinberg, *Homosexualities*, table 12, p. 338.

12. Seeking professional help were 18 percent of 105 WHM, 9 percent of 11 BHM, 12 percent of 65 WHF, and 18 percent of 11 BHF. By contrast, seeking to control their sexual orientation by having less homosexual sociosexual involvement were 39 percent of 105 WHM, 45 percent of 11 BHM, 26 percent of 65 WHF, and 55 percent of 11 BHF. Bell and Weinberg, *Homosexualities*, table 12, p. 338.

13. Identifying professional help as a means by which they made an attempt to stop being homosexual were 18 percent of 105 WHM, 9 percent of 11 BHM, 12 percent of 65 WHF, and 18 percent of 11 BHF. Bell and Weinberg, *Homosexualities*, table 12, p. 338. Responding in the affirmation to another question, "If you ever consulted a professional, was it [ever] to give up your homosexuality," were 23 percent of 334 WHM, 23 percent of 56 BHM, 18 percent of 156 WHF, and 11 percent of 37 BHF. Bell and Weinberg, *Homosexualities*, table 21.22, p. 461.

14. On which matter see Timothy F. Murphy, "Gender Identity and Gender Identity Disorder," *Encyclopedia of Bioethics*, 2d ed. (New York: Macmillan, 1995), 2:901–907.

15. Responding that they experienced no or very little regret about their homosexuality were 73 percent of 575 WHM, 80 percent of 111 BHM, 84 percent of WHF, and 90 percent of BHF. Bell and Weinberg, *Homosexualities*, table 12, p. 337.

16. Responding that they would be much or somewhat upset if their children were to become homosexual were 25 percent of 570 WHM, 26 percent of 111 BHM, 33 percent of 226 WHF, and 27 percent of 64 BHF. Bell and Weinberg, *Homosexualities*, table 12, p. 339. The other respondents said they would be not at all or only very little upset. Saying that societal rejection or punitiveness was the reason for any regret about homosexuality were 44 percent of 289 WHM, 42 percent of 45 BHM, 46 percent of 82 WHF, and 65 percent of 17 BHF. Bell and Weinberg, *Homosexualities*, table 12, p. 337.

17. Chandler Burr, "The Destiny of You," *Advocate,* December 26, pp. 36–42.

18. Ibid. Neither the geneticist quoted nor the author of the article from which this quotation was taken explore the use of the genetic probe for adults, which might offer a substantially larger market for employers (the U.S. military among them) and insurers who in wanting to know the likely health risks of their employees and policyholders could have a keen interest in the use of such a test.

19. For further discussion of this point, see Murphy, "Reproductive Controls and Sexual Destiny."

20. Stein, "Evidence for Queer Genes," p. 98.

21. See, for example, Murphy, "Homosex/Ethics," and Mohr, *A More Perfect Union.*

22. Money, *Gay, Straight, and In-Between*, p. 154.

23. The Bell and Weinberg study did ask people to imagine whether they would be upset if a child of theirs were to become homosexual. Rather than casting the issue entirely in terms of regret, I hope that future sexological surveys include the question of how many parents might actually choose to select—if it were possible—a gay or lesbian child, this in order to measure the positive value parents might attribute to having gay or lesbian children rather than only registering their anticipated regret.

24. John D'Emilio, *Making Trouble: Essays on Gay History, Politics, and the University* (New York: Routledge, 1992), pp. 3–16.

25. Robert T. Michael, John H. Gagnon, Edward O. Laumann, and Gina Kolata, *Sex in America: A Definitive Study* (Boston: Little, Brown, 1994), p. 182.

26. Chauncey, *Gay New York*.

27. Faderman, *Odd Girls and Twilight Lovers*, pp. 38–39.

28. Elizabeth Lapovsky Kennedy and Madeline D. Davis, *Boots of Leather, Slippers of Gold: The History of a Lesbian Community* (New York: Penguin, 1993), p. 9.

29. D'Emilio, *Making Trouble*, pp. 13–16.

30. Money, *Gay, Straight, and In-Between*, 71–72, 73–74, 124, 131, 134, 171, 176–177.

31. Ibid., p. 73.

32. Ibid., p. 124.

33. Ibid., pp. 73–74, 124, 131, 134, 171, 176–177. Like D'Emilio's, these claims are hard to evaluate. I note them here not to judge their conceptual or evidential adequacy but merely as a reminder that biological accounts are not the only accounts of homoeroticism and that a biological focus may in fact obscure the other factors that determine the overall incidence and prevalence of homoeroticism.

34. Hamer and Copeland, *The Science of Desire*, p. 183.

35. Despite connections that link homoeroticism to cultural decline, it is unclear that the U.S. has suffered any significant cultural decline by reason of its gay and lesbian population. If a culture like that of the United States can thrive as it ostensibly does despite the presence of gay and lesbian culture in every American city of any substantial size, it is hard to see that any easy equations can be drawn between the sheer presence of homoeroticism in a population and its economic, cultural, political, and social deficits.

36. Despite the prevalence of the view about the heightened artistic sensibilities of gay men, there is little hard evidence on the question. See Janet Demb, "Are Gay Men Artistic? A Review of the Literature," *Journal of Homosexuality* (1992), 23:83–92.

37. John Rawls, *A Theory of Justice* (Cambridge: Harvard University Press, 1971).

38. I think that using the methodology of John Rawls's original position and veil of ignorance would argue strongly for equal duty, opportunity, privacy, and protection under the law for gay people. Insofar as the original contractors under the veil of ignorance would be unaware of their sexual orientation, it would be irrational of them to argue for principles that permitted broad discrimination. For example, if people did not know what sexual orientation they would have when they were done drawing up the compact that would govern society, it is likely that they would build into that compact some measure of protection for gay people. Whether they would go so far as to protect gay people with full civic equality is another matter. Some of the decision makers might gamble that they would be straight, when the veil of ignorance is lifted, and opposed on religious grounds to homoeroticism. This possibility would seem to fracture the unanimity required in Rawls's methodology to achieve consensus about full civic rights for gay people, though it would be just as irrational to foreclose all civic protection for gay people.

39. Edward Stein raised the question of treating gay people as an endangered species in correspondence with me in the summer of 1995.

40. Schüklenk, "Does Research Into Sexual Orientation Harm Gay People?"

41. Paul Ramsey, *Fabricated Man* (New Haven: Yale University Press, 1970), p. 25.

42. See, for example, Arthur Caplan, "What's Morally Wrong with Eugenics?" in Phillip R. Sloan and Edward Manier, eds., "Controlling Our Destinies: Humanistic Perspectives

on the Human Genome Project," unpublished ms. Caplan says, "Insofar as coercion and force are absent, and individual choice is allowed to hold sway, and presuming fairness in access to the means of enhancing our offspring, it is hard to see what exactly is wrong with trying to create perfect babies."

43. I have always found it interesting that no one has advanced the right of openly gay people to serve in the United States military by calling upon the notion of a duty to serve. How is it that millions and millions of gay people have no duty to serve the military forces of their nation? Surely it is not fair to those who serve in the military, especially those who do so at risk of death, that an entire class of people has no duty whatsoever to defend the nation in a direct military role. One moral reason to include gay people in the military is to shift to them some of the burdens and risks of military efforts else they enjoy the benefit of those efforts entirely at the expense of others.

44. Frederick Suppe has rightly observed that gay researchers need to be involved in theorizing and conducting research in the study of gay people because of the way in which people not acculturated to the gay subculture may misidentify or underappreciate the issues at stake. See "The Bell and Weinberg Study: Future Priorities for Research on Homosexuality," in Koertge, *Philosophy and Homosexuality*, pp. 69–97.

EPILOGUE

1. On whether homophobic responses are rooted in the repression of homoerotic interests, see Henry E. Adams, Lester W. Wright, Jr., Bethany A. Lohr, "Is Homophobia Associated with Homosexual Arousal?" *Journal of Abnormal Psychology* (1996), 105:440–445, and Money, *Gay, Straight, and In-Between*, pp. 109–110.

2. Felix Kersten, *The Kersten Memoirs, 1940–1945* (New York: Macmillan, 1957), p. 57. A chief architect of the Nazi campaign against gay people, Himmler once observed, "The homosexual is a traitor to his own people and must be rooted out. . . . I have long been considering whether it would not be to the point to castrate every homosexual at once. That would help him and us." Instead of going forward with that idea, Himmler listened to counsel from his physician on how homosexuals could be prevented (*Kersten Memoirs*, pp. 56–60). Himmler nevertheless considered homosexuals a grave danger to the state, as did other prominent Germans, including, of course, Hitler himself. See Mosse, *Nationalism and Sexuality*, pp. 164–179.

3. Karl Menninger, "Introduction," *The Wolfenden Report: Report of the Committee on Homosexual Offenses and Prostitution* (New York: Stein and Day, 1963), p. 7.

4. James D. Watson, "The Human Genome Project: Past, Present, and Future," *Science* (1990), 248(4951):44–49. See also James D. Watson and Robert Mullan Cook-Deegan, "The Human Genome Project and International Health," *Journal of the American Medical Association* (1990), 263:3322–3324.

5. See Daniel J. Kevles, "Eugenics and the Human Genome Project: Is the Past Prologue?" in Murphy and Lappé, *Justice and the Human Genome Project*, pp. 14–29.

6. Leonard, *Sexuality and the Law*.

7. Martin Duberman, *Stonewall* (New York: Dutton, 1993).

8. Fausto-Sterling, *Myths of Gender*.

9. I owe this formulation to Wartofsky, *Conceptual Foundations of Science*, pp. 23, 415.

10. Friedrich Nietzsche, *The Gay Science*, trans. Walter Kaufmann (New York: Vintage, 1974).

11. Currently, some have seen other terms as more useful for describing personal and political homoerotic identities. That *queer* is the chief candidate in contention with *gay* and/or *lesbian* in many ways suggests that gay politics has succeeded all too well. Self-described queer men and women typically feel the need to assert their difference against social and political views that have increasingly and already accommodated gay and lesbian identities and political groups and thereby perhaps, so the argument goes, even co-opted them.

INDEX

Between Men ~ Between Women   Lesbian and Gay Studies

Lillian Faderman and Larry Gross, Editors

Noreen O'Connor and Joanna Ryan, *Wild Desires and Mistaken Identities: Lesbianism and Psychoanalysis*

Don Paulson with Roger Simpson, *An Evening in the Garden of Allah: A Gay Cabaret in Seattle*

Judith Roof, *Come As You Are: Sexuality and Narrative*

Judith Roof, *A Lure of Knowledge: Lesbian Sexuality and Theory*

Claudia Schoppmann, *Days of Masquerade: Life Stories of Lesbians During the Third Reich*

Alan Sinfield, *The Wilde Century: Effeminacy, Oscar Wilde, and the Queer Moment*

Jane McIntosh Snyder, *Lesbian Desire in the Lyrics of Sappho*

Chris Straayer: *Deviant Eyes, Deviant Bodies: Sexual Re-Orientations in Film and Video*

Thomas Waugh, *Hard to Imagine: Gay Male Eroticism in Photography and Film from Their Beginnings to Stonewall*

Kath Weston, *Families We Choose: Lesbians, Gays, Kinship*

Kath Weston, *Render me, Gender Me: Lesbians Talk Sex, Class, Color, Nation, Studmuffins . . .*

Carter Wilson, *Hidden in the Blood: A Personal Investigation of AIDS in the Yucatán*